W9-DDU-151

PANZERFAUST

VOLUME II: HOOKED

www.ShadowlineOnline.com

PETER PANZERFAUST VOLUME TWO: HOOKED

First Printing May, 2013   ISBN: 978-1-60706-728-3

Published by Image Comics, Inc. Office of publication: 2001 Center Street, Sixth Floor, Berkeley, California 94704. Copyright © 2013 KURTIS WIEBE and TYLER JENKINS. Originally published in single magazine form as PETER PANZERFAUST #6-10. All rights reserved. PETER PANZERFAUST™ (including all prominent characters featured herein), its logo and all character likenesses are trademarks of KURTIS WIEBE and TYLER JENKINS, unless otherwise noted. Image Comics® and its logos are registered trademarks of Image Comics, Inc. Shadowline and its logos are ™ and © 2013 Jim Valentino. No part of this publication may be reproduced or transmitted, in any form or by any means (except for short excerpts for review purposes) without the express written permission of Mr. Wiebe and/or Jenkins. All names, characters, events and locales in this publication are entirely fictional. Any resemblance to actual persons (living or dead), events or places, without satiric intent, is coincidental. For information regarding the CPSIA on this printed material call: 203-595-3636 and provide reference # RICH – 477194. PRINTED IN USA. International Rights / Foreign Licensing - foreignlicensing@imagecomics.com

image COMICS PRESENTS

CO-CREATORS

KURTIS WIEBE   TYLER JENKINS
WORDS   PICTURES

HEATHER BRECKEL   ED BRISSON
COLORS   LETTERS

LAURA TAVISHATI
EDITS
MARC LOMBARDI
COMMUNICATIONS
JIM VALENTINO
PUBLISHER/BOOK DESIGN

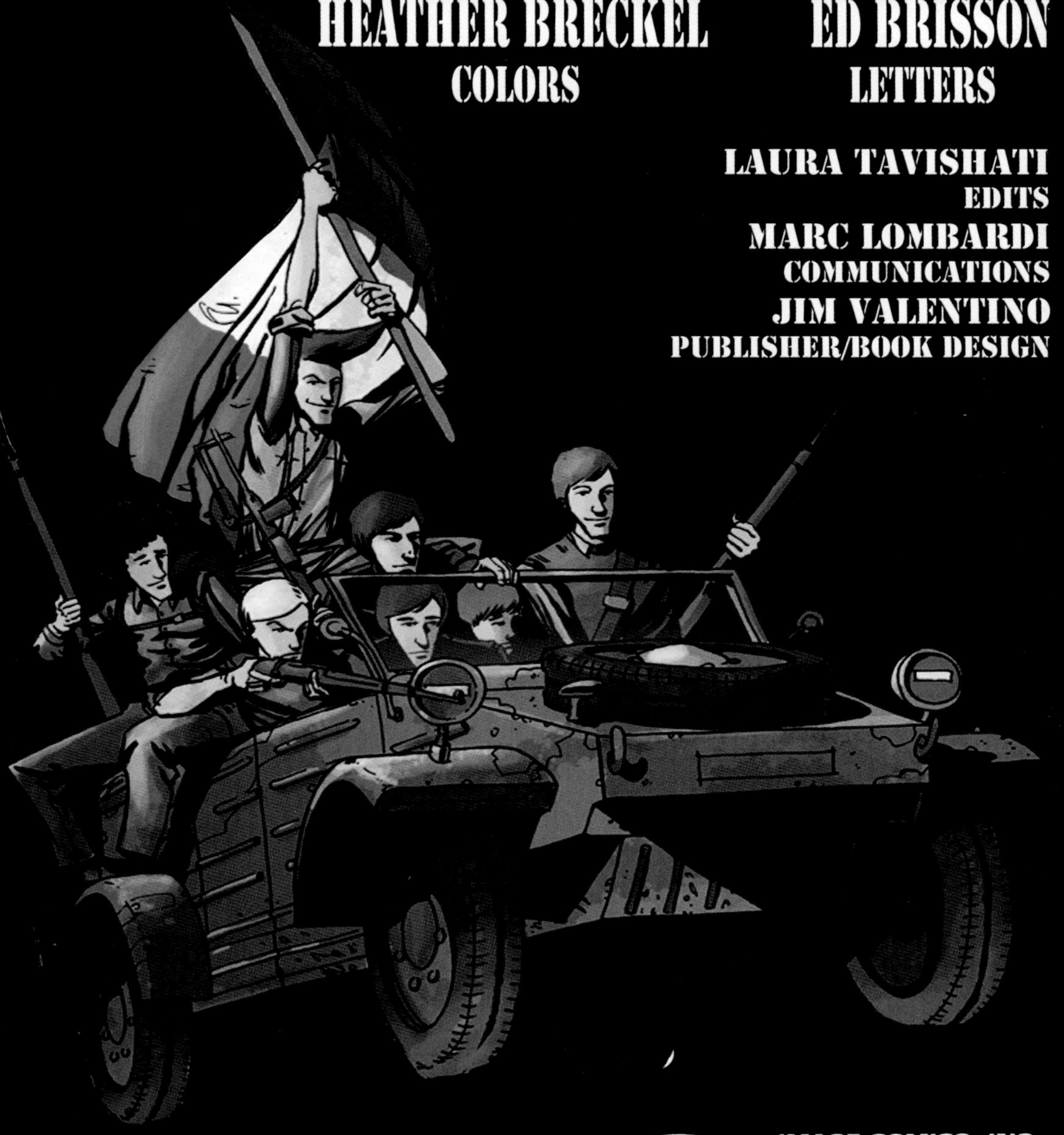

A

Shadowline™
PRODUCTION

www.ShadowlineOnline.com
Follow SHADOWLINECOMICS on [f] FACEBOOK and [t] TWITTER

IMAGE COMICS, INC.
Robert Kirkman - chief operating officer
Erik Larsen - chief financial officer
Todd McFarlane - president
Marc Silvestri - chief executive officer
Jim Valentino - vice-president
Eric Stephenson - publisher
Ron Richards - director of business development
Jennifer de Guzman - pr & marketing director
Branwyn Bigglestone - accounts manager
Emily Miller - accounting assistant
Jamie Parreno - marketing assistant
Jenna Savage - administrative assistant
Kevin Yuen - digital rights coordinator
Jonathan Chan - production manager
Drew Gill - art director
Monica Garcia - production artist
Vincent Kukua - production artist
Jana Cook - production artist
www.imagecomics.com

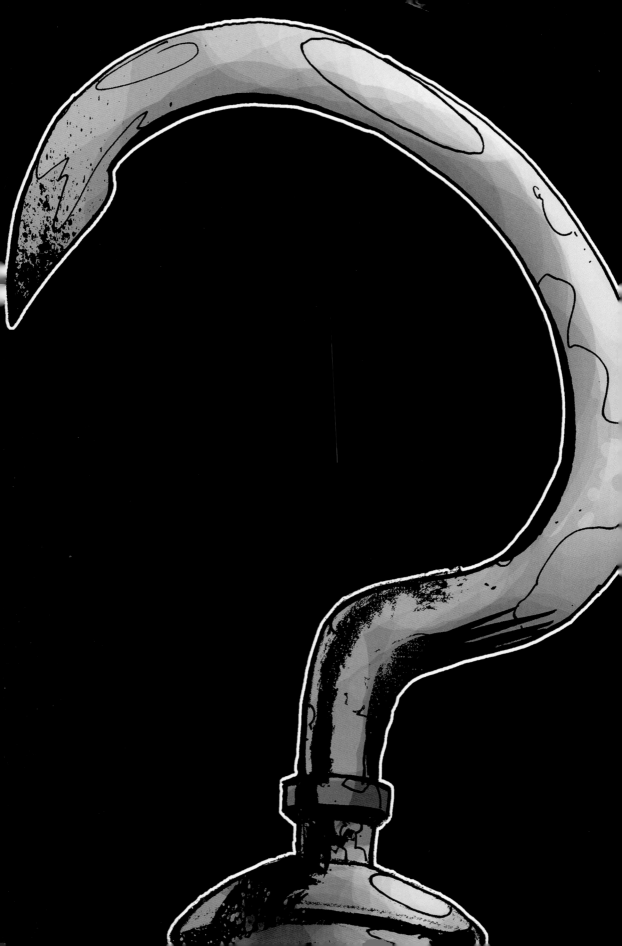

CHAPTER SIX

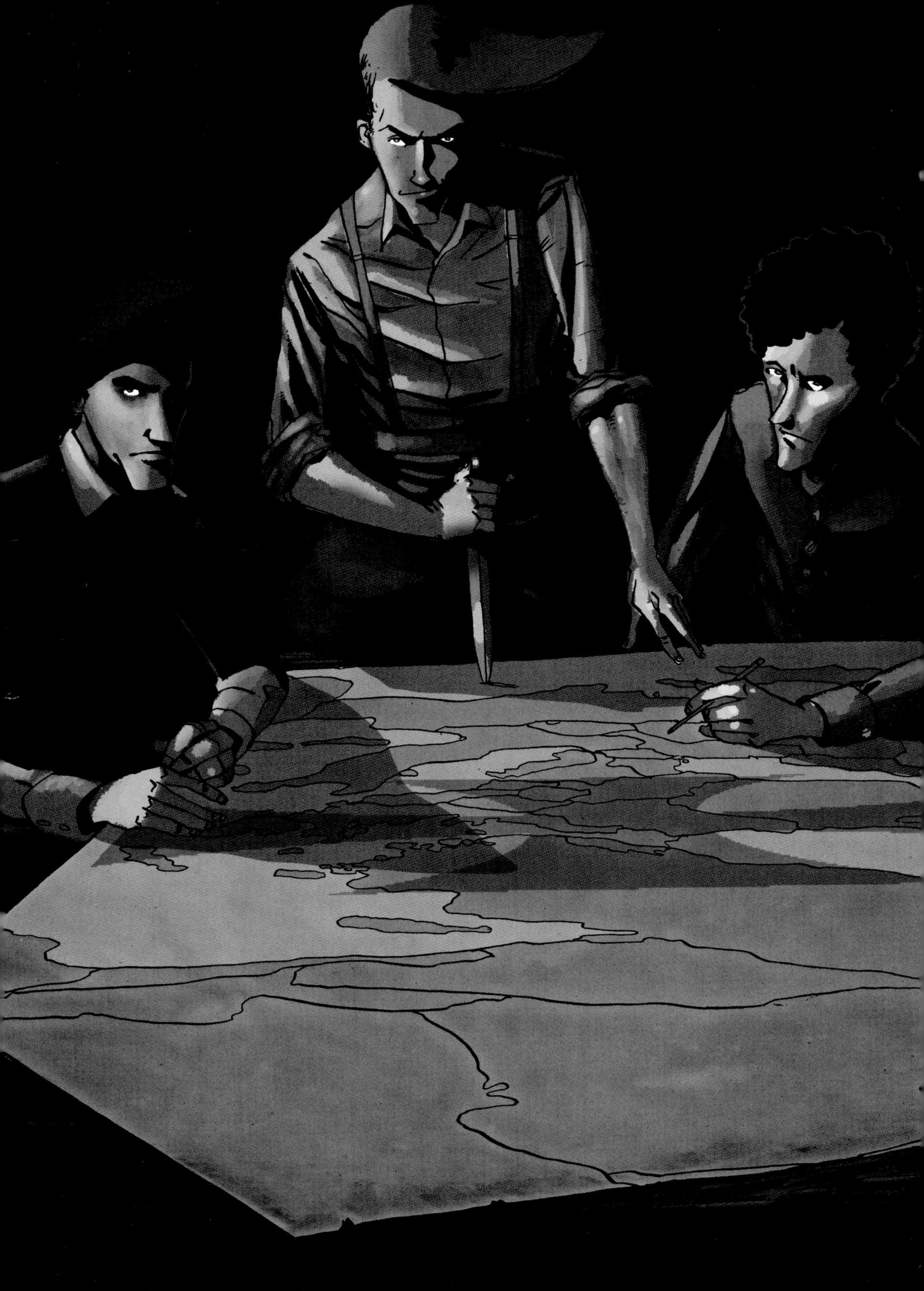

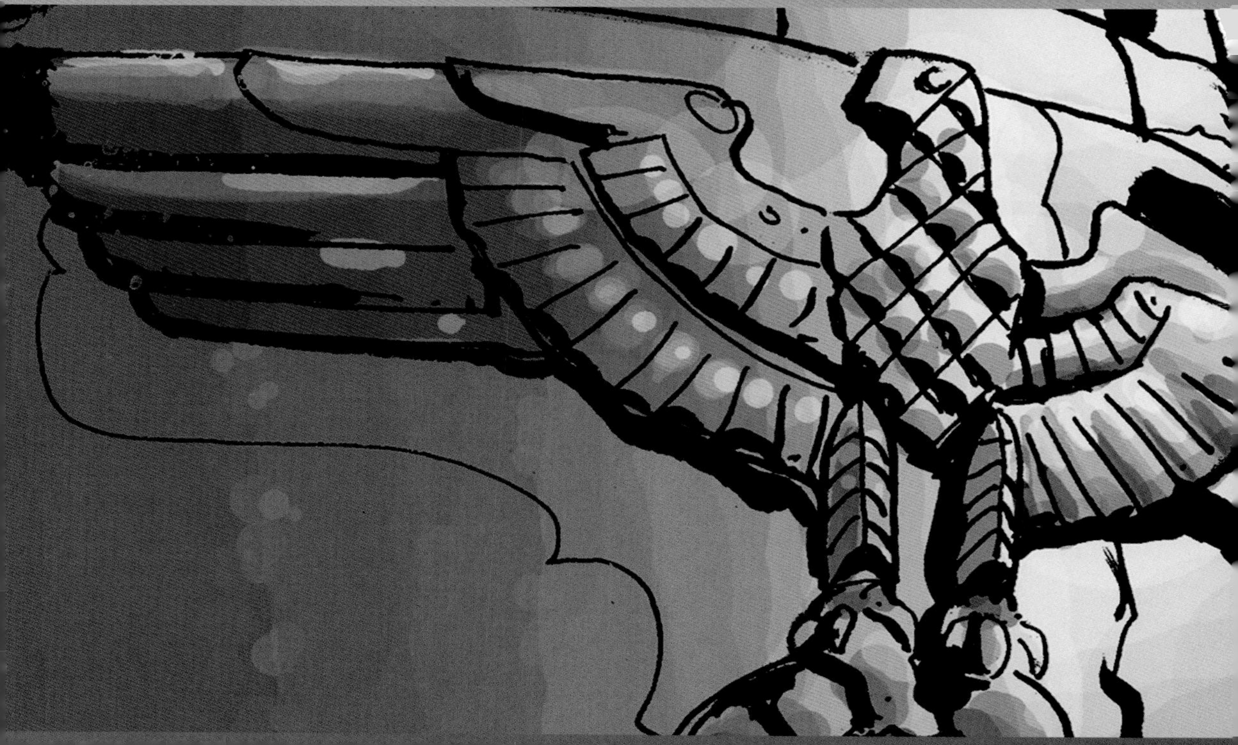

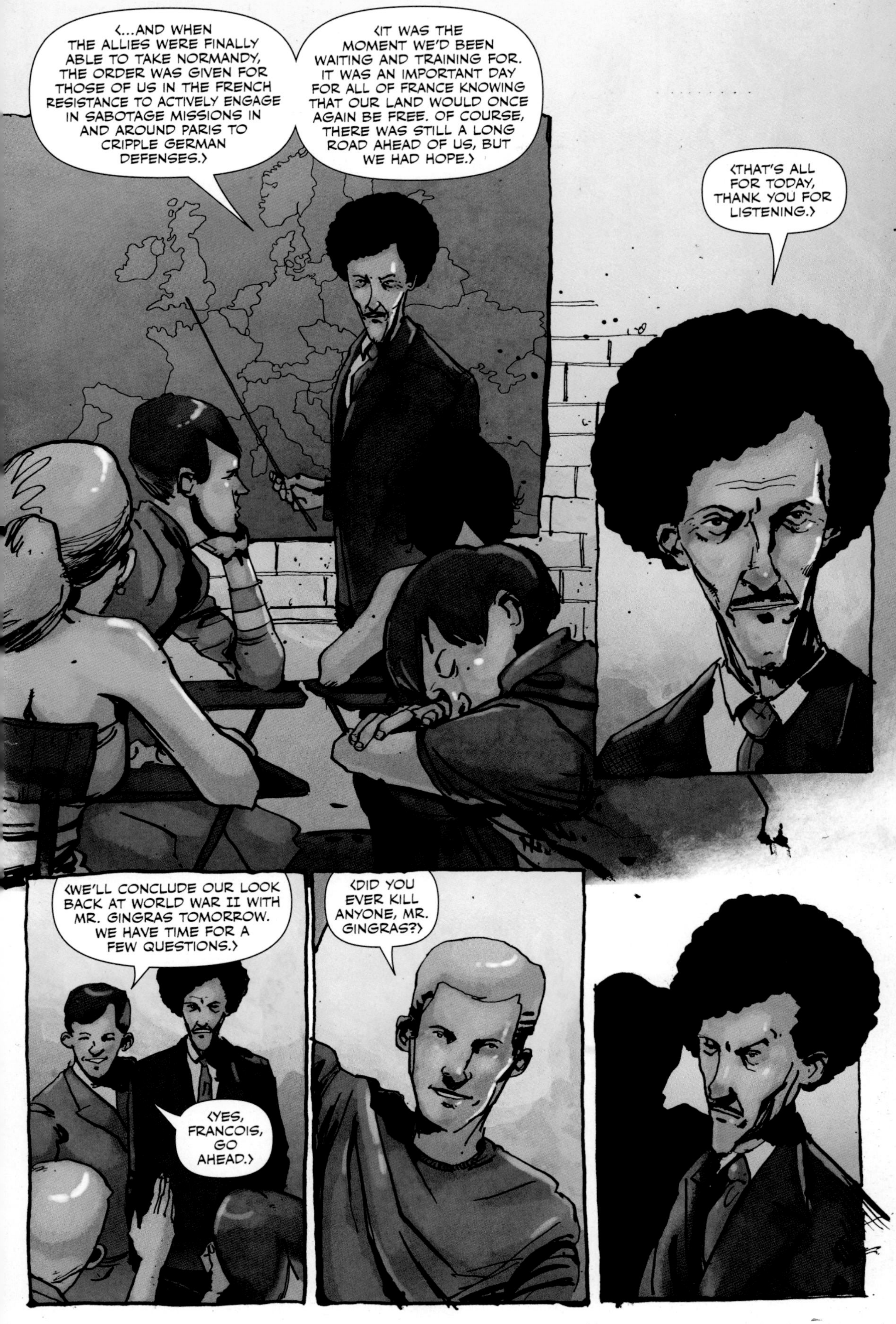
<...AND WHEN THE ALLIES WERE FINALLY ABLE TO TAKE NORMANDY, THE ORDER WAS GIVEN FOR THOSE OF US IN THE FRENCH RESISTANCE TO ACTIVELY ENGAGE IN SABOTAGE MISSIONS IN AND AROUND PARIS TO CRIPPLE GERMAN DEFENSES.>
<IT WAS THE MOMENT WE'D BEEN WAITING AND TRAINING FOR. IT WAS AN IMPORTANT DAY FOR ALL OF FRANCE KNOWING THAT OUR LAND WOULD ONCE AGAIN BE FREE. OF COURSE, THERE WAS STILL A LONG ROAD AHEAD OF US, BUT WE HAD HOPE.>
<THAT'S ALL FOR TODAY, THANK YOU FOR LISTENING.>
<WE'LL CONCLUDE OUR LOOK BACK AT WORLD WAR II WITH MR. GINGRAS TOMORROW. WE HAVE TIME FOR A FEW QUESTIONS.>
<YES, FRANCOIS, GO AHEAD.>
<DID YOU EVER KILL ANYONE, MR. GINGRAS?>

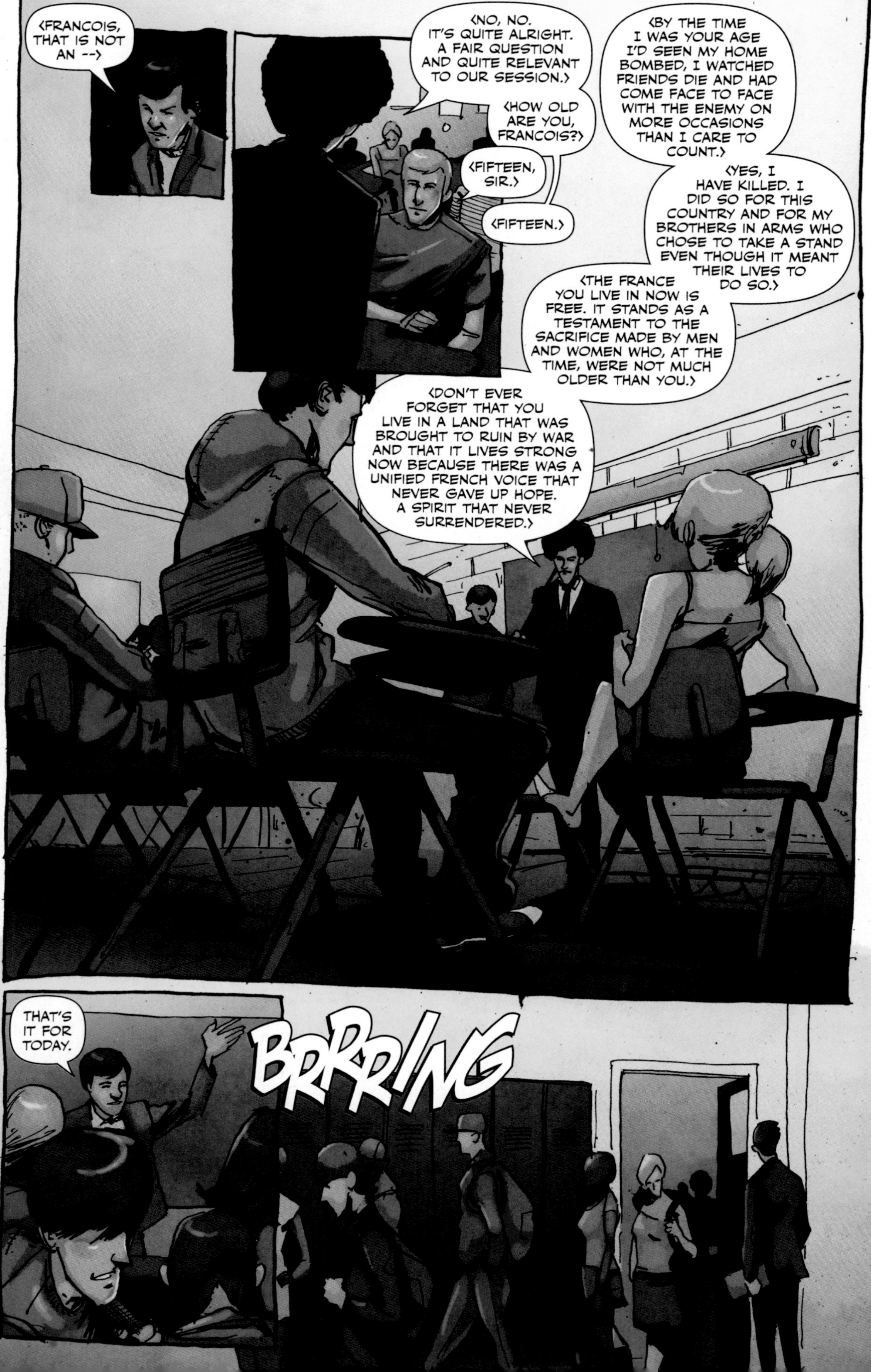
<FRANCOIS, THAT IS NOT AN -->
<NO, NO. IT'S QUITE ALRIGHT. A FAIR QUESTION AND QUITE RELEVANT TO OUR SESSION.>
<HOW OLD ARE YOU, FRANCOIS?>
<FIFTEEN, SIR.>
<FIFTEEN.>
<BY THE TIME I WAS YOUR AGE I'D SEEN MY HOME BOMBED, I WATCHED FRIENDS DIE AND HAD COME FACE TO FACE WITH THE ENEMY ON MORE OCCASIONS THAN I CARE TO COUNT.>
<YES, I HAVE KILLED. I DID SO FOR THIS COUNTRY AND FOR MY BROTHERS IN ARMS WHO CHOSE TO TAKE A STAND EVEN THOUGH IT MEANT THEIR LIVES TO DO SO.>
<THE FRANCE YOU LIVE IN NOW IS FREE. IT STANDS AS A TESTAMENT TO THE SACRIFICE MADE BY MEN AND WOMEN WHO, AT THE TIME, WERE NOT MUCH OLDER THAN YOU.>
<DON'T EVER FORGET THAT YOU LIVE IN A LAND THAT WAS BROUGHT TO RUIN BY WAR AND THAT IT LIVES STRONG NOW BECAUSE THERE WAS A UNIFIED FRENCH VOICE THAT NEVER GAVE UP HOPE. A SPIRIT THAT NEVER SURRENDERED.>
THAT'S IT FOR TODAY.
BRRRING

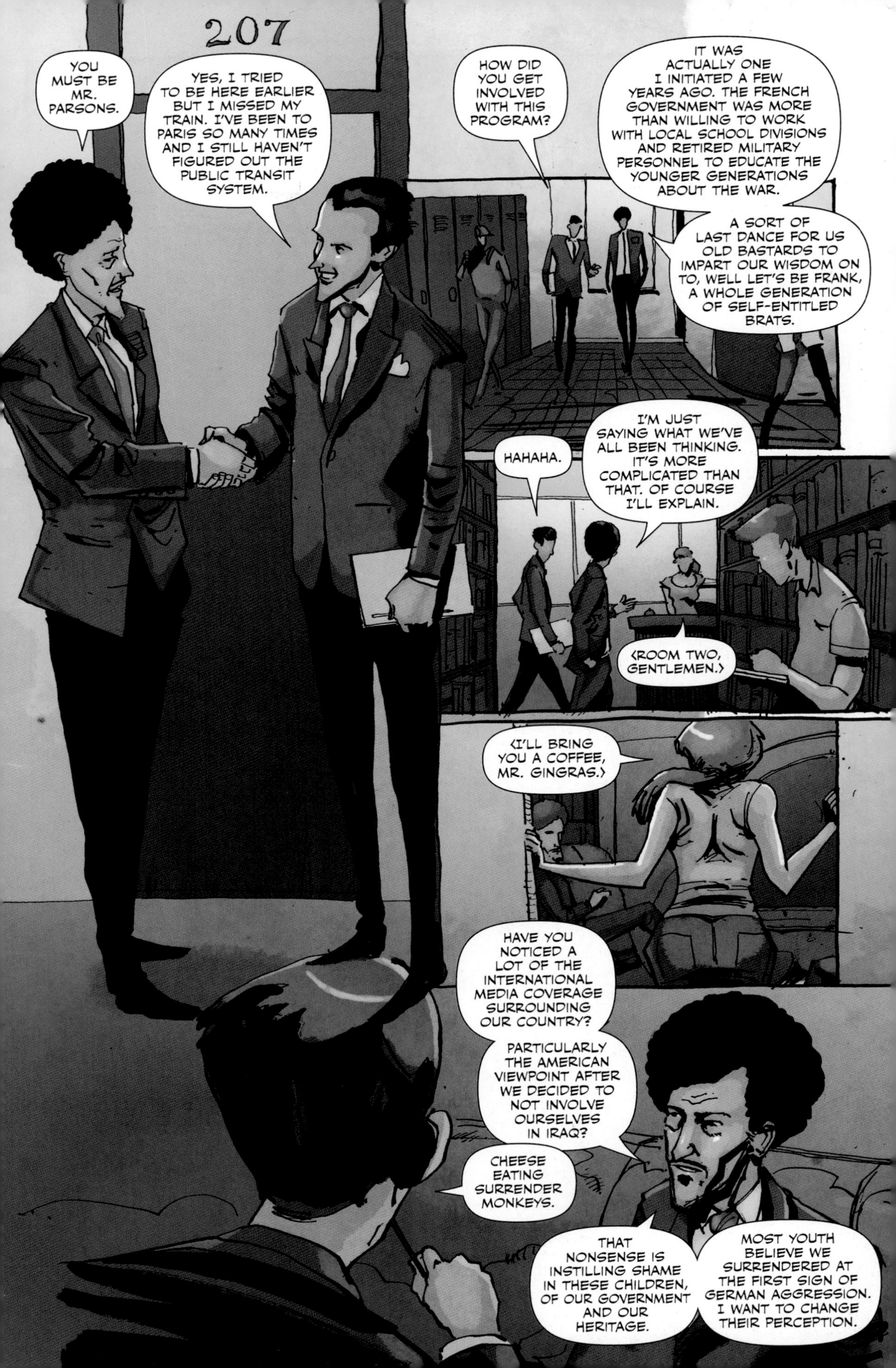
207
YOU MUST BE MR. PARSONS.
YES, I TRIED TO BE HERE EARLIER BUT I MISSED MY TRAIN. I'VE BEEN TO PARIS SO MANY TIMES AND I STILL HAVEN'T FIGURED OUT THE PUBLIC TRANSIT SYSTEM.
HOW DID YOU GET INVOLVED WITH THIS PROGRAM?
IT WAS ACTUALLY ONE I INITIATED A FEW YEARS AGO. THE FRENCH GOVERNMENT WAS MORE THAN WILLING TO WORK WITH LOCAL SCHOOL DIVISIONS AND RETIRED MILITARY PERSONNEL TO EDUCATE THE YOUNGER GENERATIONS ABOUT THE WAR.
A SORT OF LAST DANCE FOR US OLD BASTARDS TO IMPART OUR WISDOM ON TO, WELL LET'S BE FRANK, A WHOLE GENERATION OF SELF-ENTITLED BRATS.
HAHAHA.
I'M JUST SAYING WHAT WE'VE ALL BEEN THINKING. IT'S MORE COMPLICATED THAN THAT. OF COURSE I'LL EXPLAIN.
<ROOM TWO, GENTLEMEN.>
<I'LL BRING YOU A COFFEE, MR. GINGRAS.>
HAVE YOU NOTICED A LOT OF THE INTERNATIONAL MEDIA COVERAGE SURROUNDING OUR COUNTRY?
PARTICULARLY THE AMERICAN VIEWPOINT AFTER WE DECIDED TO NOT INVOLVE OURSELVES IN IRAQ?
CHEESE EATING SURRENDER MONKEYS.
MOST YOUTH BELIEVE WE SURRENDERED AT THE FIRST SIGN OF GERMAN AGGRESSION. I WANT TO CHANGE THEIR PERCEPTION.
THAT NONSENSE IS INSTILLING SHAME IN THESE CHILDREN, OF OUR GOVERNMENT AND OUR HERITAGE.

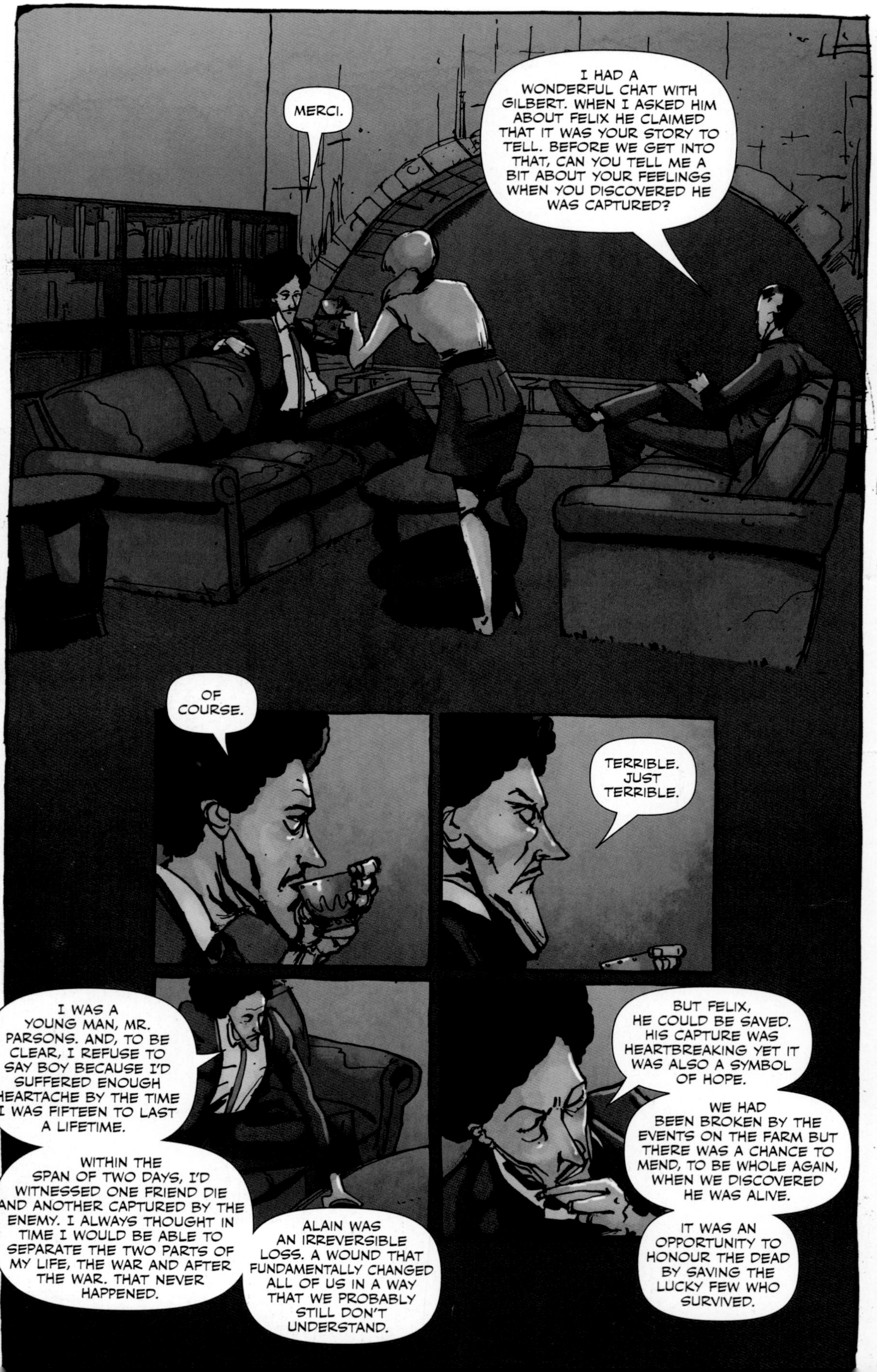
MERCI.
I HAD A WONDERFUL CHAT WITH GILBERT. WHEN I ASKED HIM ABOUT FELIX HE CLAIMED THAT IT WAS YOUR STORY TO TELL. BEFORE WE GET INTO THAT, CAN YOU TELL ME A BIT ABOUT YOUR FEELINGS WHEN YOU DISCOVERED HE WAS CAPTURED?
OF COURSE.
TERRIBLE. JUST TERRIBLE.
I WAS A YOUNG MAN, MR. PARSONS. AND, TO BE CLEAR, I REFUSE TO SAY BOY BECAUSE I'D SUFFERED ENOUGH HEARTACHE BY THE TIME I WAS FIFTEEN TO LAST A LIFETIME.
WITHIN THE SPAN OF TWO DAYS, I'D WITNESSED ONE FRIEND DIE AND ANOTHER CAPTURED BY THE ENEMY. I ALWAYS THOUGHT IN TIME I WOULD BE ABLE TO SEPARATE THE TWO PARTS OF MY LIFE, THE WAR AND AFTER THE WAR. THAT NEVER HAPPENED.
ALAIN WAS AN IRREVERSIBLE LOSS. A WOUND THAT FUNDAMENTALLY CHANGED ALL OF US IN A WAY THAT WE PROBABLY STILL DON'T UNDERSTAND.
BUT FELIX, HE COULD BE SAVED. HIS CAPTURE WAS HEARTBREAKING YET IT WAS ALSO A SYMBOL OF HOPE.
WE HAD BEEN BROKEN BY THE EVENTS ON THE FARM BUT THERE WAS A CHANCE TO MEND, TO BE WHOLE AGAIN, WHEN WE DISCOVERED HE WAS ALIVE.
IT WAS AN OPPORTUNITY TO HONOUR THE DEAD BY SAVING THE LUCKY FEW WHO SURVIVED.

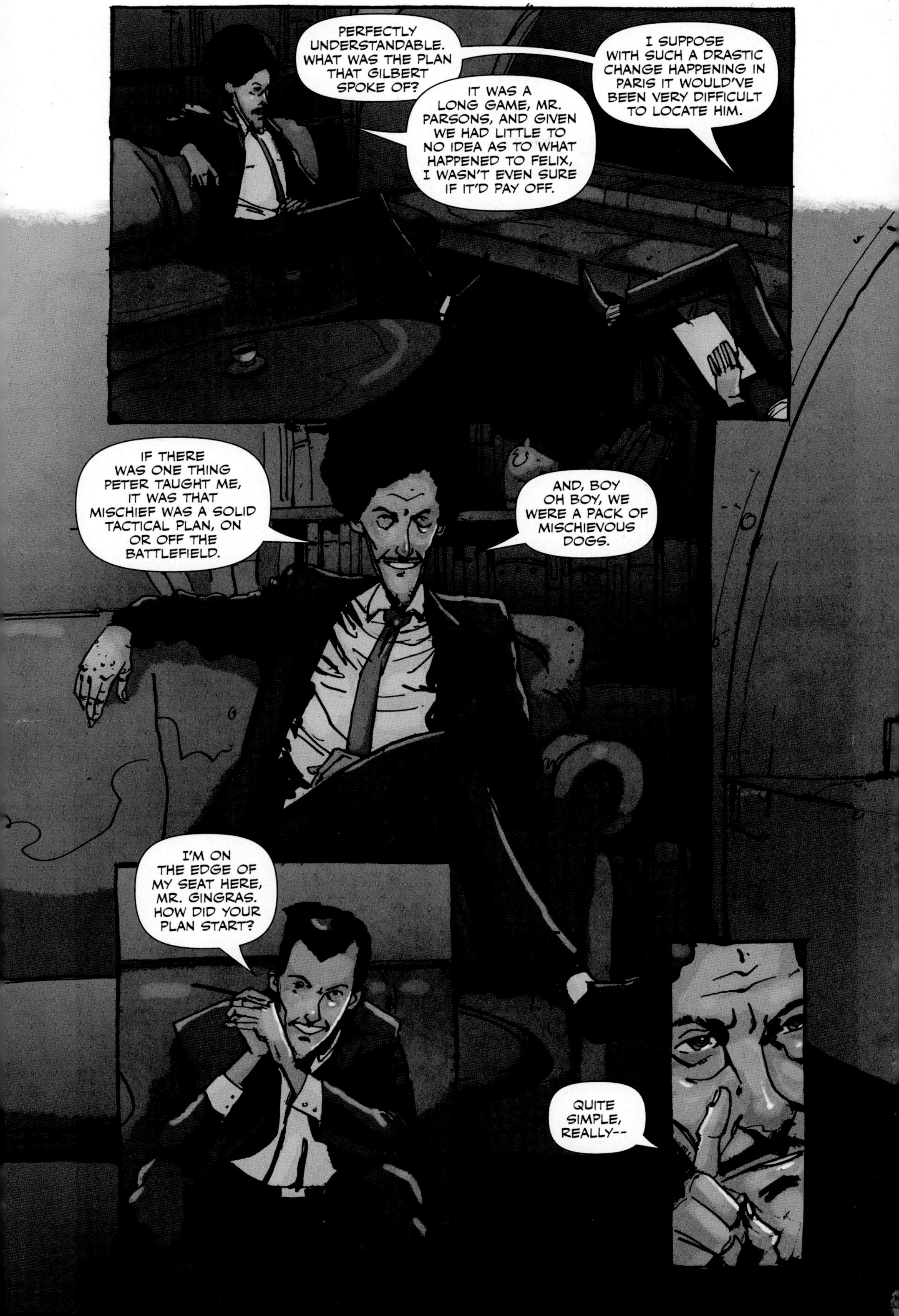
PERFECTLY UNDERSTANDABLE. WHAT WAS THE PLAN THAT GILBERT SPOKE OF?
IT WAS A LONG GAME, MR. PARSONS, AND GIVEN WE HAD LITTLE TO NO IDEA AS TO WHAT HAPPENED TO FELIX, I WASN'T EVEN SURE IF IT'D PAY OFF.
I SUPPOSE WITH SUCH A DRASTIC CHANGE HAPPENING IN PARIS IT WOULD'VE BEEN VERY DIFFICULT TO LOCATE HIM.
IF THERE WAS ONE THING PETER TAUGHT ME, IT WAS THAT MISCHIEF WAS A SOLID TACTICAL PLAN, ON OR OFF THE BATTLEFIELD.
AND, BOY OH BOY, WE WERE A PACK OF MISCHIEVOUS DOGS.
I'M ON THE EDGE OF MY SEAT HERE, MR. GINGRAS. HOW DID YOUR PLAN START?
QUITE SIMPLE, REALLY--

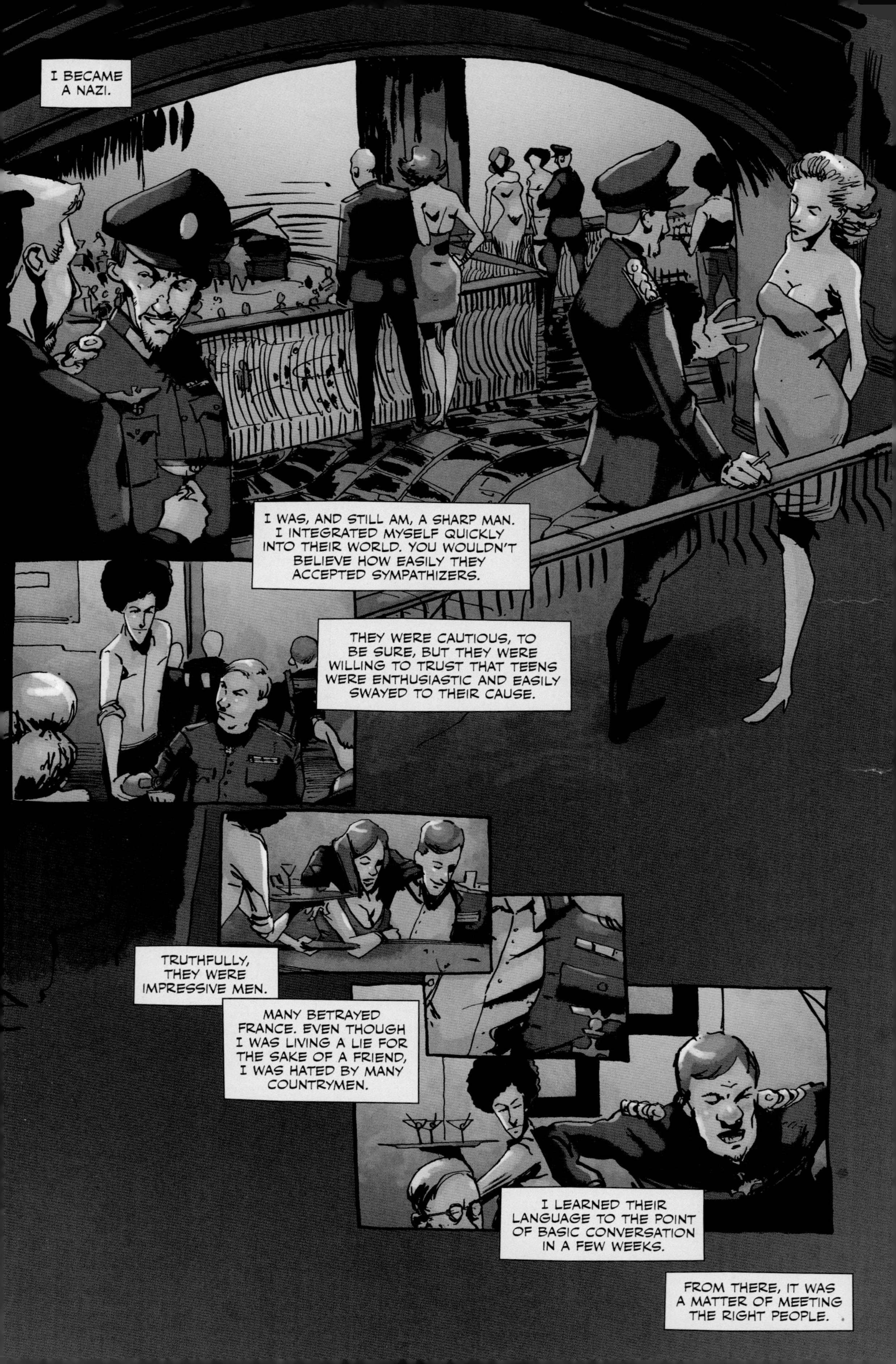
I BECAME A NAZI.
I WAS, AND STILL AM, A SHARP MAN. I INTEGRATED MYSELF QUICKLY INTO THEIR WORLD. YOU WOULDN'T BELIEVE HOW EASILY THEY ACCEPTED SYMPATHIZERS.
THEY WERE CAUTIOUS, TO BE SURE, BUT THEY WERE WILLING TO TRUST THAT TEENS WERE ENTHUSIASTIC AND EASILY SWAYED TO THEIR CAUSE.
TRUTHFULLY, THEY WERE IMPRESSIVE MEN.
MANY BETRAYED FRANCE. EVEN THOUGH I WAS LIVING A LIE FOR THE SAKE OF A FRIEND, I WAS HATED BY MANY COUNTRYMEN.
I LEARNED THEIR LANGUAGE TO THE POINT OF BASIC CONVERSATION IN A FEW WEEKS.
FROM THERE, IT WAS A MATTER OF MEETING THE RIGHT PEOPLE.

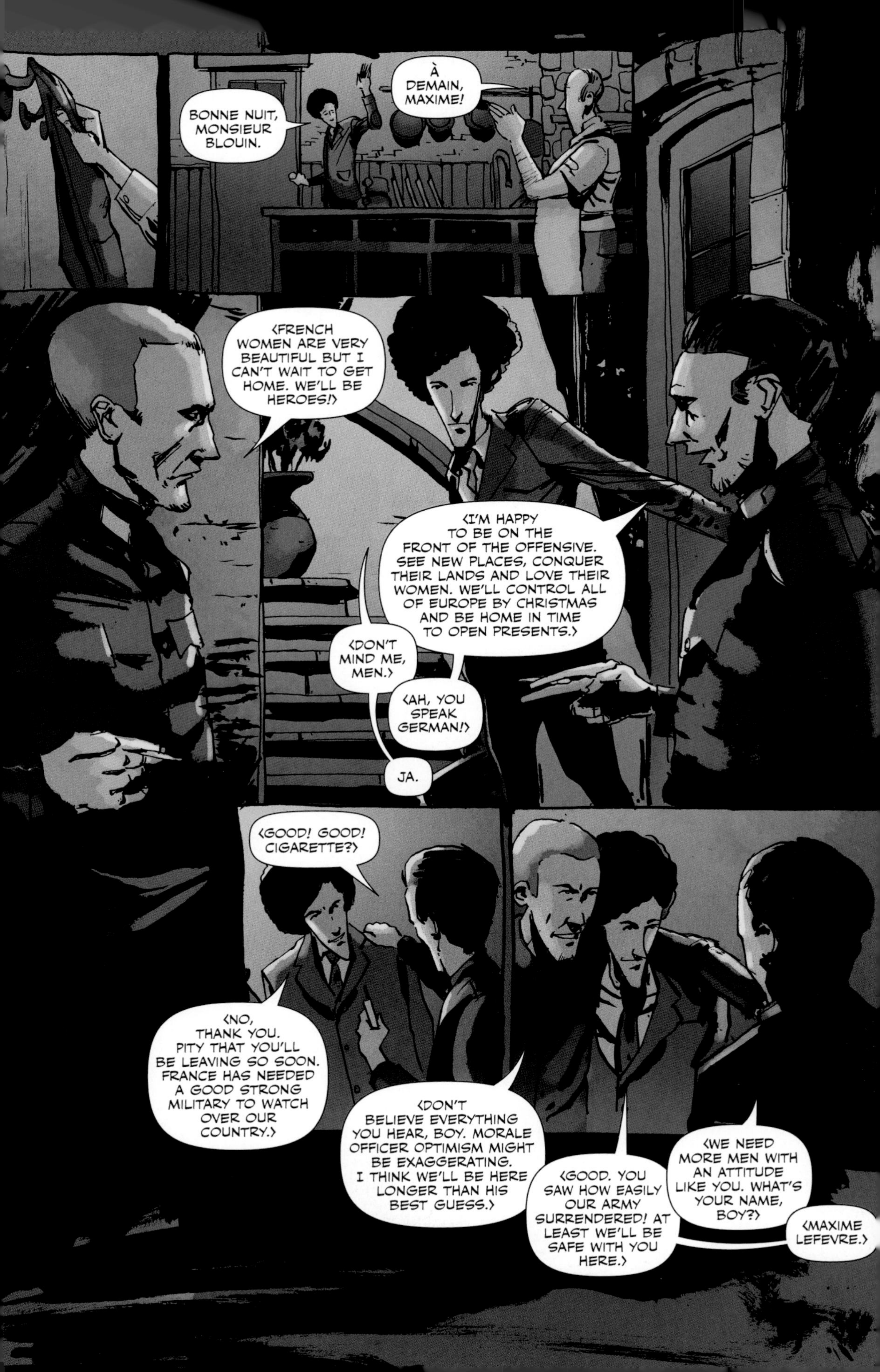
BONNE NUIT, MONSIEUR BLOUIN.
À DEMAIN, MAXIME!
‹FRENCH WOMEN ARE VERY BEAUTIFUL BUT I CAN'T WAIT TO GET HOME. WE'LL BE HEROES!›
‹I'M HAPPY TO BE ON THE FRONT OF THE OFFENSIVE. SEE NEW PLACES, CONQUER THEIR LANDS AND LOVE THEIR WOMEN. WE'LL CONTROL ALL OF EUROPE BY CHRISTMAS AND BE HOME IN TIME TO OPEN PRESENTS.›
‹DON'T MIND ME, MEN.›
‹AH, YOU SPEAK GERMAN!›
JA.
‹GOOD! GOOD! CIGARETTE?›
‹NO, THANK YOU. PITY THAT YOU'LL BE LEAVING SO SOON. FRANCE HAS NEEDED A GOOD STRONG MILITARY TO WATCH OVER OUR COUNTRY.›
‹DON'T BELIEVE EVERYTHING YOU HEAR, BOY. MORALE OFFICER OPTIMISM MIGHT BE EXAGGERATING. I THINK WE'LL BE HERE LONGER THAN HIS BEST GUESS.›
‹GOOD. YOU SAW HOW EASILY OUR ARMY SURRENDERED! AT LEAST WE'LL BE SAFE WITH YOU HERE.›
‹WE NEED MORE MEN WITH AN ATTITUDE LIKE YOU. WHAT'S YOUR NAME, BOY?›
‹MAXIME LEFEVRE.›

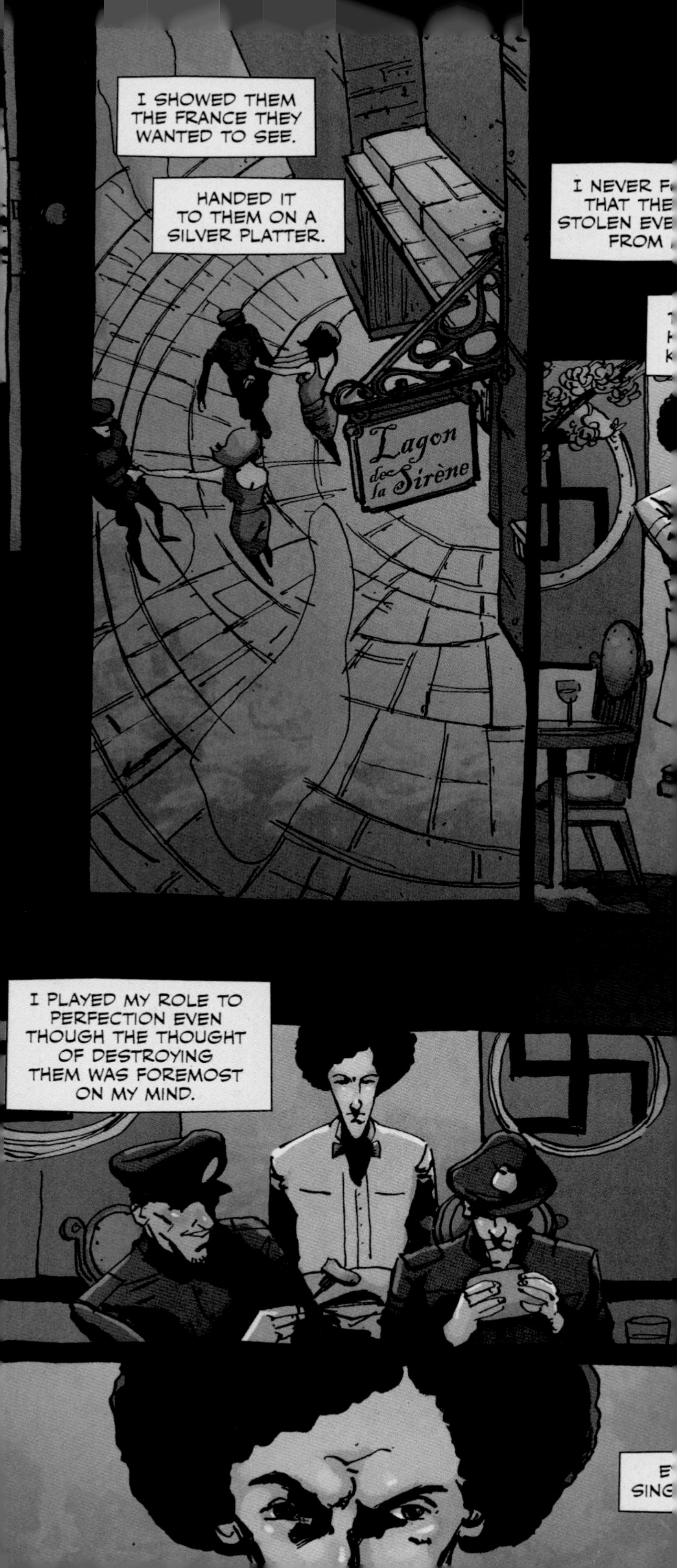
I SHOWED THEM THE FRANCE THEY WANTED TO SEE.
HANDED IT TO THEM ON A SILVER PLATTER.
Lagon de la Sirène
I NEVER
THAT
STOLEN
FROM
I PLAYED MY ROLE TO PERFECTION EVEN THOUGH THE THOUGHT OF DESTROYING THEM WAS FOREMOST ON MY MIND.

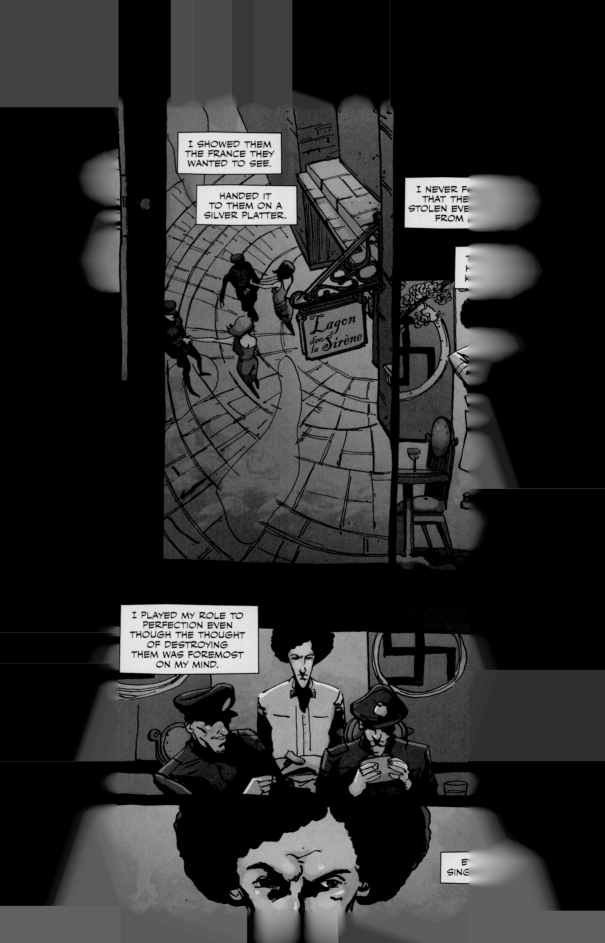

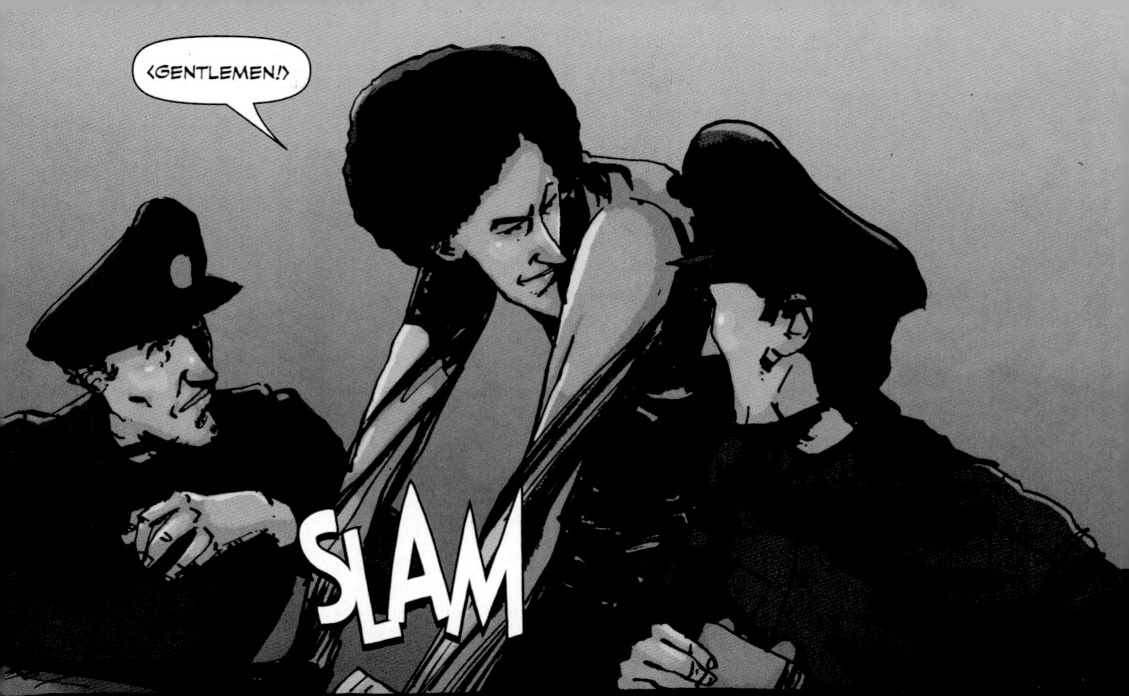

<GENTLEMEN!>
SLAM

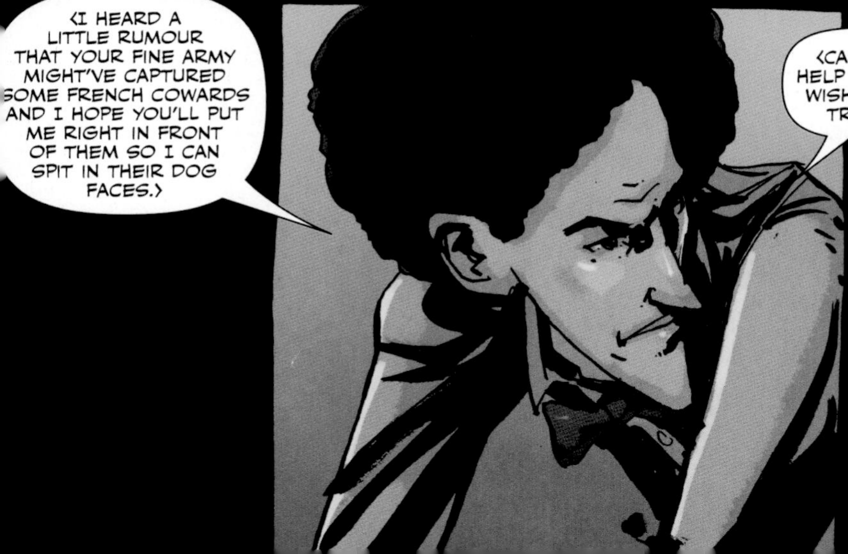

<I HEARD A LITTLE RUMOUR THAT YOUR FINE ARMY MIGHT'VE CAPTURED SOME FRENCH COWARDS AND I HOPE YOU'LL PUT ME RIGHT IN FRONT OF THEM SO I CAN SPIT IN THEIR DOG FACES.>
<CARE TO HELP MAKE A WISH COME TRUE?>

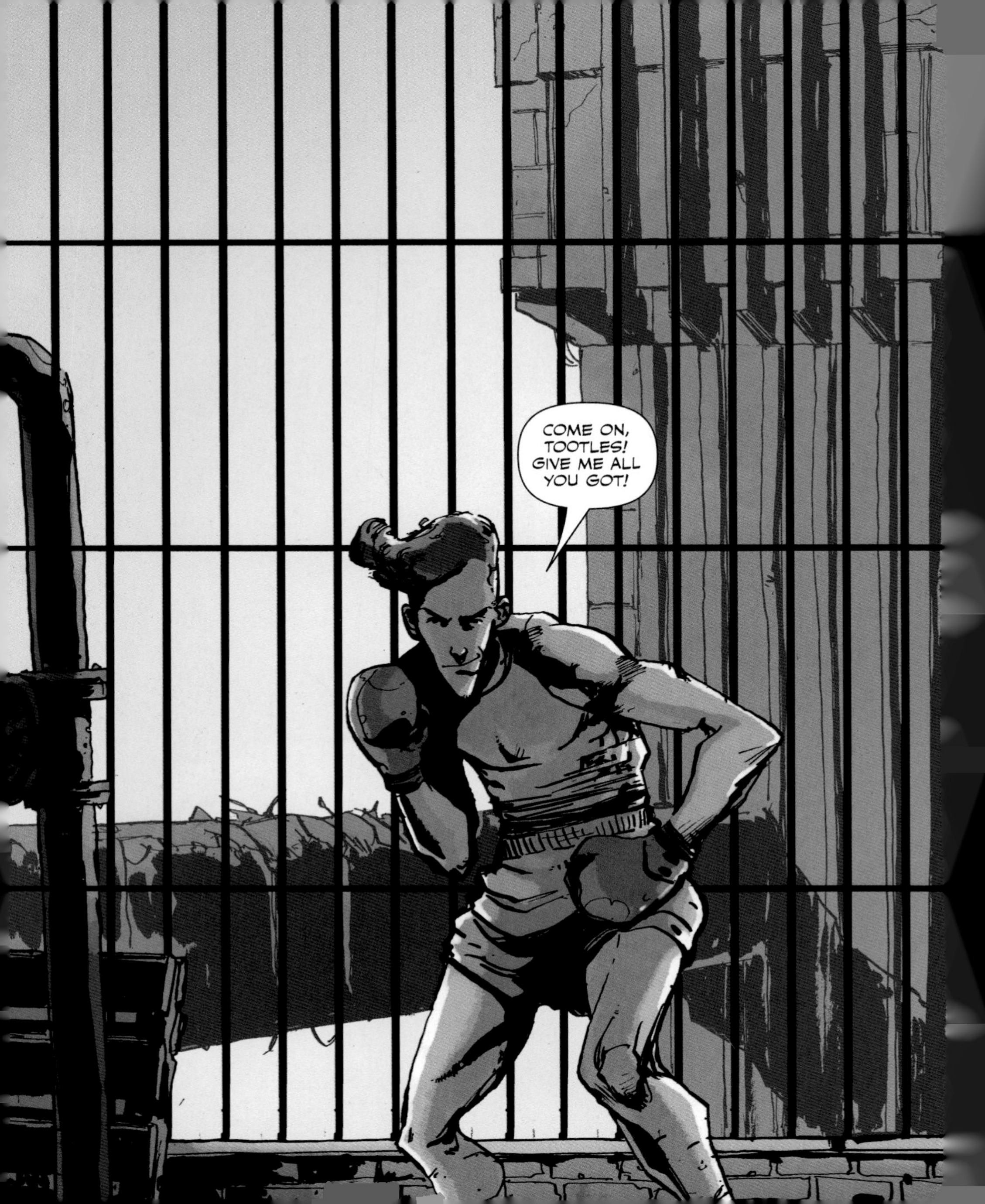
COME ON, TOOTLES! GIVE ME ALL YOU GOT!

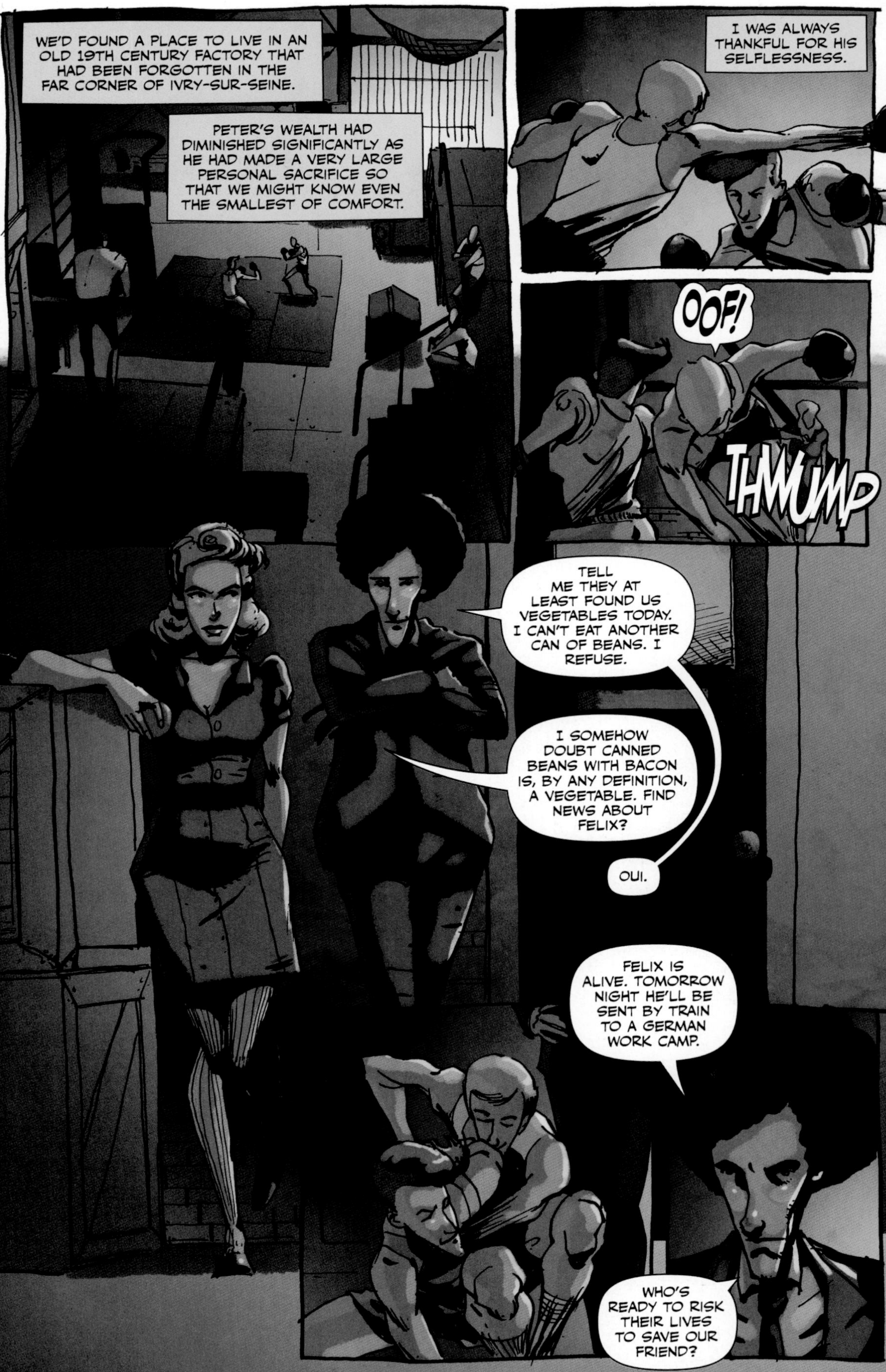
WE'D FOUND A PLACE TO LIVE IN AN OLD 19TH CENTURY FACTORY THAT HAD BEEN FORGOTTEN IN THE FAR CORNER OF IVRY-SUR-SEINE.
PETER'S WEALTH HAD DIMINISHED SIGNIFICANTLY AS HE HAD MADE A VERY LARGE PERSONAL SACRIFICE SO THAT WE MIGHT KNOW EVEN THE SMALLEST OF COMFORT.
I WAS ALWAYS THANKFUL FOR HIS SELFLESSNESS.
OOF!
THWUMP
TELL ME THEY AT LEAST FOUND US VEGETABLES TODAY. I CAN'T EAT ANOTHER CAN OF BEANS. I REFUSE.
I SOMEHOW DOUBT CANNED BEANS WITH BACON IS, BY ANY DEFINITION, A VEGETABLE. FIND NEWS ABOUT FELIX?
OUI.
FELIX IS ALIVE. TOMORROW NIGHT HE'LL BE SENT BY TRAIN TO A GERMAN WORK CAMP.
WHO'S READY TO RISK THEIR LIVES TO SAVE OUR FRIEND?

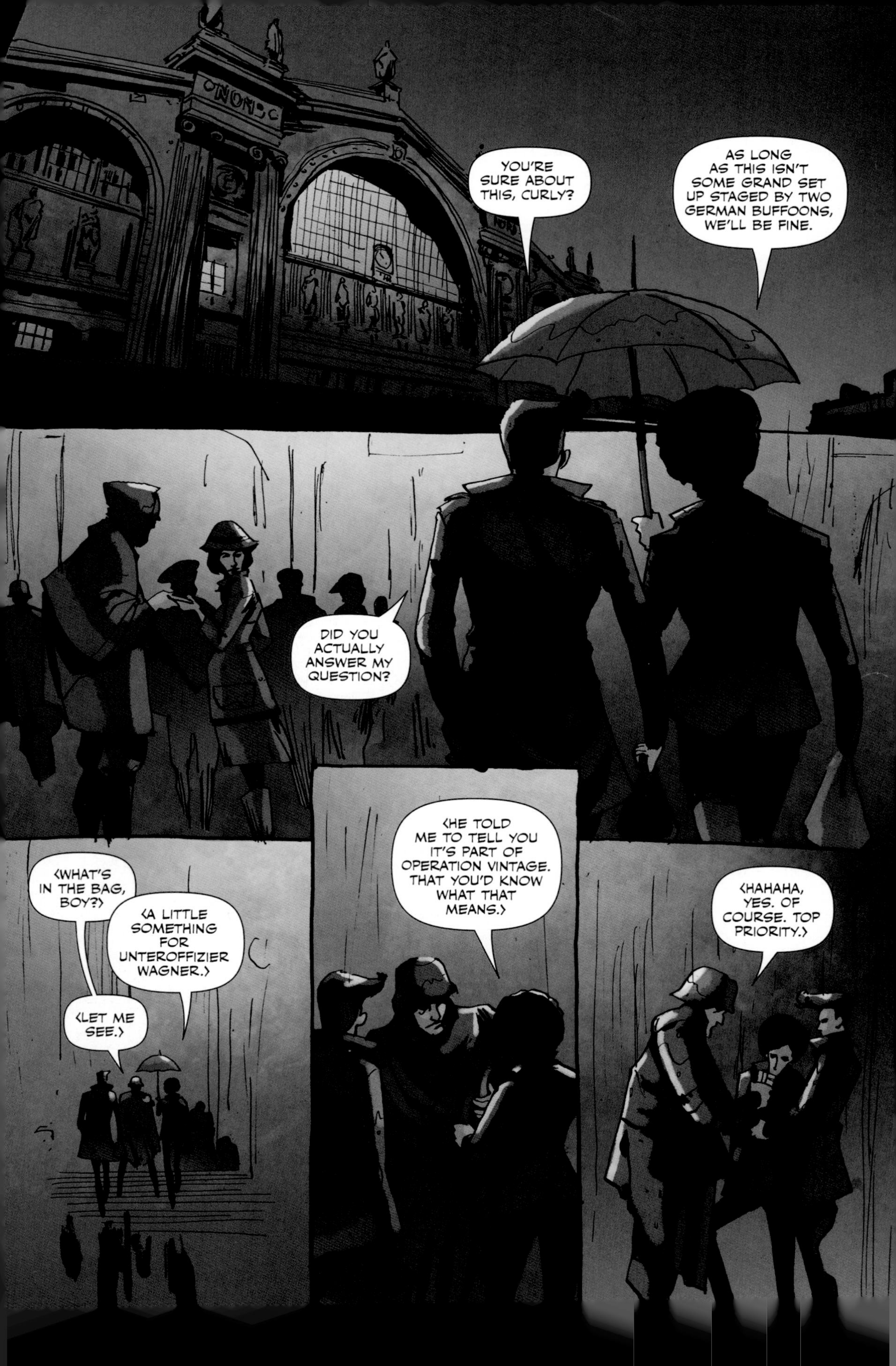
YOU'RE SURE ABOUT THIS, CURLY?
AS LONG AS THIS ISN'T SOME GRAND SET UP STAGED BY TWO GERMAN BUFFOONS, WE'LL BE FINE.
DID YOU ACTUALLY ANSWER MY QUESTION?
<WHAT'S IN THE BAG, BOY?>
<A LITTLE SOMETHING FOR UNTEROFFIZIER WAGNER.>
<LET ME SEE.>
<HE TOLD ME TO TELL YOU IT'S PART OF OPERATION VINTAGE. THAT YOU'D KNOW WHAT THAT MEANS.>
<HAHAHA, YES. OF COURSE. TOP PRIORITY.>

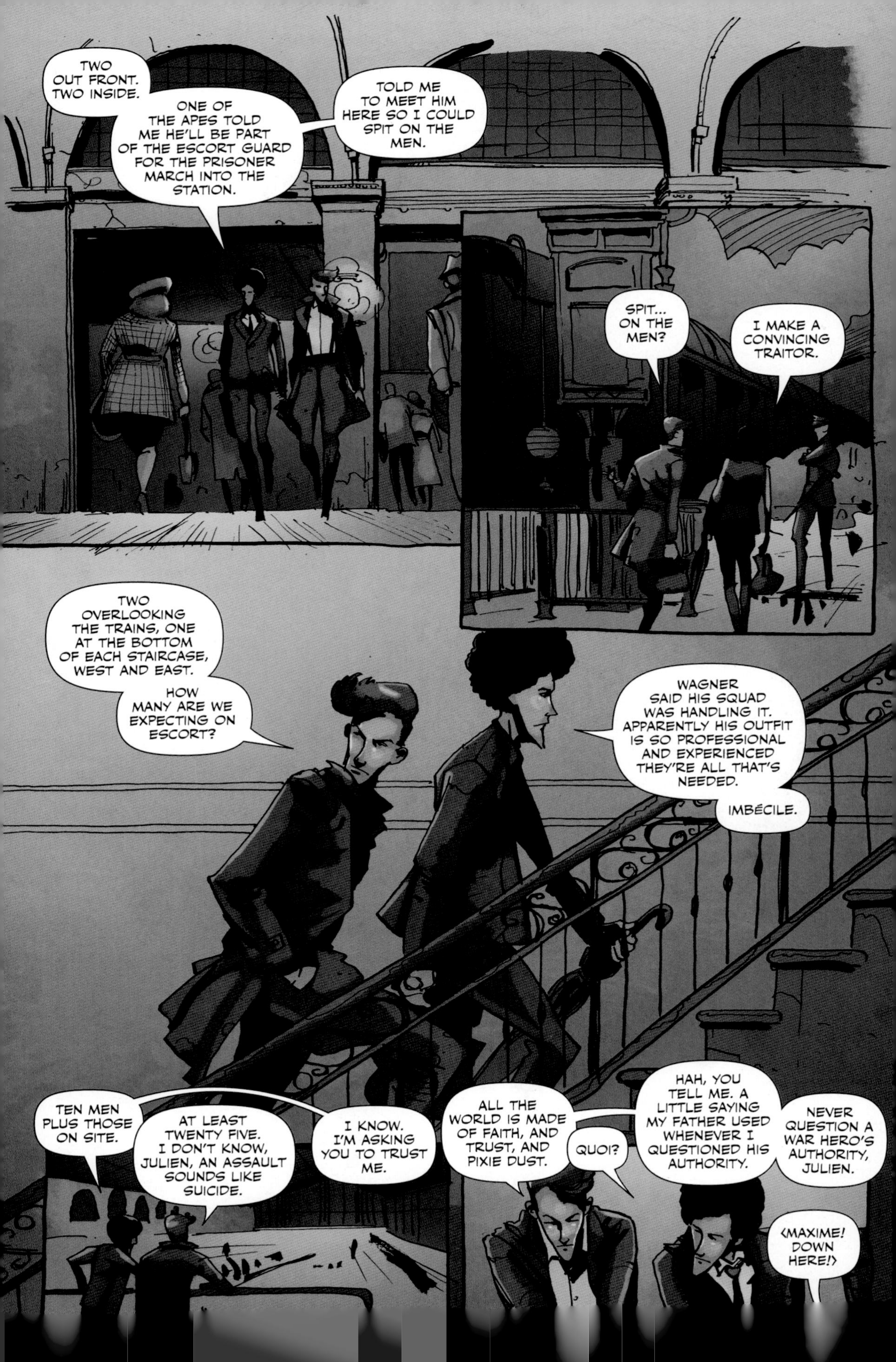
TWO OUT FRONT. TWO INSIDE.
ONE OF THE APES TOLD ME HE'LL BE PART OF THE ESCORT GUARD FOR THE PRISONER MARCH INTO THE STATION.
TOLD ME TO MEET HIM HERE SO I COULD SPIT ON THE MEN.
SPIT... ON THE MEN?
I MAKE A CONVINCING TRAITOR.
TWO OVERLOOKING THE TRAINS, ONE AT THE BOTTOM OF EACH STAIRCASE, WEST AND EAST.
HOW MANY ARE WE EXPECTING ON ESCORT?
WAGNER SAID HIS SQUAD WAS HANDLING IT. APPARENTLY HIS OUTFIT IS SO PROFESSIONAL AND EXPERIENCED THEY'RE ALL THAT'S NEEDED.
IMBÉCILE.
TEN MEN PLUS THOSE ON SITE.
AT LEAST TWENTY FIVE. I DON'T KNOW, JULIEN, AN ASSAULT SOUNDS LIKE SUICIDE.
I KNOW. I'M ASKING YOU TO TRUST ME.
ALL THE WORLD IS MADE OF FAITH, AND TRUST, AND PIXIE DUST.
QUOI?
HAH, YOU TELL ME. A LITTLE SAYING MY FATHER USED WHENEVER I QUESTIONED HIS AUTHORITY.
NEVER QUESTION A WAR HERO'S AUTHORITY, JULIEN.
<MAXIME! DOWN HERE!>

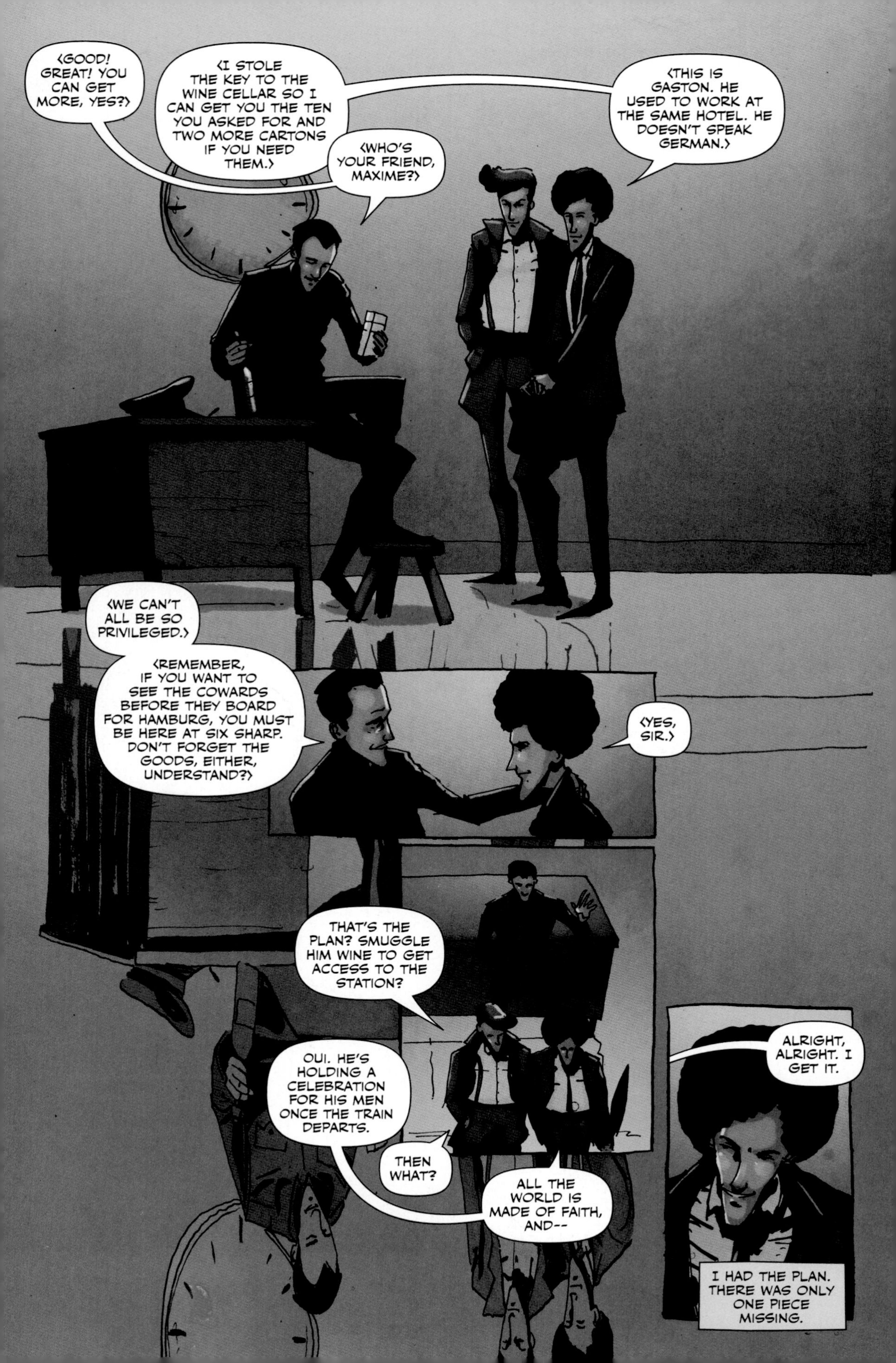

‹GOOD! GREAT! YOU CAN GET MORE, YES?›
‹I STOLE THE KEY TO THE WINE CELLAR SO I CAN GET YOU THE TEN YOU ASKED FOR AND TWO MORE CARTONS IF YOU NEED THEM.›
‹WHO'S YOUR FRIEND, MAXIME?›
‹THIS IS GASTON. HE USED TO WORK AT THE SAME HOTEL. HE DOESN'T SPEAK GERMAN.›
‹WE CAN'T ALL BE SO PRIVILEGED.›
‹REMEMBER, IF YOU WANT TO SEE THE COWARDS BEFORE THEY BOARD FOR HAMBURG, YOU MUST BE HERE AT SIX SHARP. DON'T FORGET THE GOODS, EITHER, UNDERSTAND?›
‹YES, SIR.›
THAT'S THE PLAN? SMUGGLE HIM WINE TO GET ACCESS TO THE STATION?
OUI. HE'S HOLDING A CELEBRATION FOR HIS MEN ONCE THE TRAIN DEPARTS.
THEN WHAT?
ALL THE WORLD IS MADE OF FAITH, AND--
ALRIGHT, ALRIGHT. I GET IT.
I HAD THE PLAN. THERE WAS ONLY ONE PIECE MISSING.

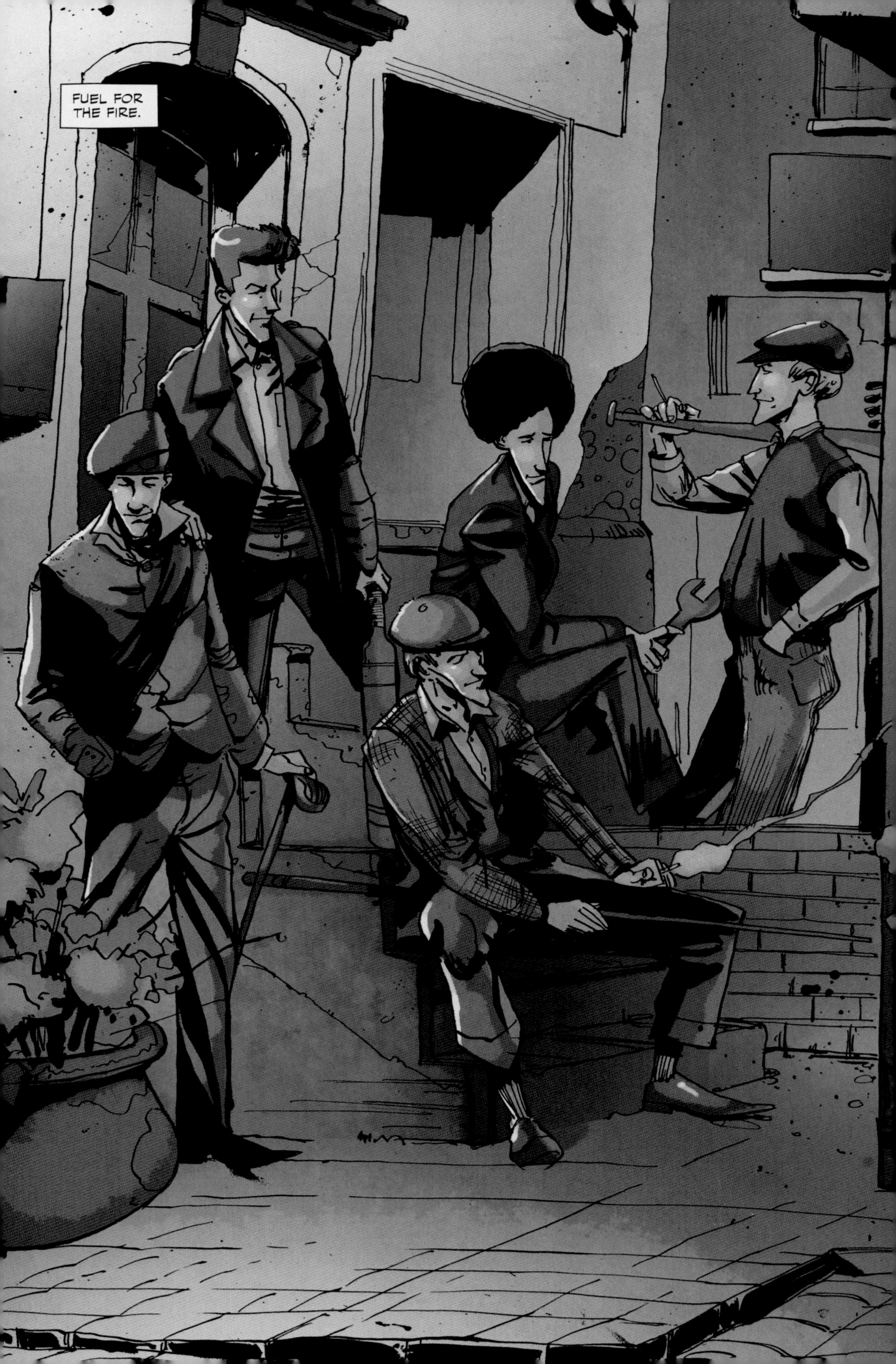
FUEL FOR THE FIRE.

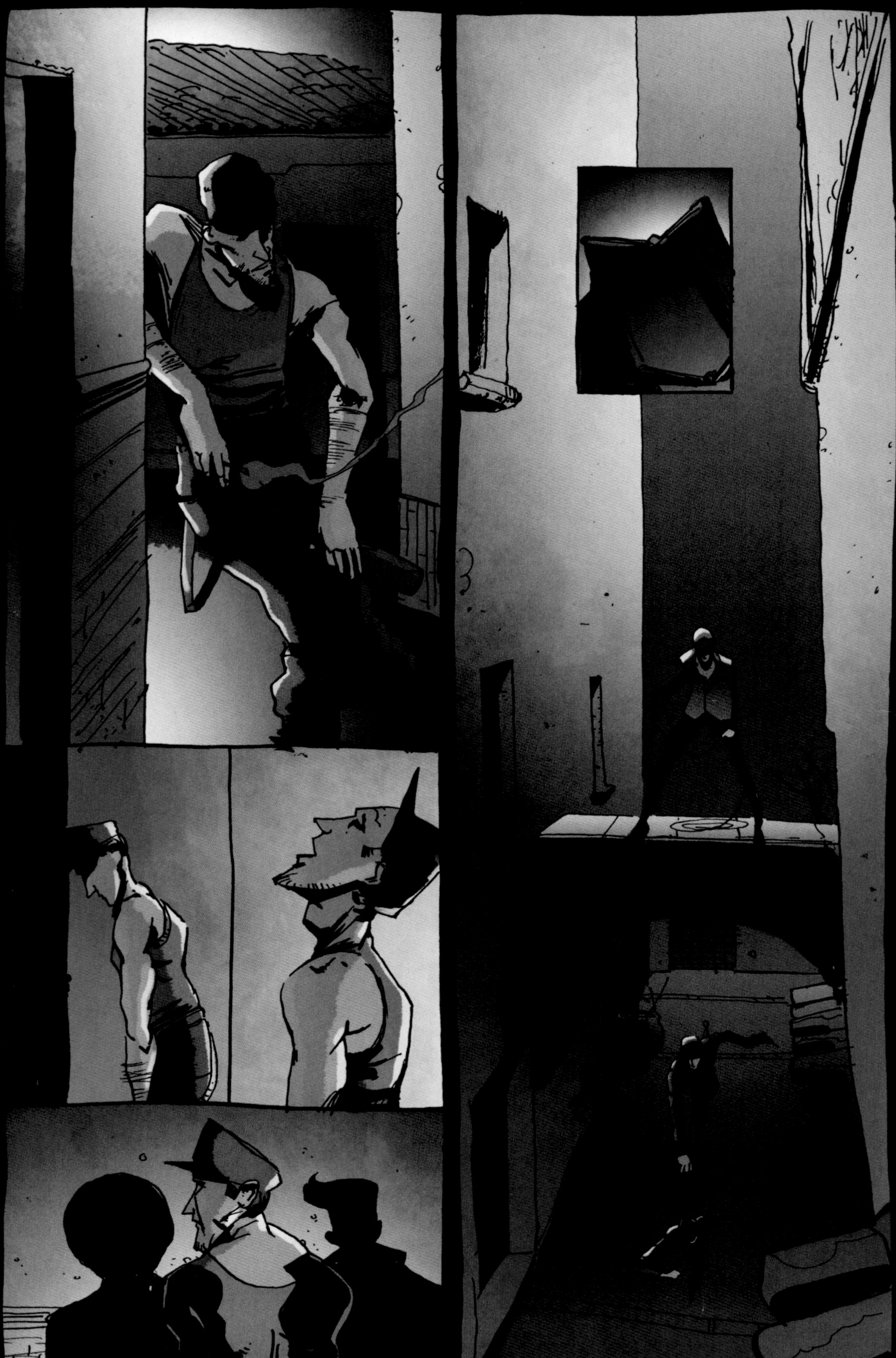

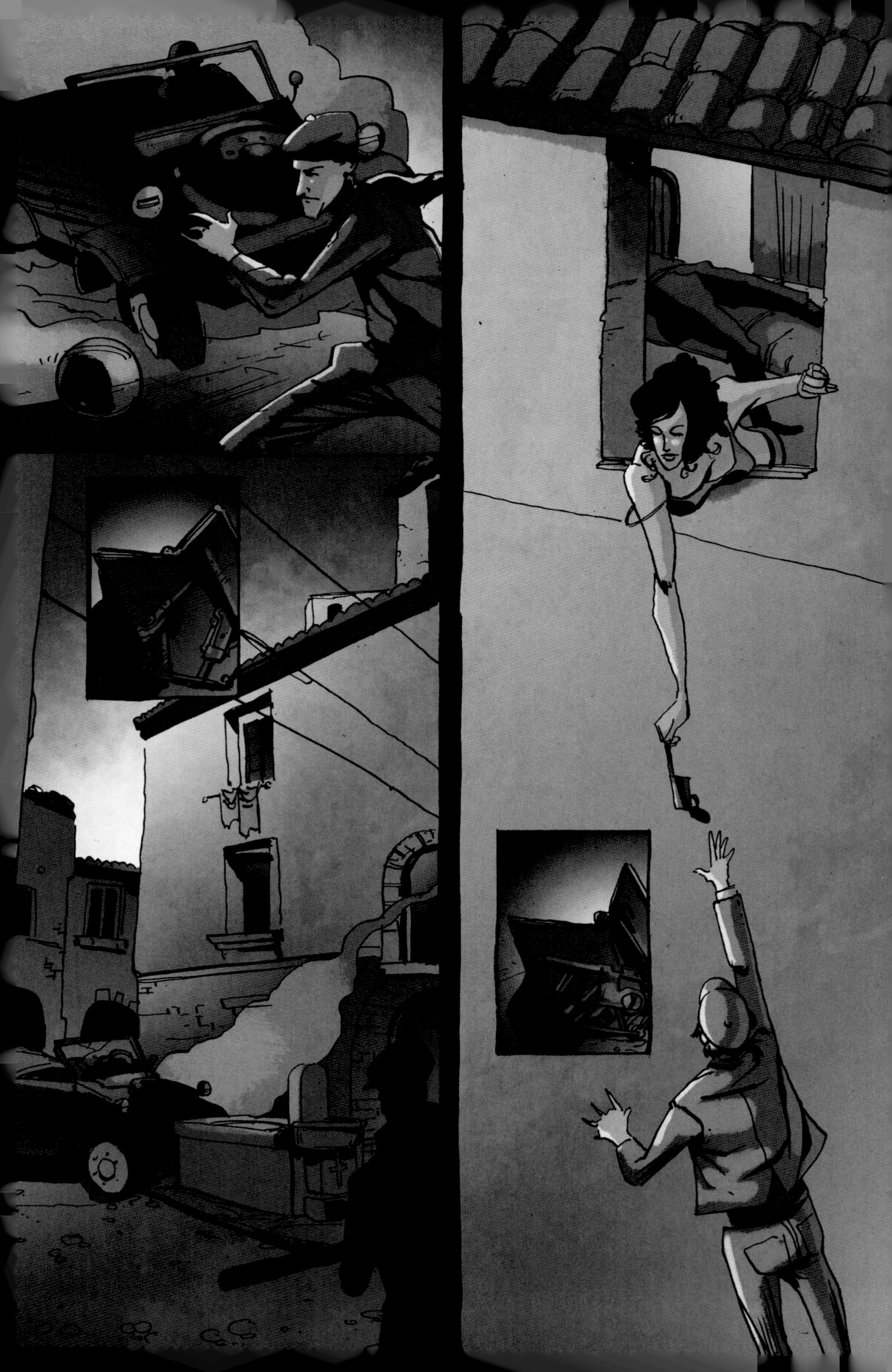

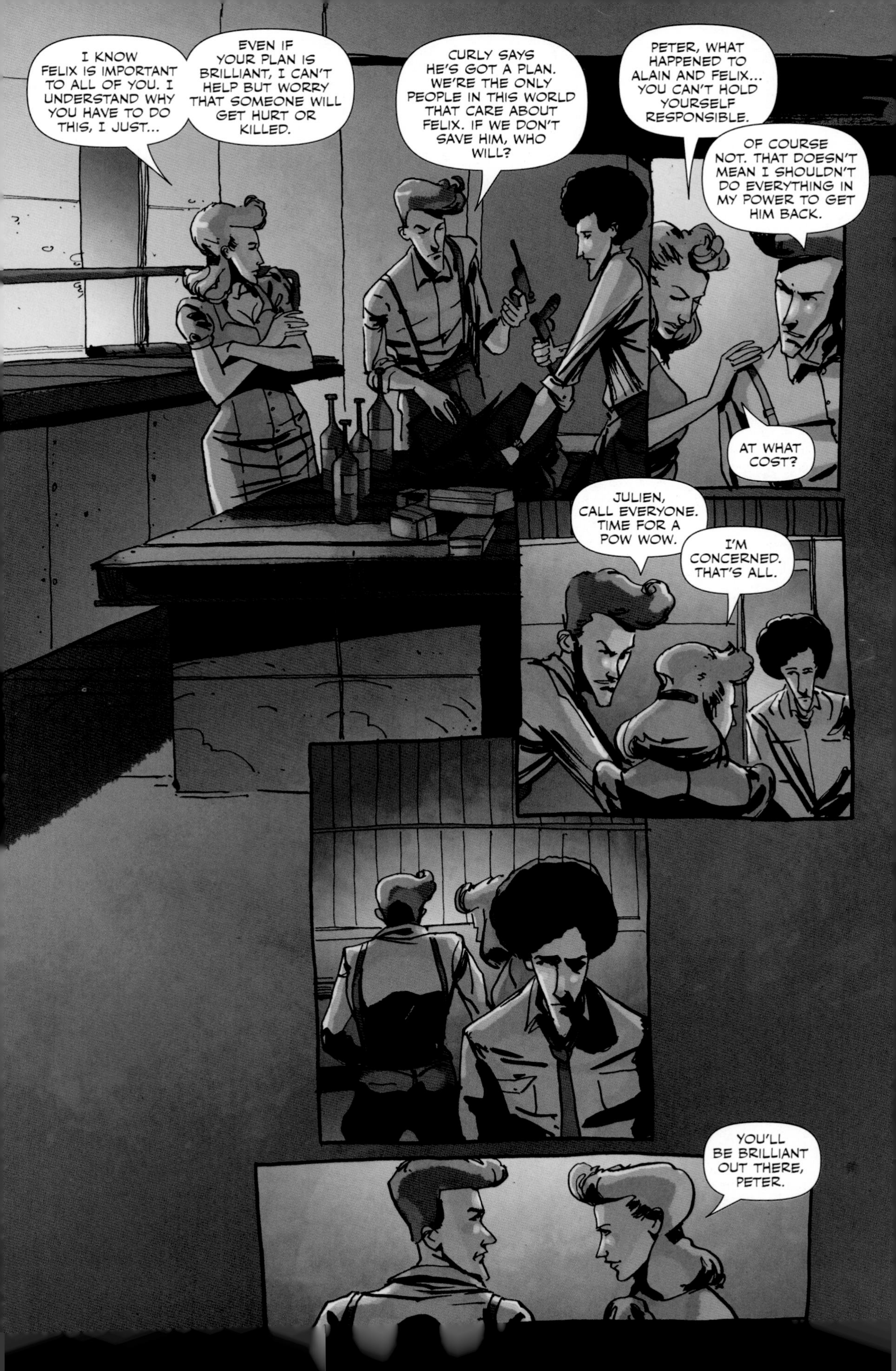
I KNOW FELIX IS IMPORTANT TO ALL OF YOU. I UNDERSTAND WHY YOU HAVE TO DO THIS, I JUST...
EVEN IF YOUR PLAN IS BRILLIANT, I CAN'T HELP BUT WORRY THAT SOMEONE WILL GET HURT OR KILLED.
CURLY SAYS HE'S GOT A PLAN. WE'RE THE ONLY PEOPLE IN THIS WORLD THAT CARE ABOUT FELIX. IF WE DON'T SAVE HIM, WHO WILL?
PETER, WHAT HAPPENED TO ALAIN AND FELIX... YOU CAN'T HOLD YOURSELF RESPONSIBLE.
OF COURSE NOT. THAT DOESN'T MEAN I SHOULDN'T DO EVERYTHING IN MY POWER TO GET HIM BACK.
AT WHAT COST?
JULIEN, CALL EVERYONE. TIME FOR A POW WOW.
I'M CONCERNED. THAT'S ALL.
YOU'LL BE BRILLIANT OUT THERE, PETER.

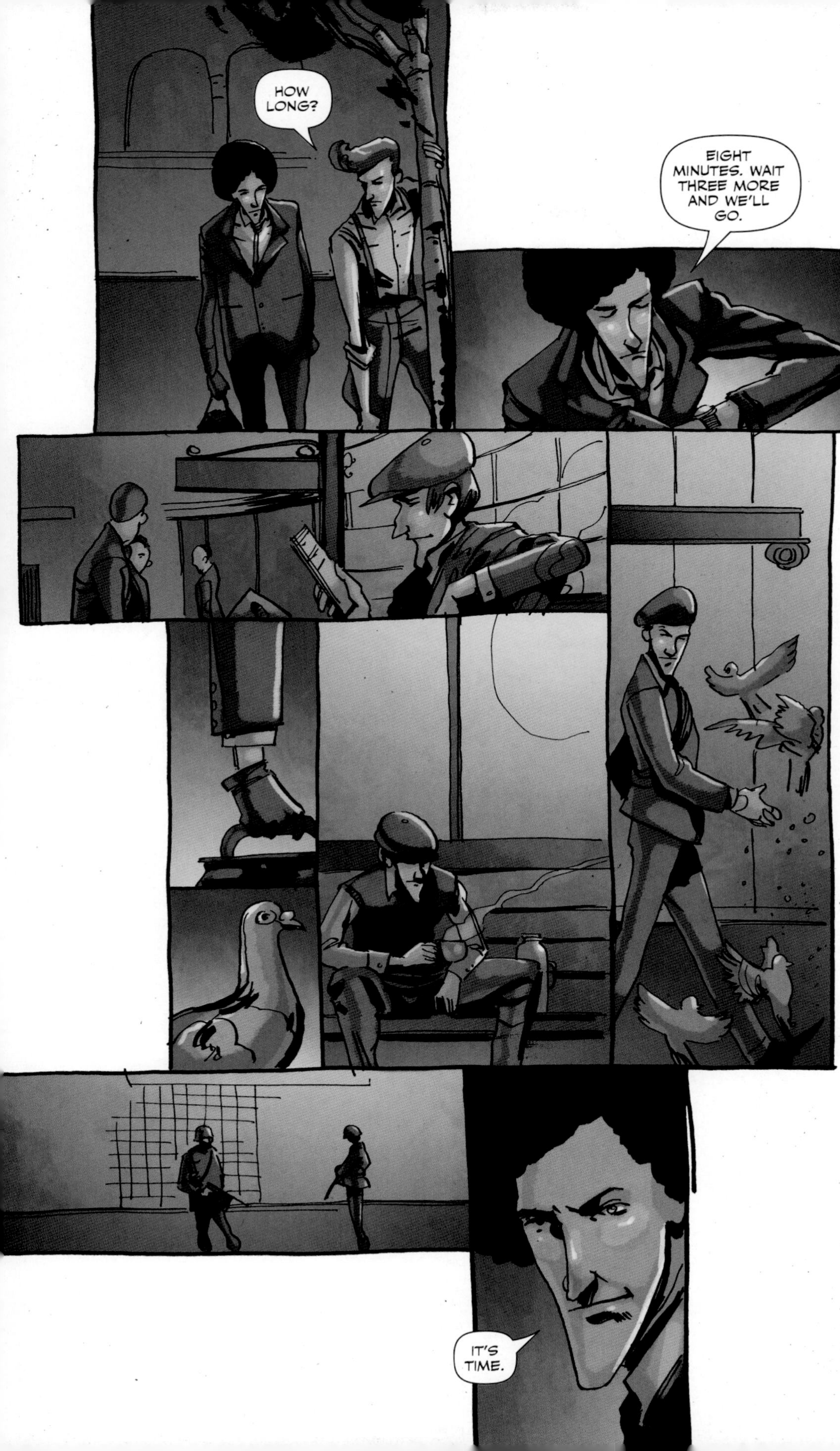
HOW LONG?
EIGHT MINUTES. WAIT THREE MORE AND WE'LL GO.
IT'S TIME.

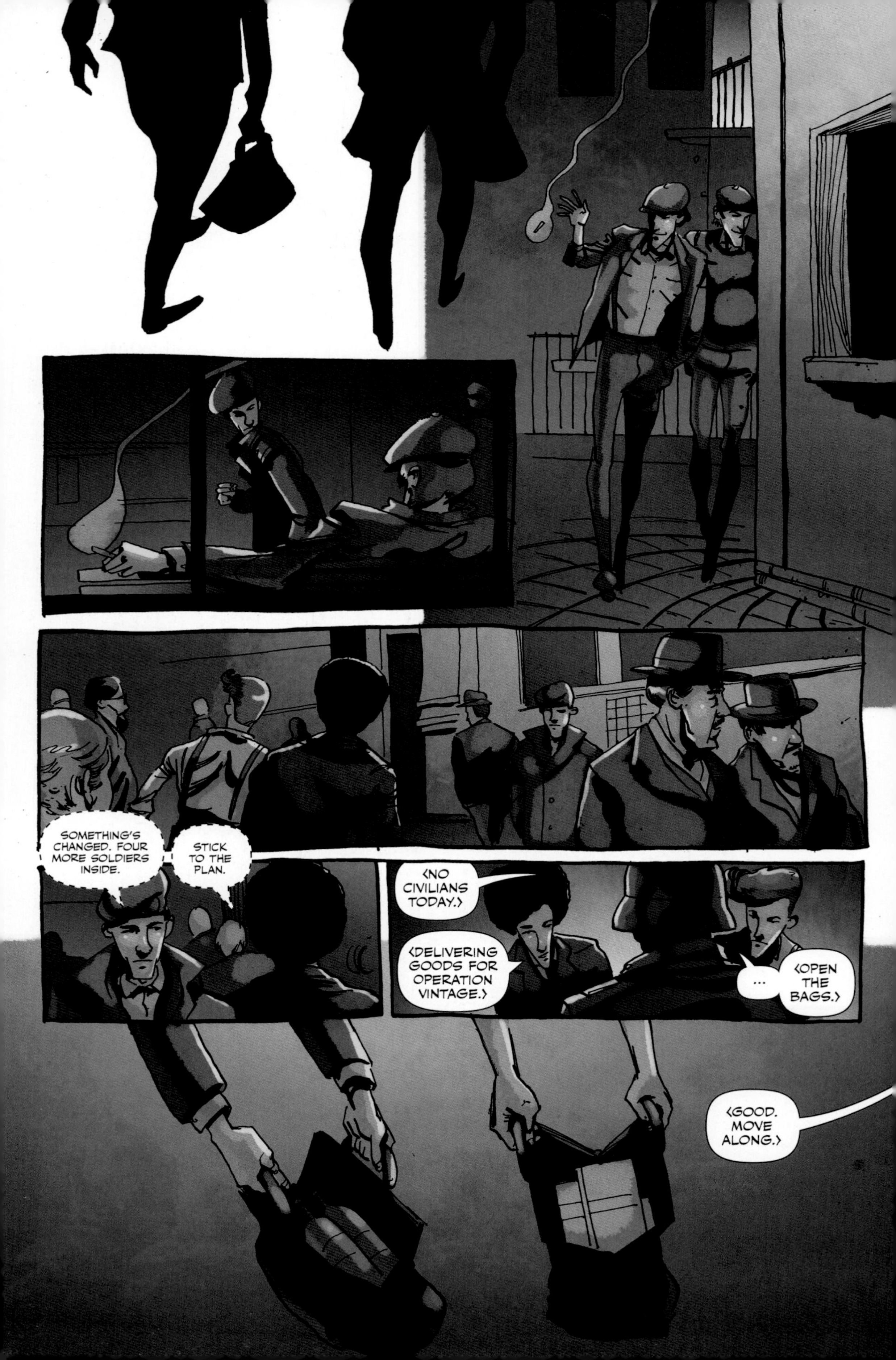
SOMETHING'S CHANGED. FOUR MORE SOLDIERS INSIDE.
STICK TO THE PLAN.
‹NO CIVILIANS TODAY.›
‹DELIVERING GOODS FOR OPERATION VINTAGE.›
...
‹OPEN THE BAGS.›
‹GOOD. MOVE ALONG.›

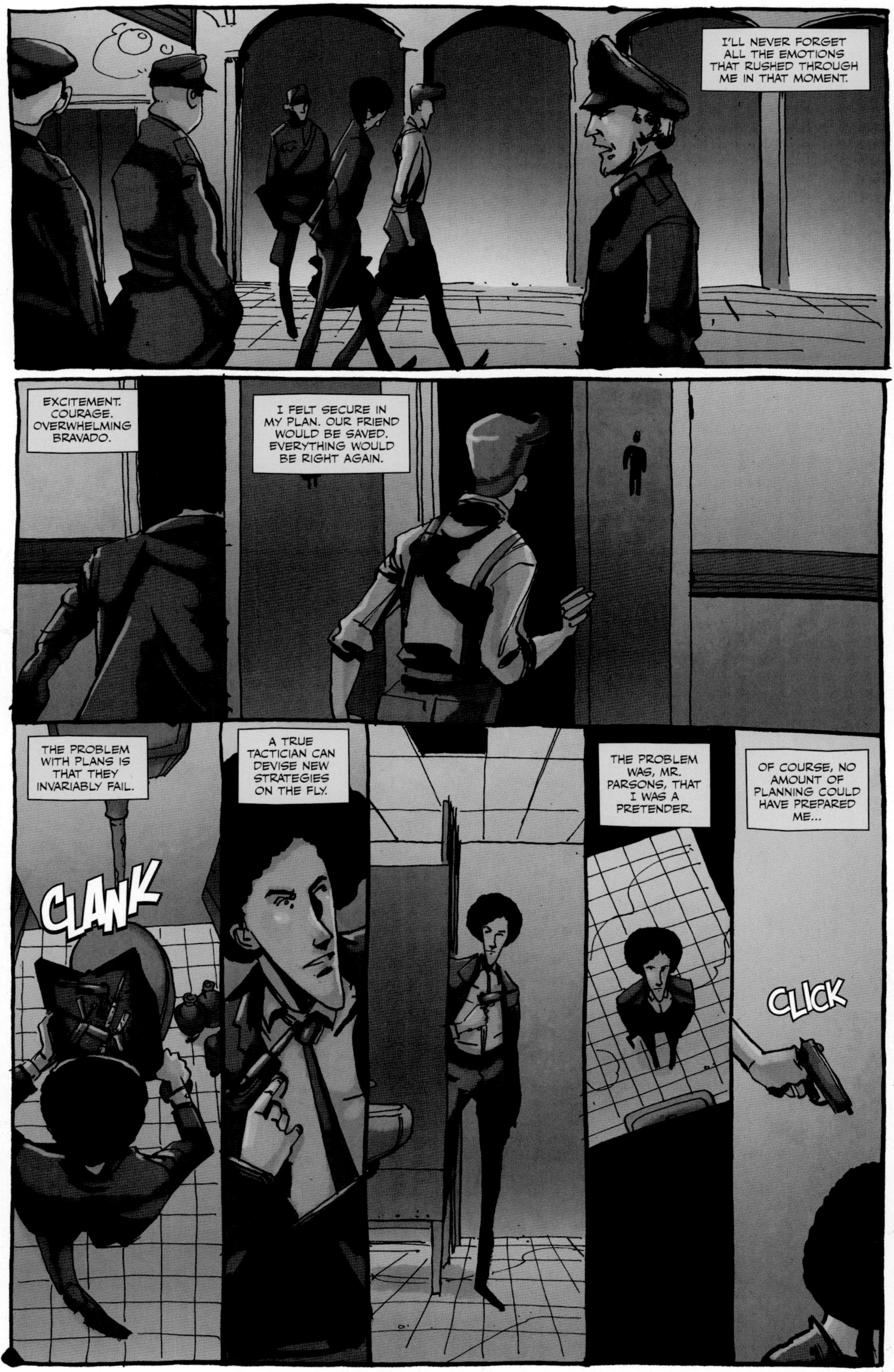
I'LL NEVER FORGET ALL THE EMOTIONS THAT RUSHED THROUGH ME IN THAT MOMENT.
EXCITEMENT. COURAGE. OVERWHELMING BRAVADO.
I FELT SECURE IN MY PLAN. OUR FRIEND WOULD BE SAVED. EVERYTHING WOULD BE RIGHT AGAIN.
THE PROBLEM WITH PLANS IS THAT THEY INVARIABLY FAIL.
CLANK
A TRUE TACTICIAN CAN DEVISE NEW STRATEGIES ON THE FLY.
THE PROBLEM WAS, MR. PARSONS, THAT I WAS A PRETENDER.
OF COURSE, NO AMOUNT OF PLANNING COULD HAVE PREPARED ME...
CLICK

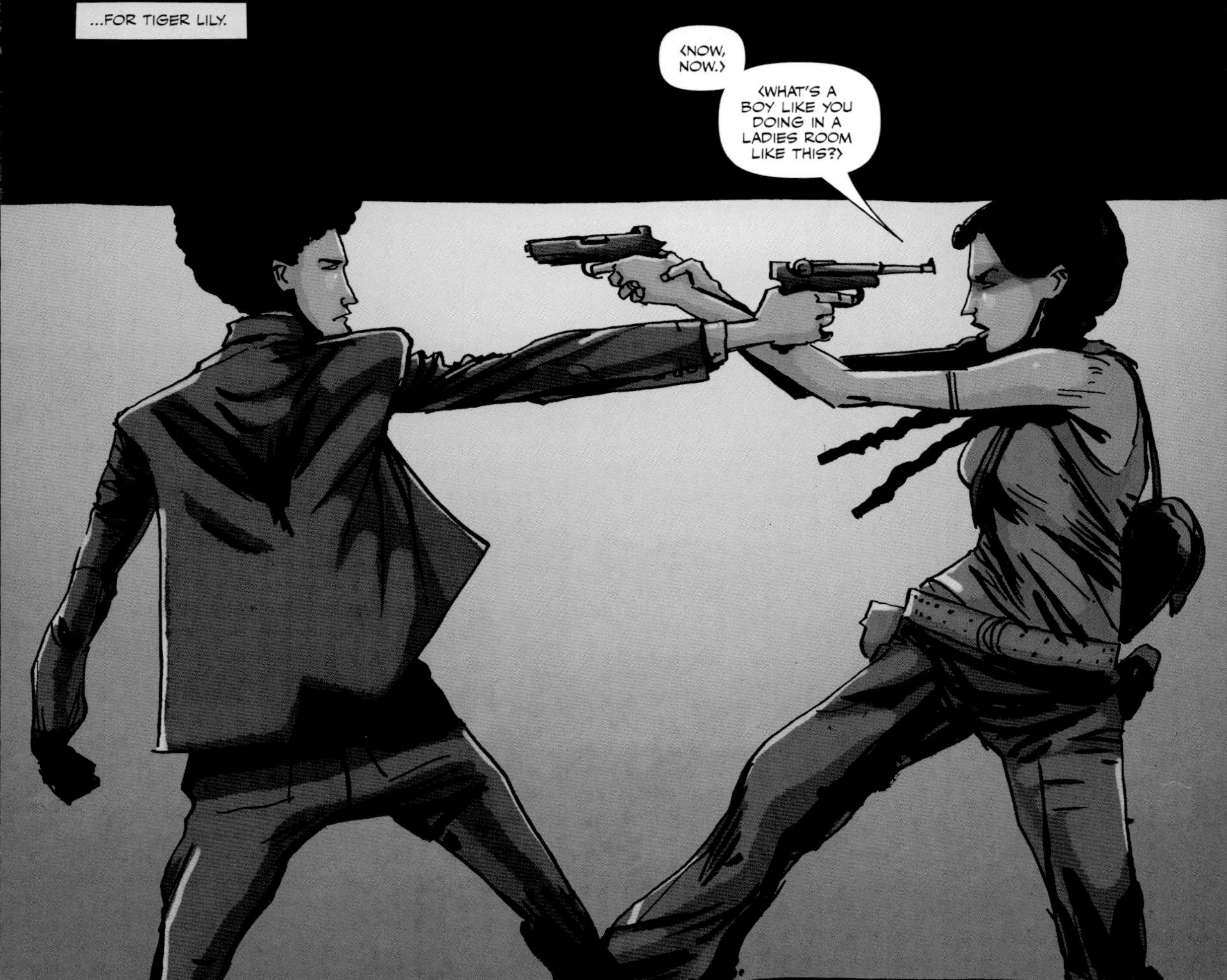
...FOR TIGER LILY.
<NOW, NOW.>
<WHAT'S A BOY LIKE YOU DOING IN A LADIES ROOM LIKE THIS?>

CHAPTER SEVEN

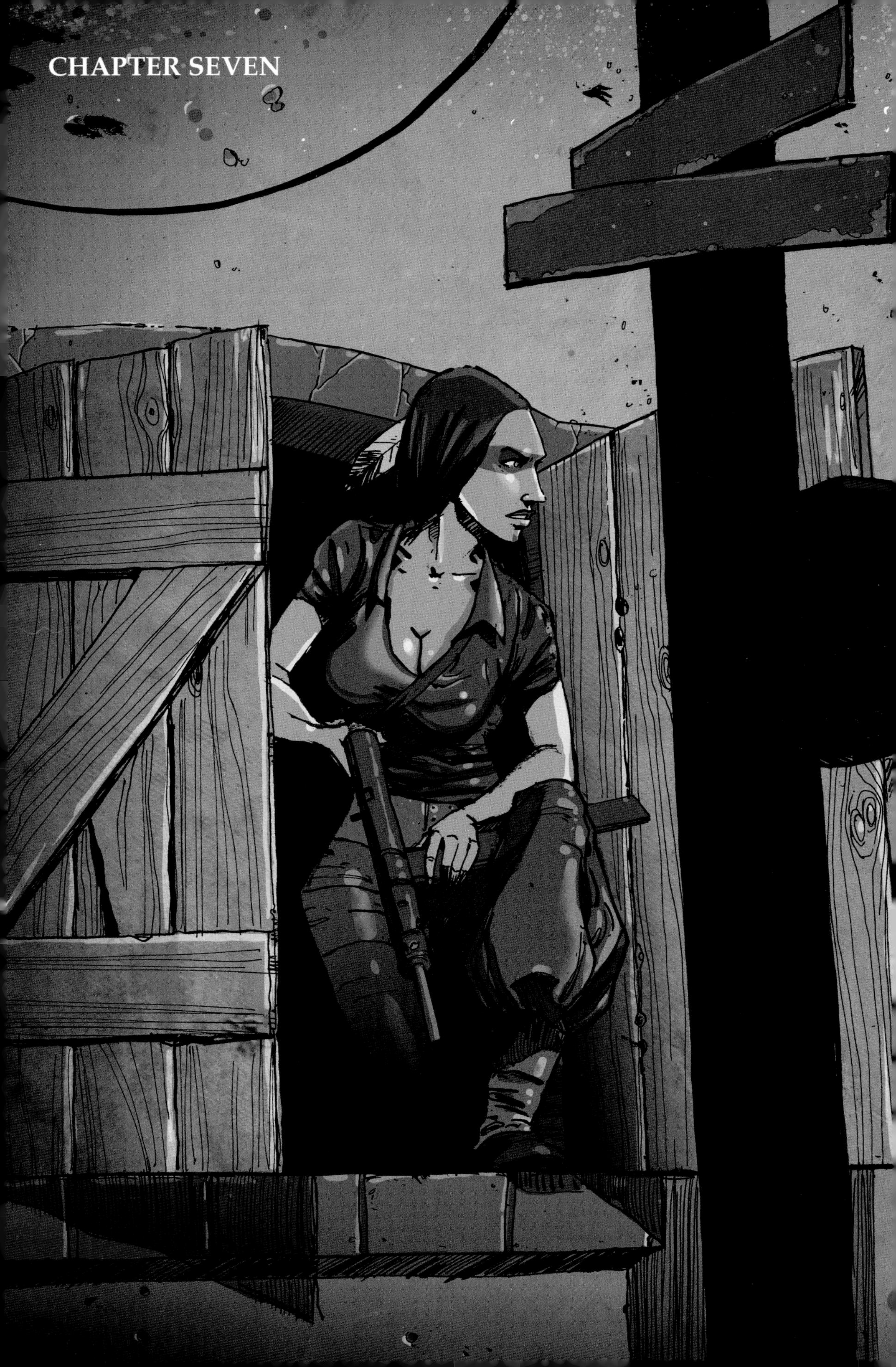

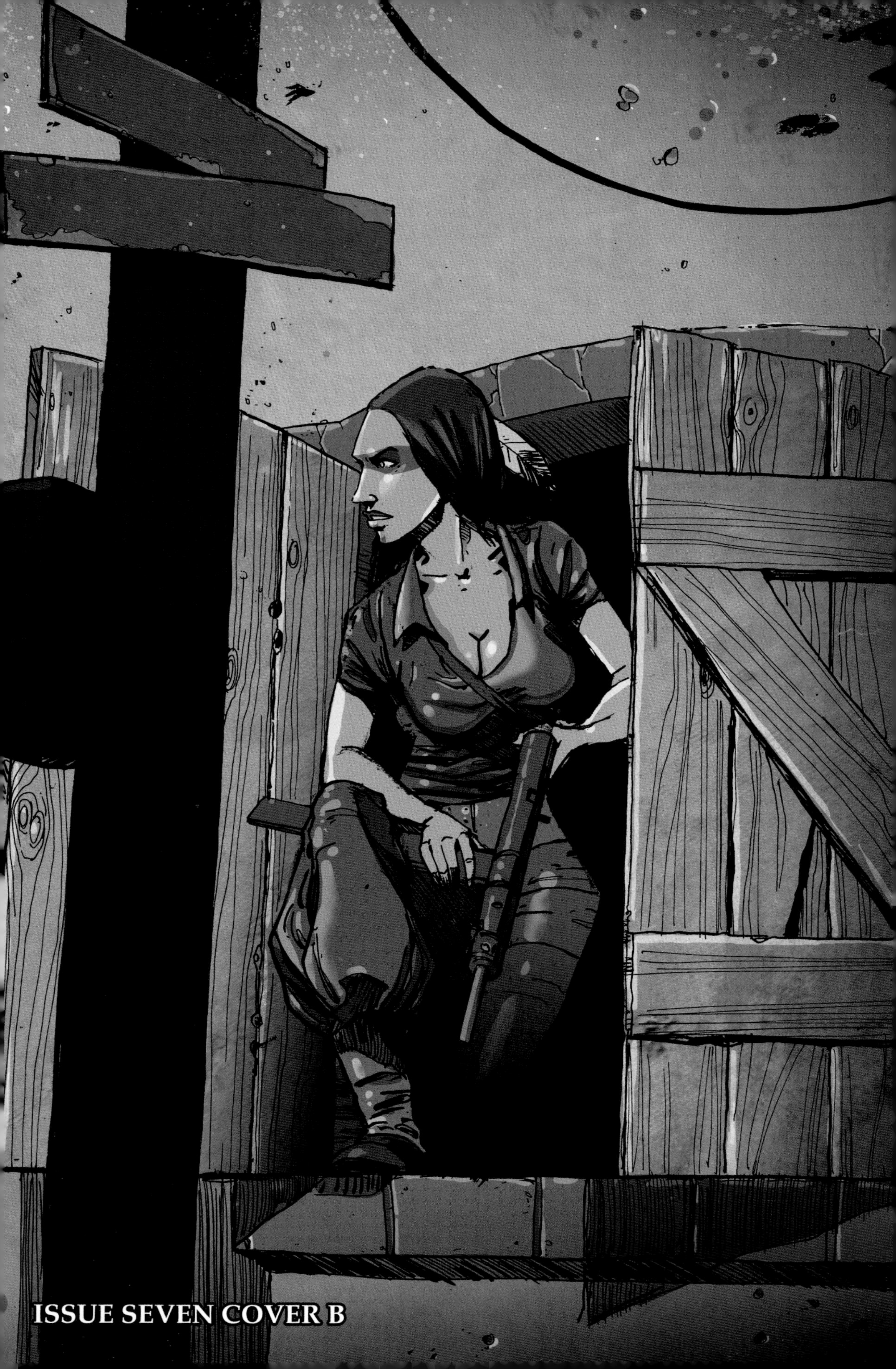

ISSUE SEVEN COVER B

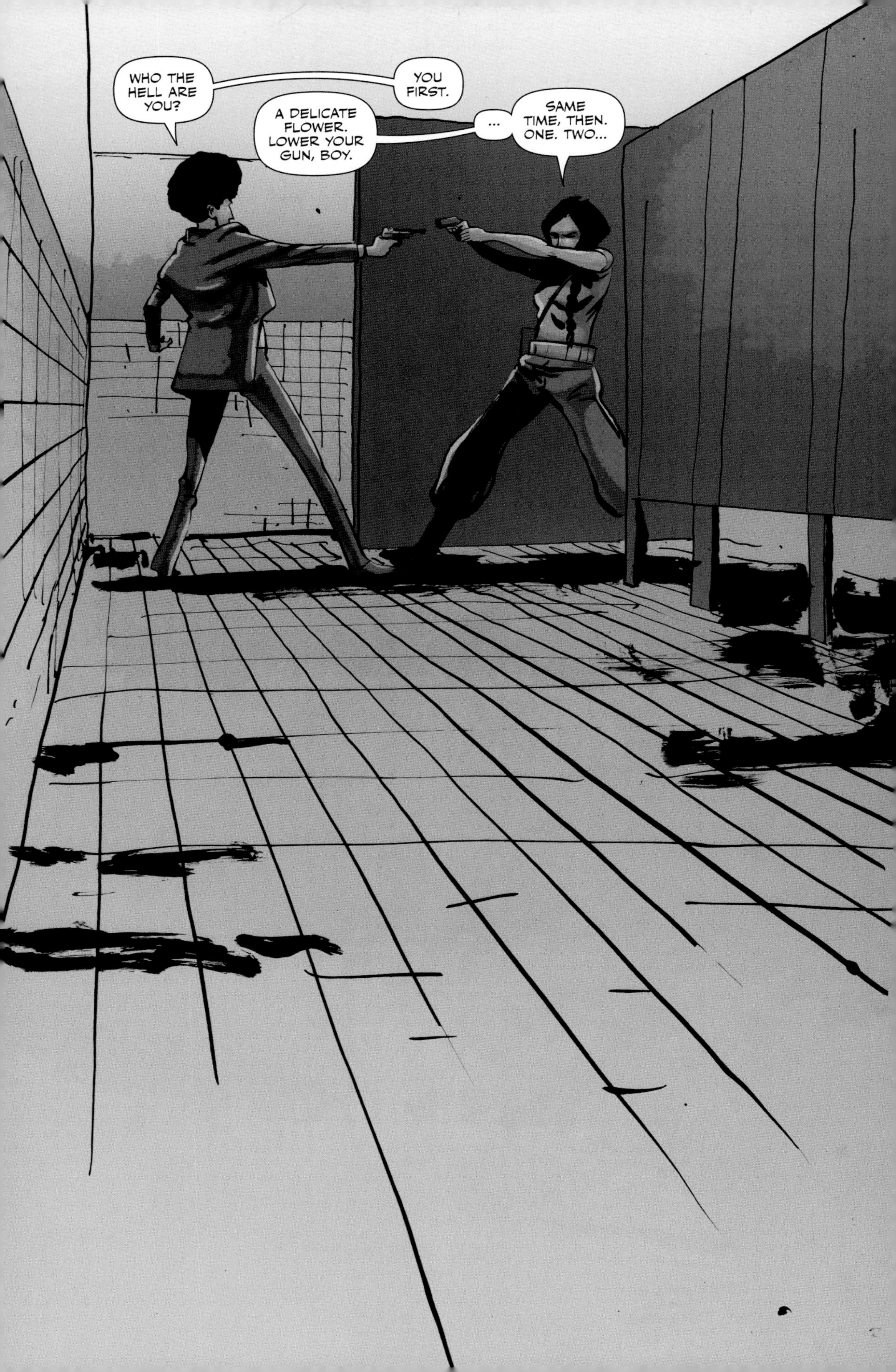
WHO THE HELL ARE YOU?
YOU FIRST.
A DELICATE FLOWER. LOWER YOUR GUN, BOY.
...
SAME TIME, THEN. ONE. TWO...

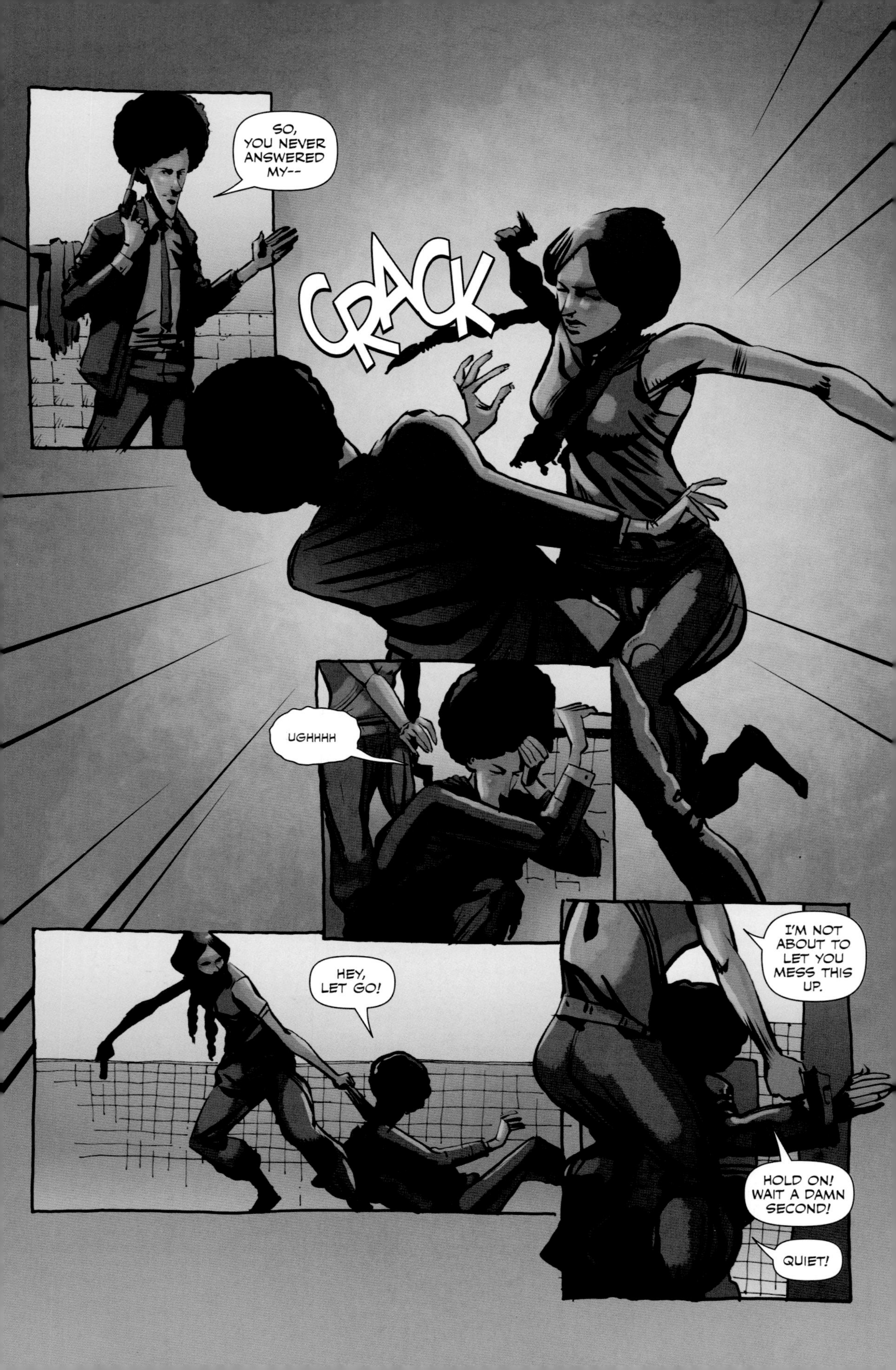
SO, YOU NEVER ANSWERED MY--
CRACK
UGHHHH
HEY, LET GO!
I'M NOT ABOUT TO LET YOU MESS THIS UP.
HOLD ON! WAIT A DAMN SECOND!
QUIET!

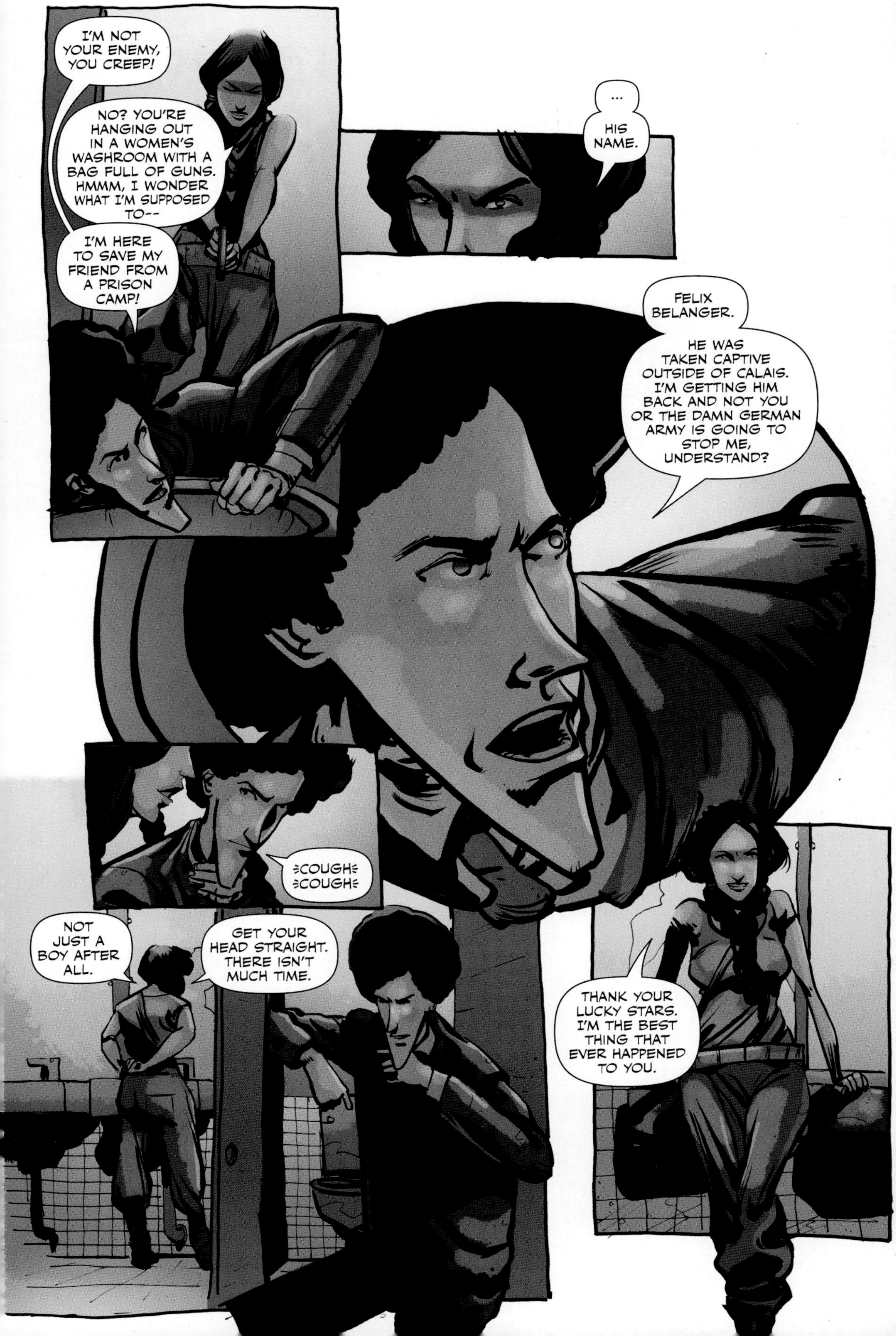
I'M NOT YOUR ENEMY, YOU CREEP!
NO? YOU'RE HANGING OUT IN A WOMEN'S WASHROOM WITH A BAG FULL OF GUNS. HMMM, I WONDER WHAT I'M SUPPOSED TO--
I'M HERE TO SAVE MY FRIEND FROM A PRISON CAMP!
...
HIS NAME.
FELIX BELANGER.
HE WAS TAKEN CAPTIVE OUTSIDE OF CALAIS. I'M GETTING HIM BACK AND NOT YOU OR THE DAMN GERMAN ARMY IS GOING TO STOP ME, UNDERSTAND?
COUGH COUGH
NOT JUST A BOY AFTER ALL.
GET YOUR HEAD STRAIGHT. THERE ISN'T MUCH TIME.
THANK YOUR LUCKY STARS. I'M THE BEST THING THAT EVER HAPPENED TO YOU.

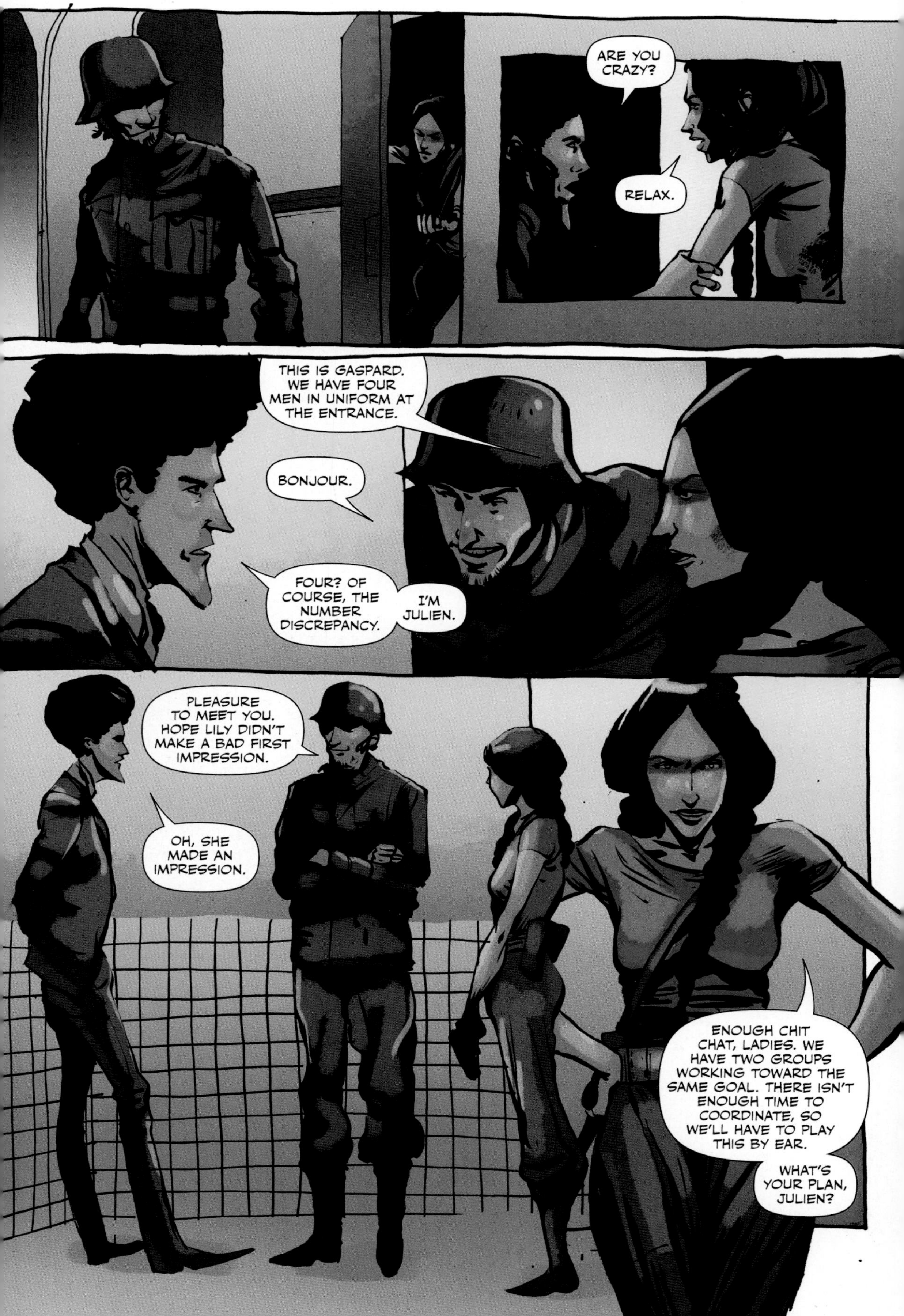
ARE YOU CRAZY?
RELAX.
THIS IS GASPARD. WE HAVE FOUR MEN IN UNIFORM AT THE ENTRANCE.
BONJOUR.
FOUR? OF COURSE, THE NUMBER DISCREPANCY.
I'M JULIEN.
PLEASURE TO MEET YOU. HOPE LILY DIDN'T MAKE A BAD FIRST IMPRESSION.
OH, SHE MADE AN IMPRESSION.
ENOUGH CHIT CHAT, LADIES. WE HAVE TWO GROUPS WORKING TOWARD THE SAME GOAL. THERE ISN'T ENOUGH TIME TO COORDINATE, SO WE'LL HAVE TO PLAY THIS BY EAR.
WHAT'S YOUR PLAN, JULIEN?

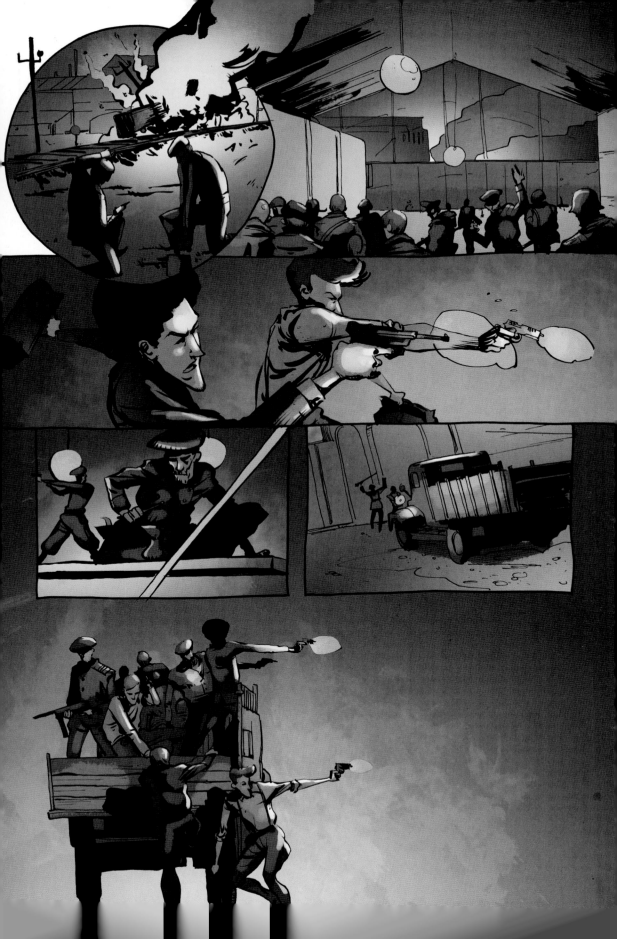

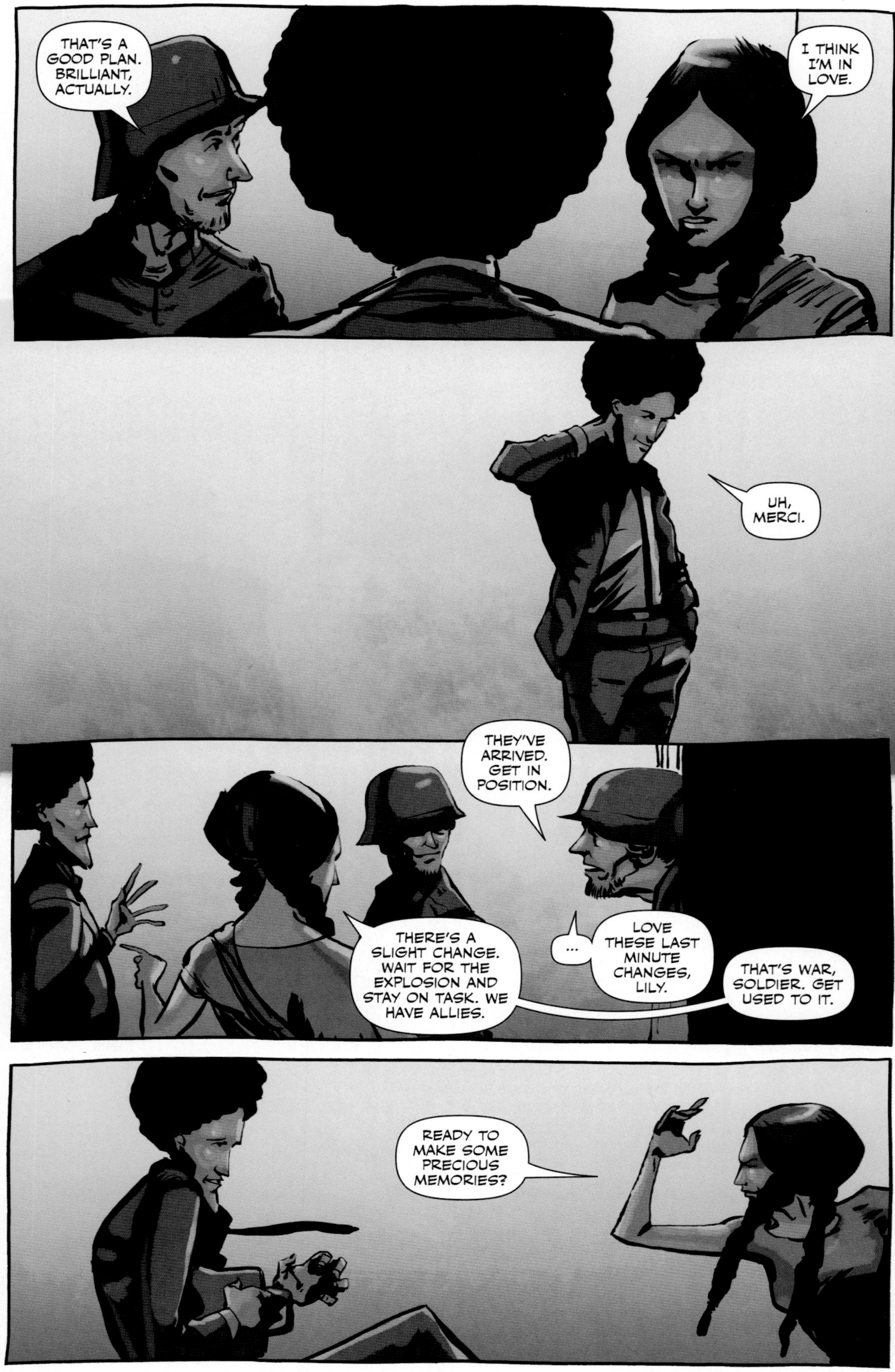
THAT'S A GOOD PLAN. BRILLIANT, ACTUALLY.
I THINK I'M IN LOVE.
UH, MERCI.
THEY'VE ARRIVED. GET IN POSITION.
THERE'S A SLIGHT CHANGE. WAIT FOR THE EXPLOSION AND STAY ON TASK. WE HAVE ALLIES.
...
LOVE THESE LAST MINUTE CHANGES, LILY.
THAT'S WAR, SOLDIER. GET USED TO IT.
READY TO MAKE SOME PRECIOUS MEMORIES?

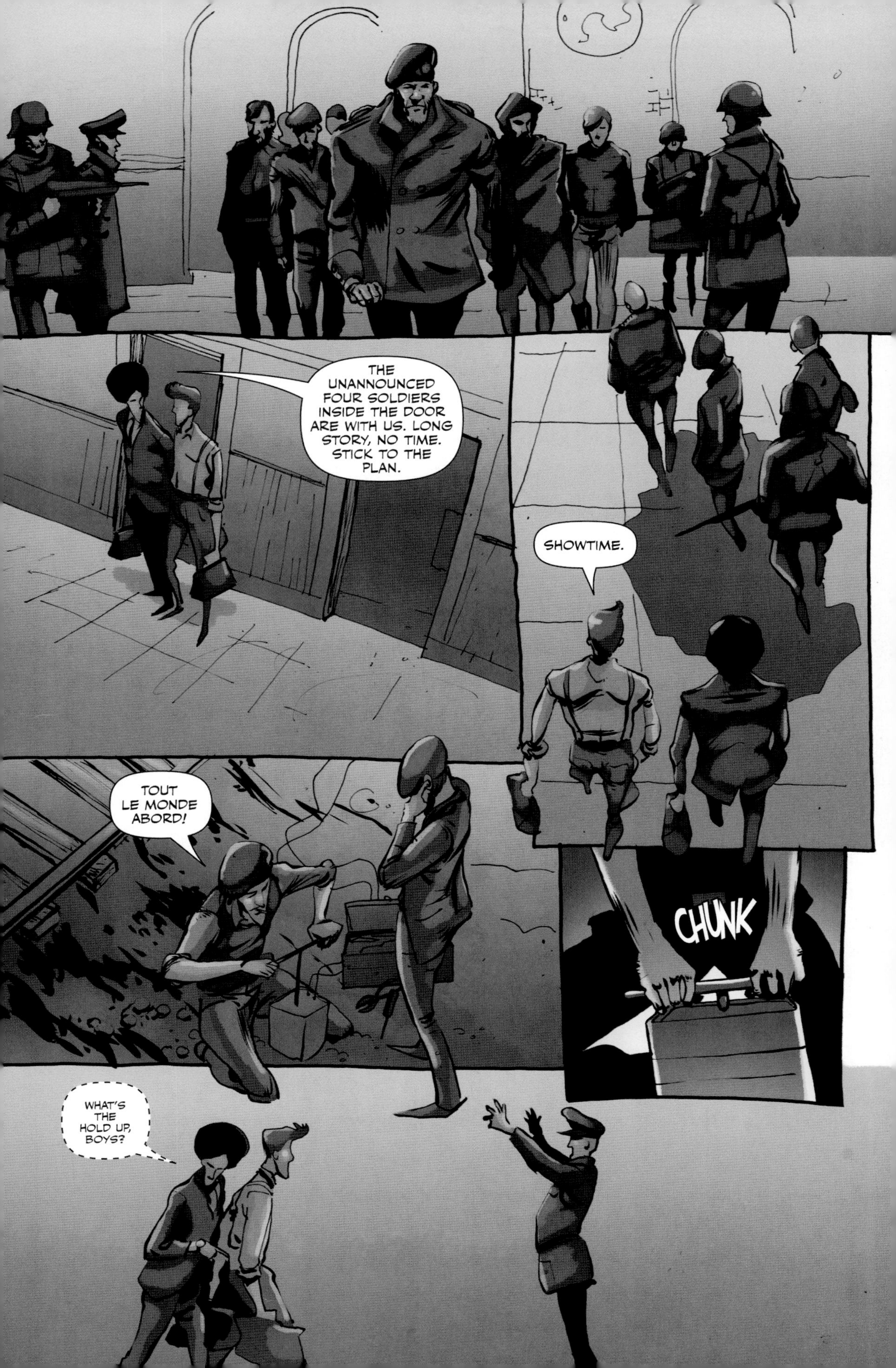
THE UNANNOUNCED FOUR SOLDIERS INSIDE THE DOOR ARE WITH US. LONG STORY, NO TIME. STICK TO THE PLAN.
SHOWTIME.
TOUT LE MONDE ABORD!
CHUNK
WHAT'S THE HOLD UP, BOYS?

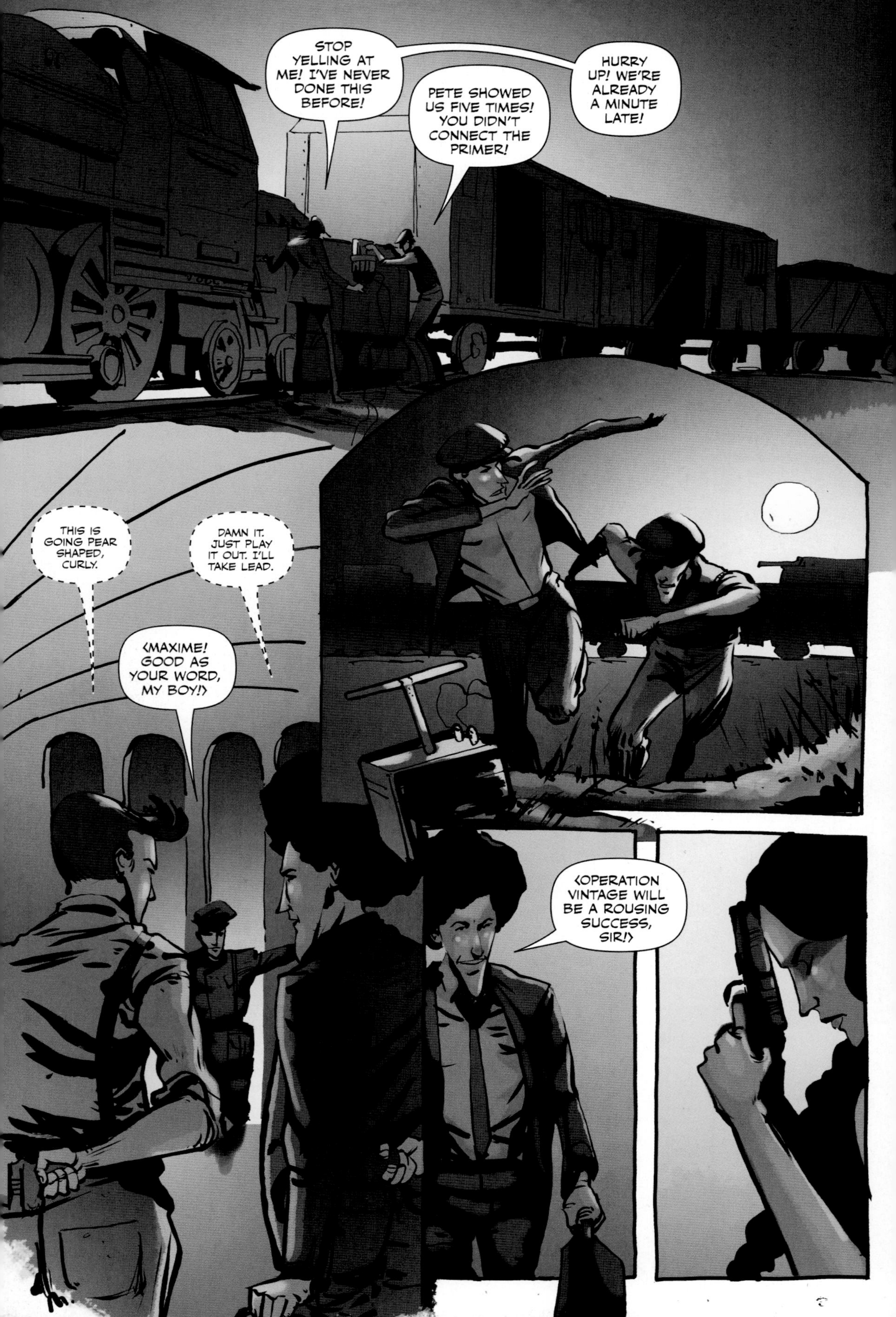
STOP YELLING AT ME! I'VE NEVER DONE THIS BEFORE!
PETE SHOWED US FIVE TIMES! YOU DIDN'T CONNECT THE PRIMER!
HURRY UP! WE'RE ALREADY A MINUTE LATE!
THIS IS GOING PEAR SHAPED, CURLY.
DAMN IT. JUST PLAY IT OUT. I'LL TAKE LEAD.
‹MAXIME! GOOD AS YOUR WORD, MY BOY!›
‹OPERATION VINTAGE WILL BE A ROUSING SUCCESS, SIR!›

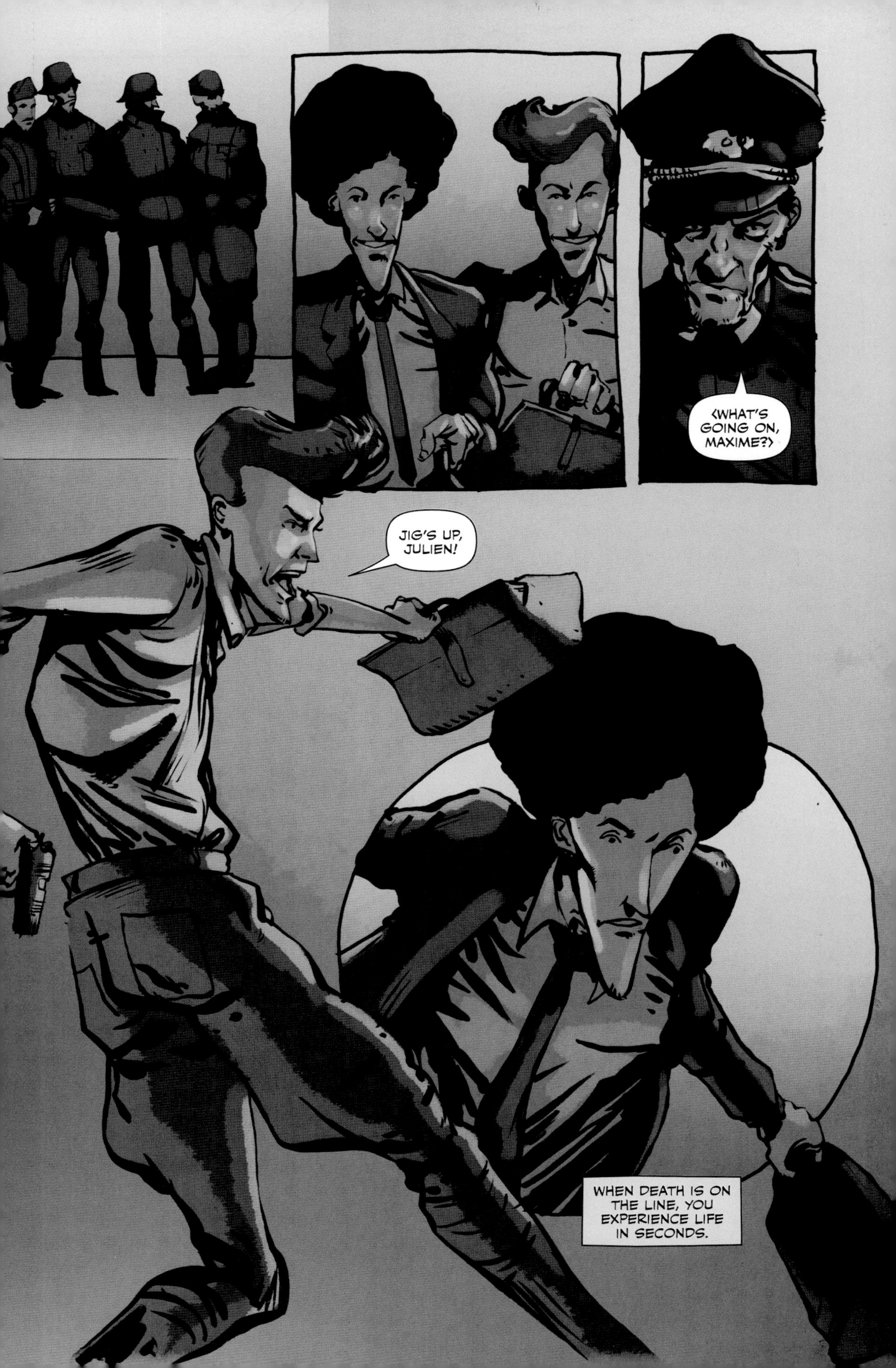
<WHAT'S GOING ON, MAXIME?>
JIG'S UP, JULIEN!
WHEN DEATH IS ON THE LINE, YOU EXPERIENCE LIFE IN SECONDS.

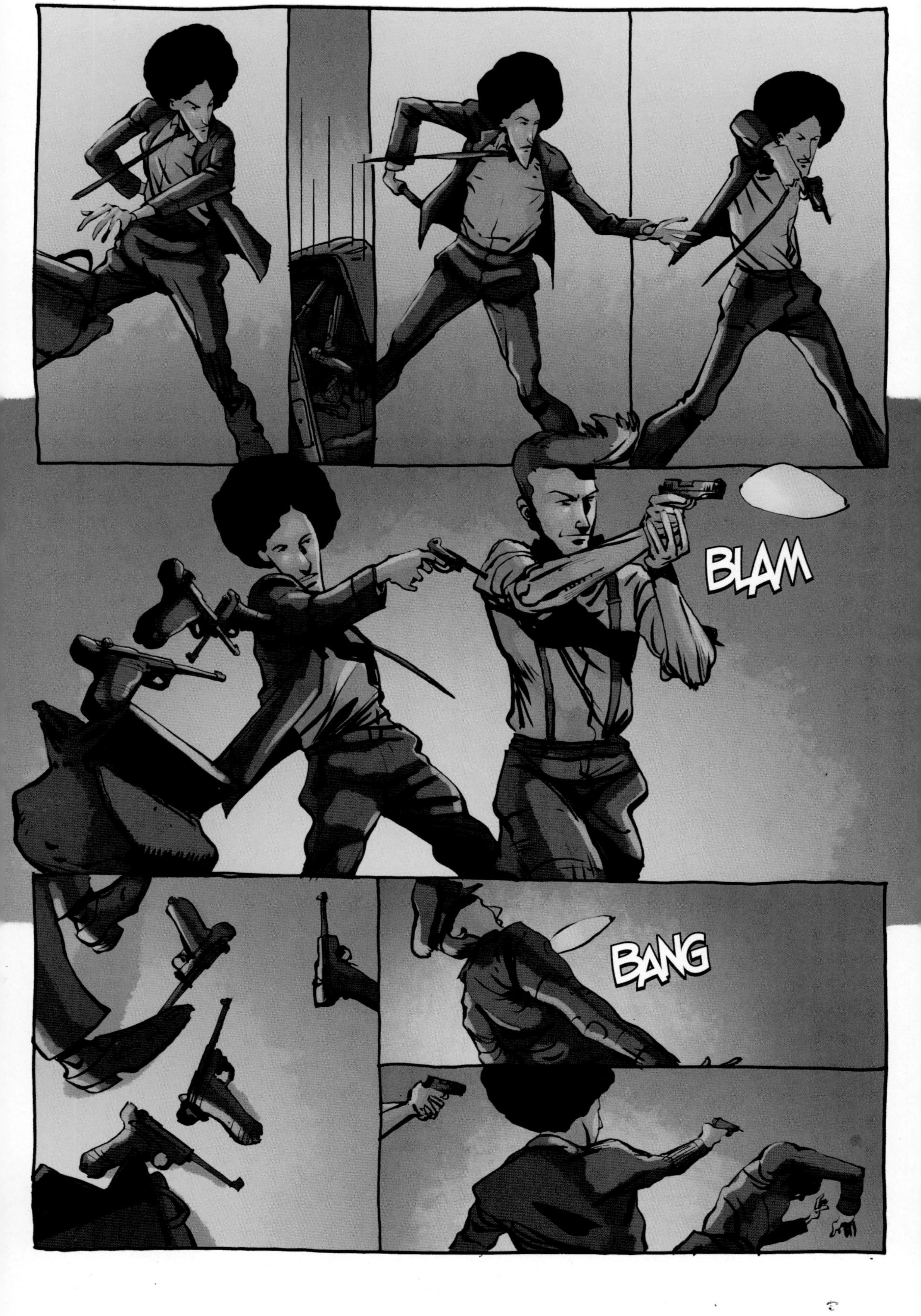
BLAM
BANG

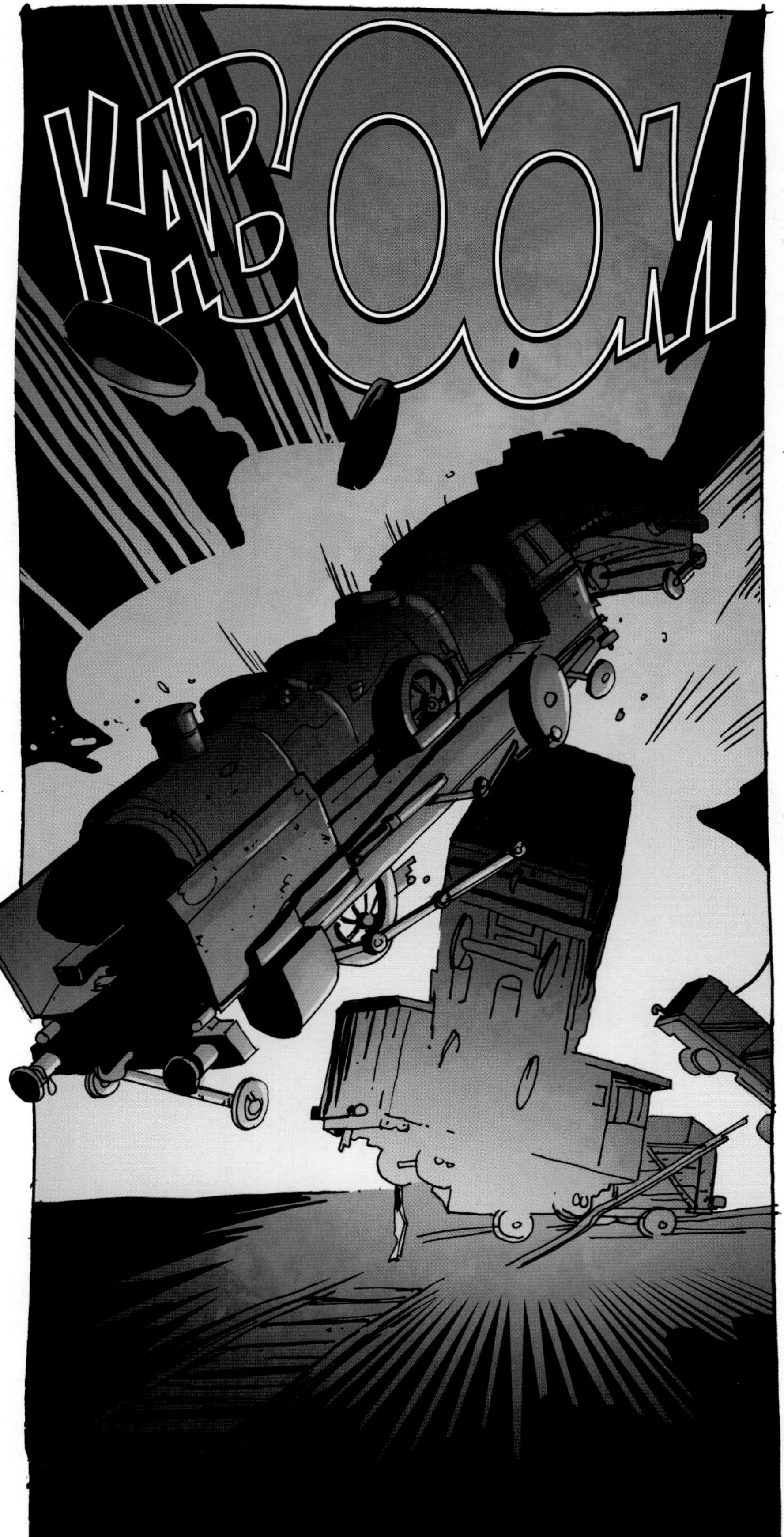
KABOOM

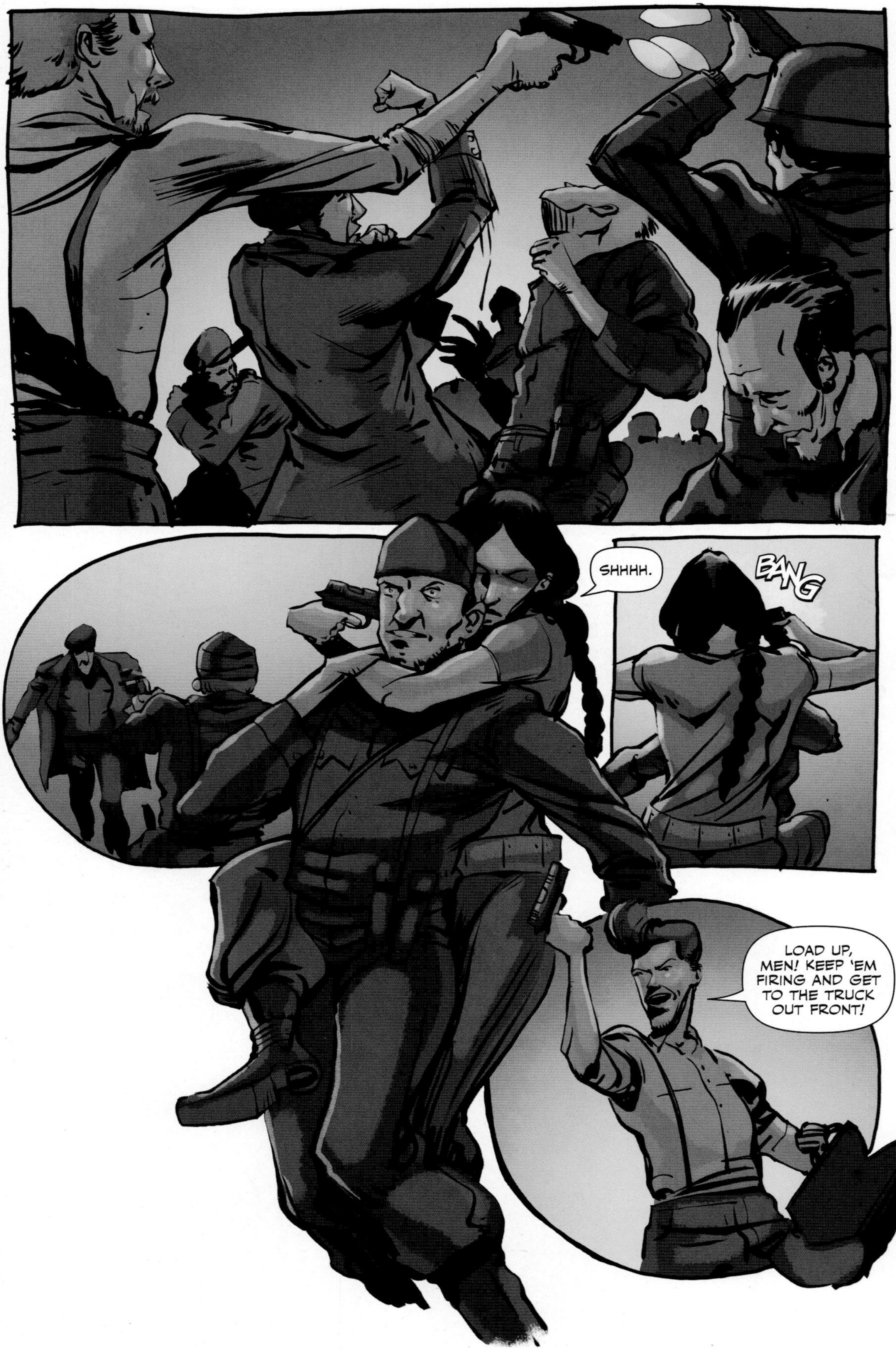
SHHHH.
BANG
LOAD UP, MEN! KEEP 'EM FIRING AND GET TO THE TRUCK OUT FRONT!

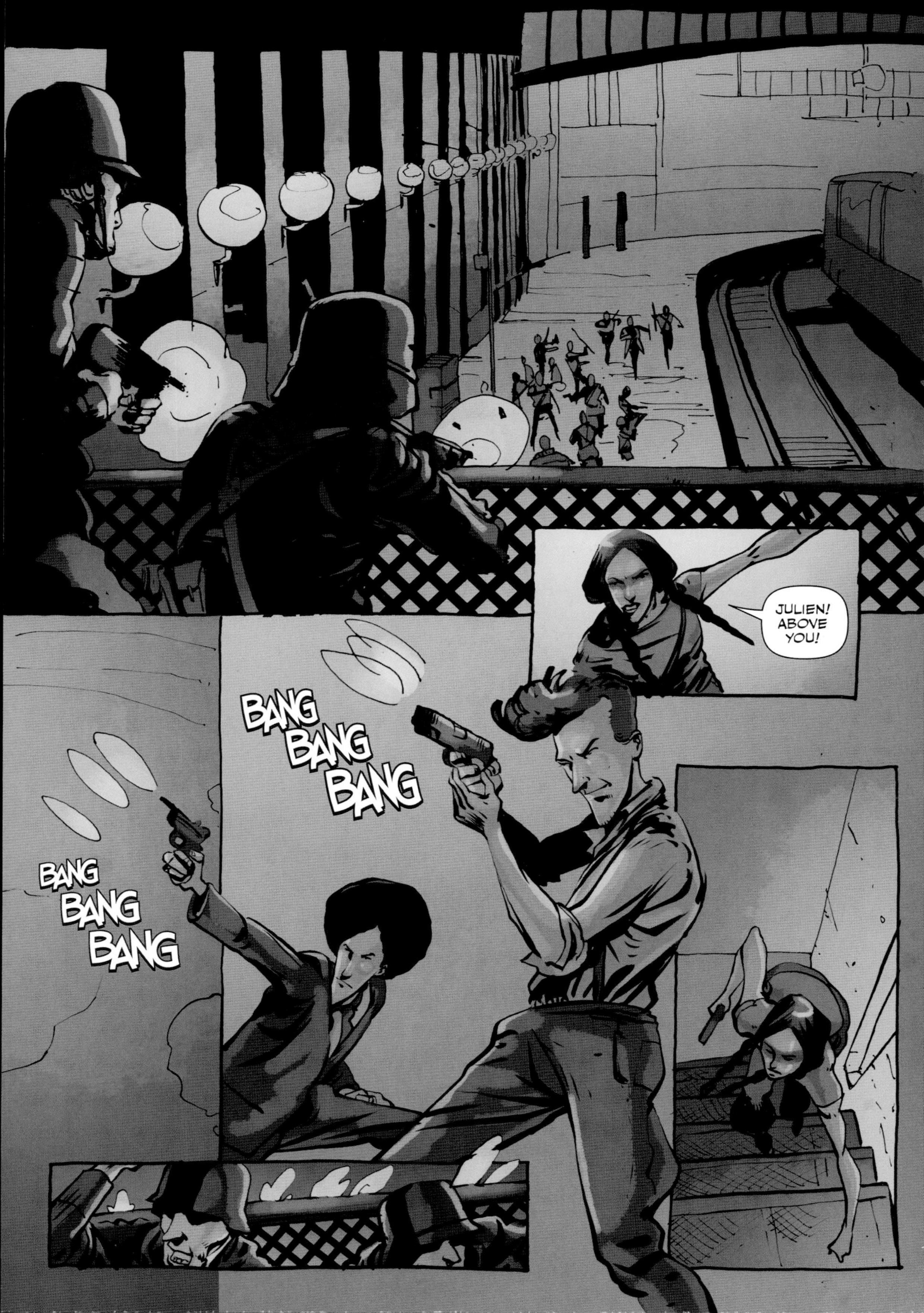
JULIEN! ABOVE YOU!
BANG BANG BANG
BANG BANG BANG

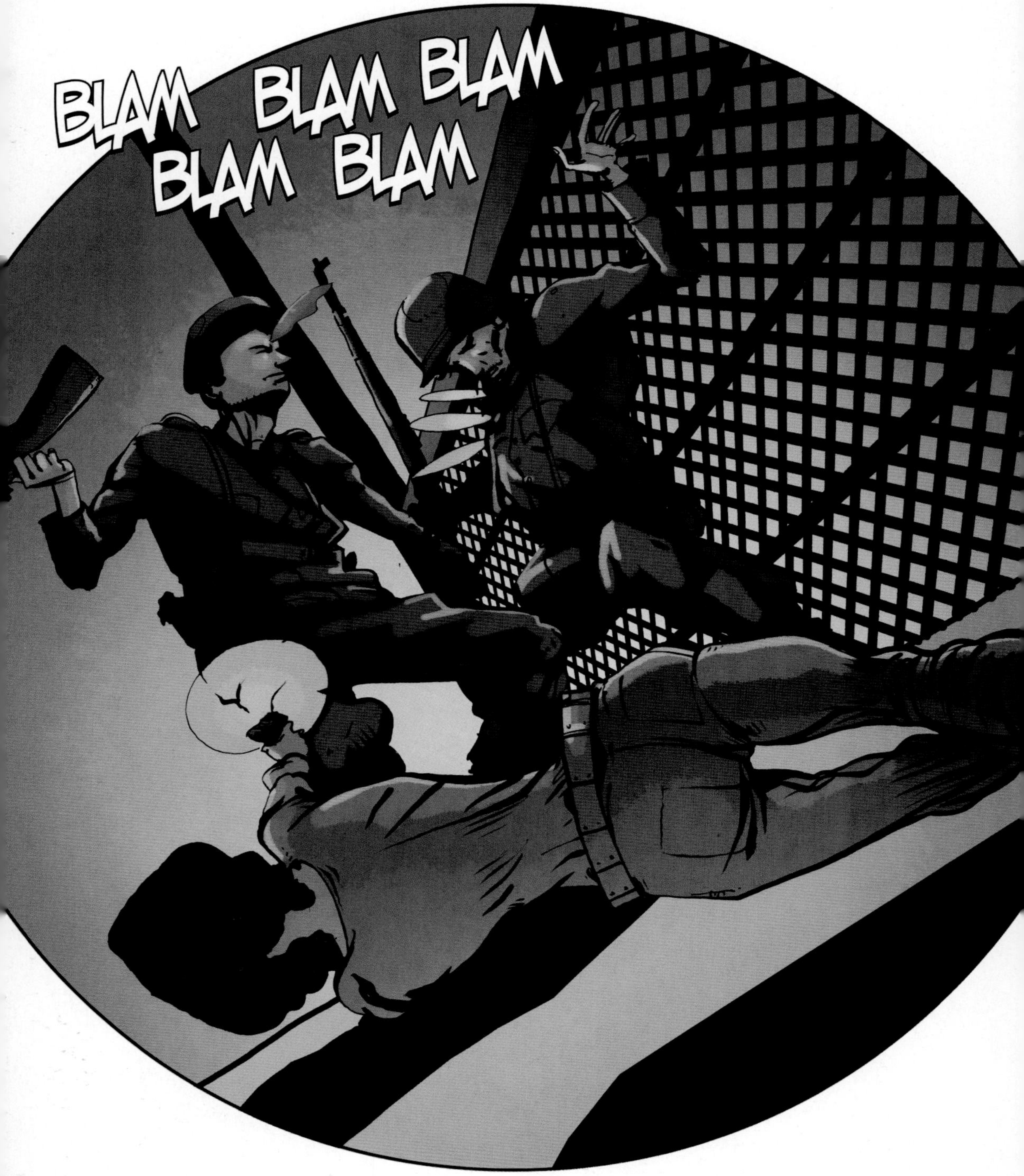
BLAM BLAM BLAM
BLAM BLAM

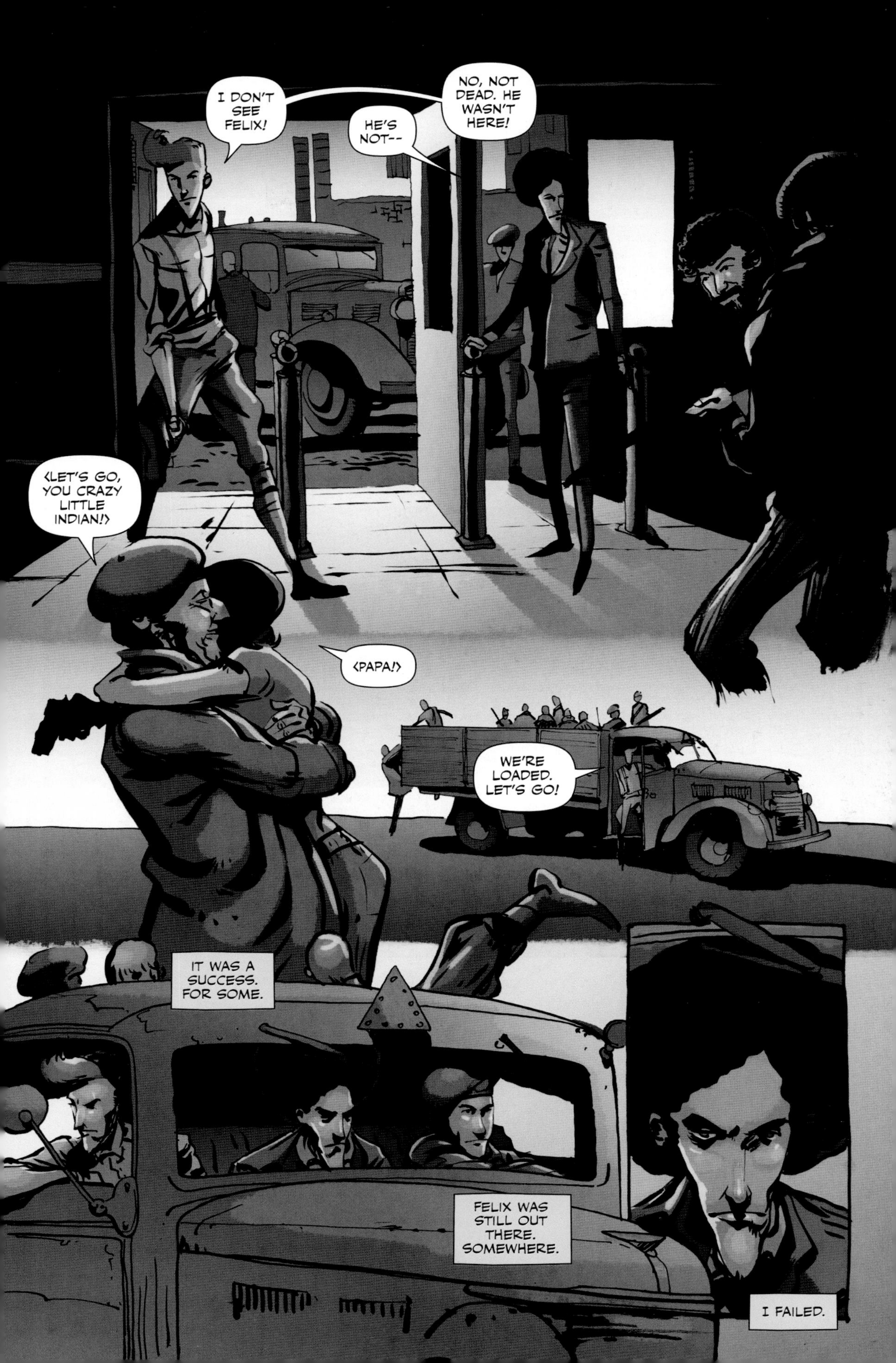
I DON'T SEE FELIX!
HE'S NOT--
NO, NOT DEAD. HE WASN'T HERE!
<LET'S GO, YOU CRAZY LITTLE INDIAN!>
<PAPA!>
WE'RE LOADED. LET'S GO!
IT WAS A SUCCESS. FOR SOME.
FELIX WAS STILL OUT THERE. SOMEWHERE.
I FAILED.

I WOULDN'T SAY YOU FAILED, MR. GINGRAS. IT SOUNDS LIKE YOU WERE ABLE TO SAVE MANY FRENCH P.O.W.'S WITH VERY FEW CASUALTIES.

OUI. I'M STILL PROUD OF THAT MISSION. FOR THE OUTSIDERS LOOKING IN, GERMAN AND FRENCH ALIKE, IT HAD BEEN AN IMMACULATELY EXECUTED RESCUE OPERATION.

FOR ME, AND MAYBE EVEN TO THE REST OF THE BOYS, IT ENDED WITH THIS... EMPTY FEELING.

WHAT DID YOU THINK HAPPENED TO FELIX?

PETER WAS QUICK TO ENCOURAGE US. HE KEPT SAYING THAT FELIX WAS A FIGHTER AND WE'D FIND HIM IF WE NEVER GAVE UP HOPE.

SOMETIMES I WANTED TO PUNCH HIM IN HIS OPTIMISTIC FACE. WE ALL BELIEVED FELIX TO BE DEAD. HOW WERE WE SUPPOSED TO BUCK UP AND CARRY ON?

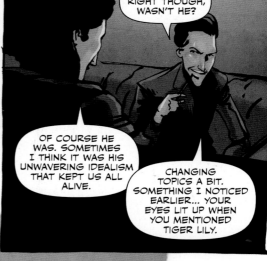

PETER WAS RIGHT THOUGH, WASN'T HE?

OF COURSE HE WAS. SOMETIMES I THINK IT WAS HIS UNWAVERING IDEALISM THAT KEPT US ALL ALIVE.

CHANGING TOPICS A BIT. SOMETHING I NOTICED EARLIER... YOUR EYES LIT UP WHEN YOU MENTIONED TIGER LILY.

WHAT CAN I SAY, MR. PARSONS...

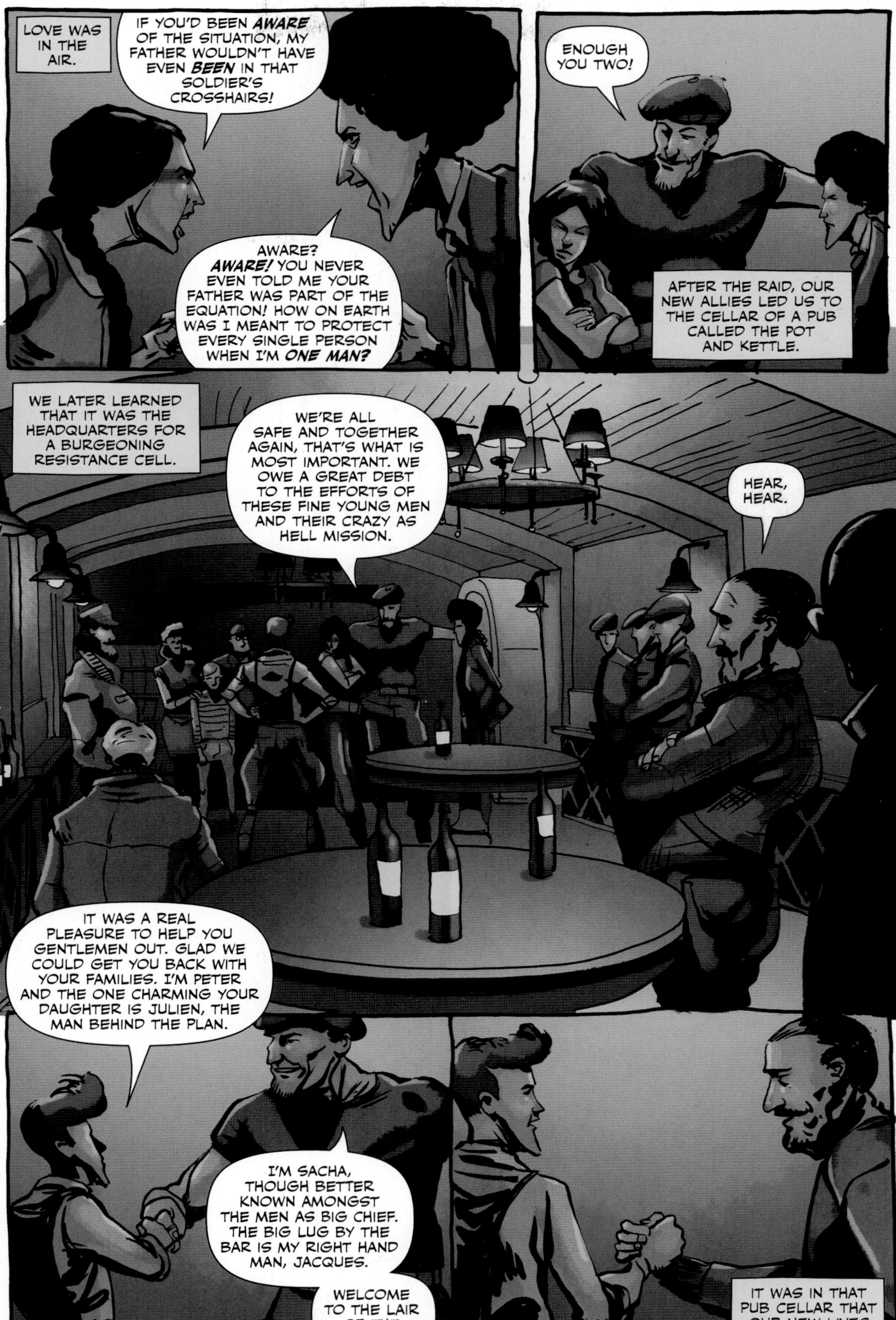
LOVE WAS IN THE AIR.
IF YOU'D BEEN AWARE OF THE SITUATION, MY FATHER WOULDN'T HAVE EVEN BEEN IN THAT SOLDIER'S CROSSHAIRS!
AWARE? AWARE! YOU NEVER EVEN TOLD ME YOUR FATHER WAS PART OF THE EQUATION! HOW ON EARTH WAS I MEANT TO PROTECT EVERY SINGLE PERSON WHEN I'M ONE MAN?
ENOUGH YOU TWO!
AFTER THE RAID, OUR NEW ALLIES LED US TO THE CELLAR OF A PUB CALLED THE POT AND KETTLE.
WE LATER LEARNED THAT IT WAS THE HEADQUARTERS FOR A BURGEONING RESISTANCE CELL.
WE'RE ALL SAFE AND TOGETHER AGAIN, THAT'S WHAT IS MOST IMPORTANT. WE OWE A GREAT DEBT TO THE EFFORTS OF THESE FINE YOUNG MEN AND THEIR CRAZY AS HELL MISSION.
HEAR, HEAR.
IT WAS A REAL PLEASURE TO HELP YOU GENTLEMEN OUT. GLAD WE COULD GET YOU BACK WITH YOUR FAMILIES. I'M PETER AND THE ONE CHARMING YOUR DAUGHTER IS JULIEN, THE MAN BEHIND THE PLAN.
I'M SACHA, THOUGH BETTER KNOWN AMONGST THE MEN AS BIG CHIEF. THE BIG LUG BY THE BAR IS MY RIGHT HAND MAN, JACQUES.
WELCOME TO THE LAIR OF THE BRAVES.
IT WAS IN THAT PUB CELLAR THAT OUR NEW LIVES BEGAN.

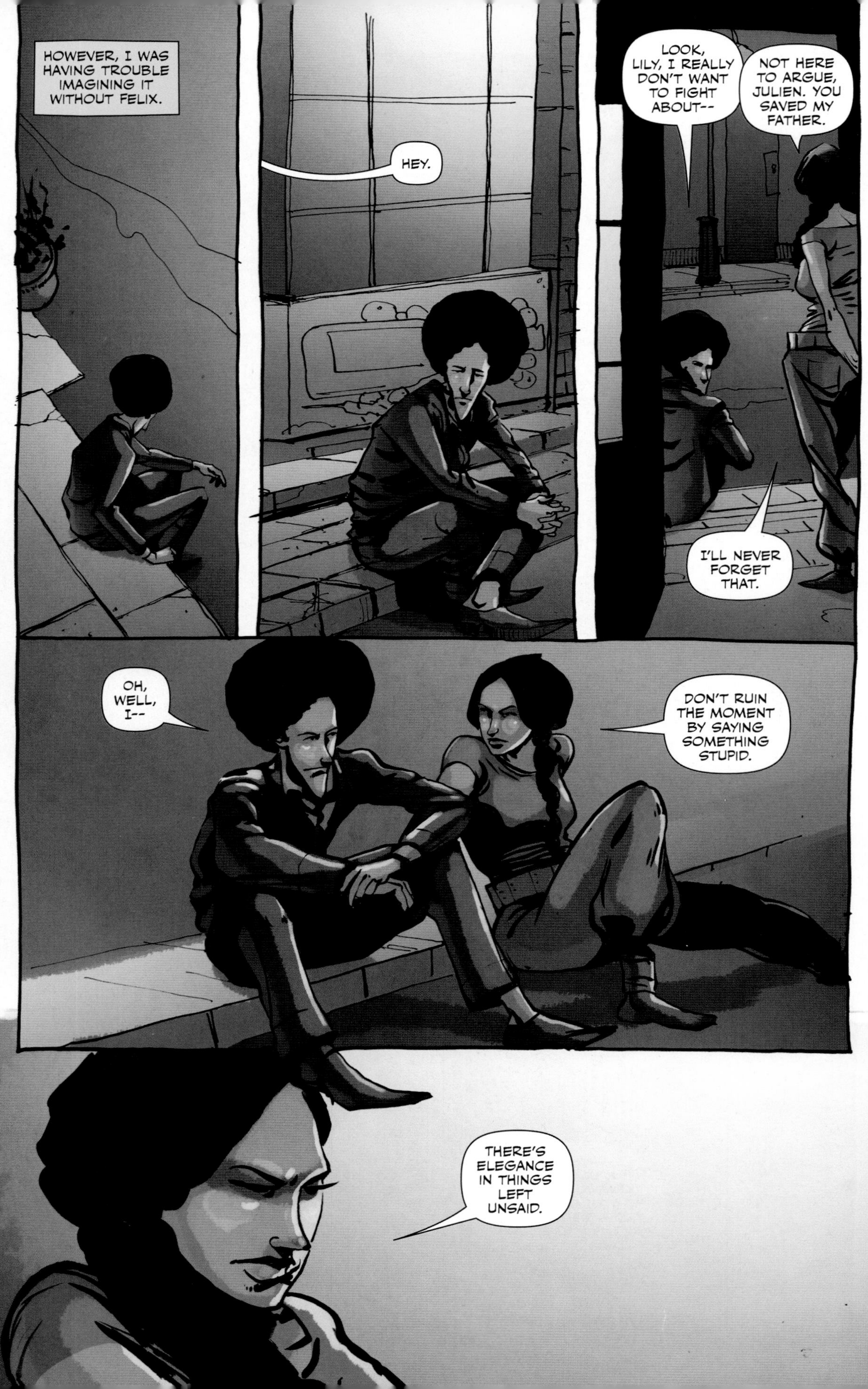
HOWEVER, I WAS HAVING TROUBLE IMAGINING IT WITHOUT FELIX.
HEY.
LOOK, LILY, I REALLY DON'T WANT TO FIGHT ABOUT--
NOT HERE TO ARGUE, JULIEN. YOU SAVED MY FATHER.
I'LL NEVER FORGET THAT.
OH, WELL, I--
DON'T RUIN THE MOMENT BY SAYING SOMETHING STUPID.
THERE'S ELEGANCE IN THINGS LEFT UNSAID.

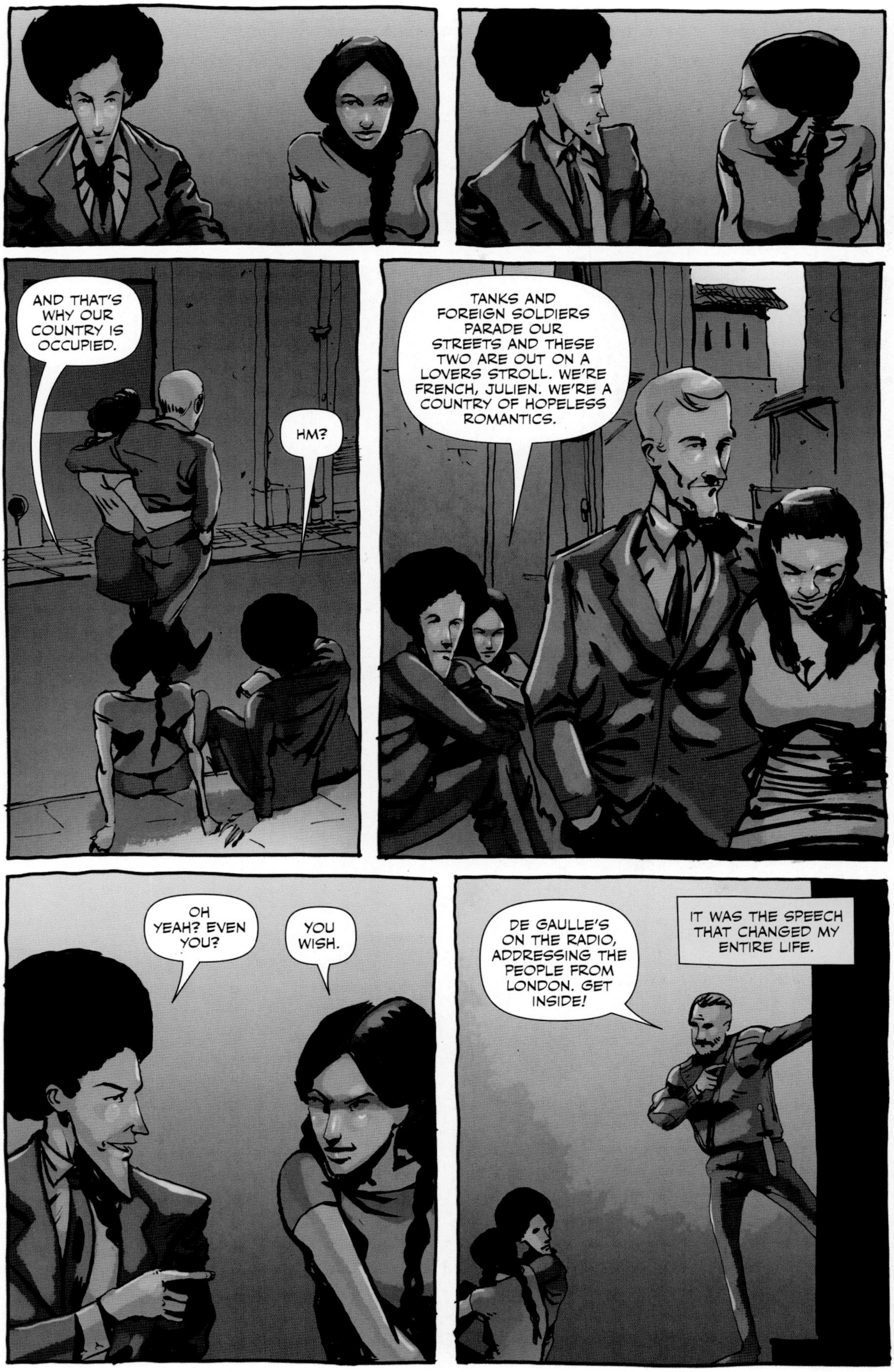
AND THAT'S WHY OUR COUNTRY IS OCCUPIED.
HM?
TANKS AND FOREIGN SOLDIERS PARADE OUR STREETS AND THESE TWO ARE OUT ON A LOVERS STROLL. WE'RE FRENCH, JULIEN. WE'RE A COUNTRY OF HOPELESS ROMANTICS.
OH YEAH? EVEN YOU?
YOU WISH.
DE GAULLE'S ON THE RADIO, ADDRESSING THE PEOPLE FROM LONDON. GET INSIDE!
IT WAS THE SPEECH THAT CHANGED MY ENTIRE LIFE.

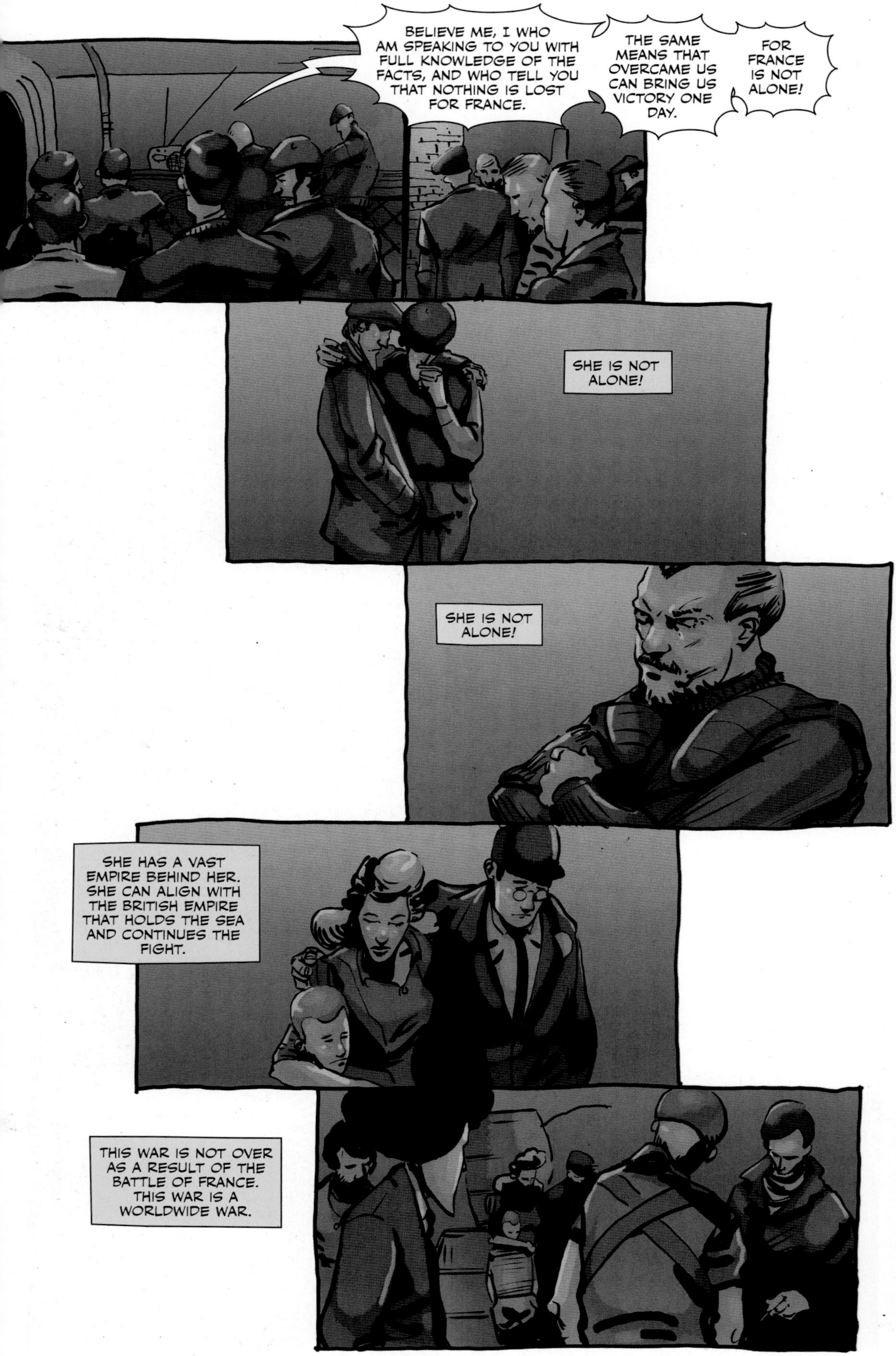
BELIEVE ME, I WHO AM SPEAKING TO YOU WITH FULL KNOWLEDGE OF THE FACTS, AND WHO TELL YOU THAT NOTHING IS LOST FOR FRANCE.
THE SAME MEANS THAT OVERCAME US CAN BRING US VICTORY ONE DAY.
FOR FRANCE IS NOT ALONE!
SHE IS NOT ALONE!
SHE IS NOT ALONE!
SHE HAS A VAST EMPIRE BEHIND HER. SHE CAN ALIGN WITH THE BRITISH EMPIRE THAT HOLDS THE SEA AND CONTINUES THE FIGHT.
THIS WAR IS NOT OVER AS A RESULT OF THE BATTLE OF FRANCE. THIS WAR IS A WORLDWIDE WAR.

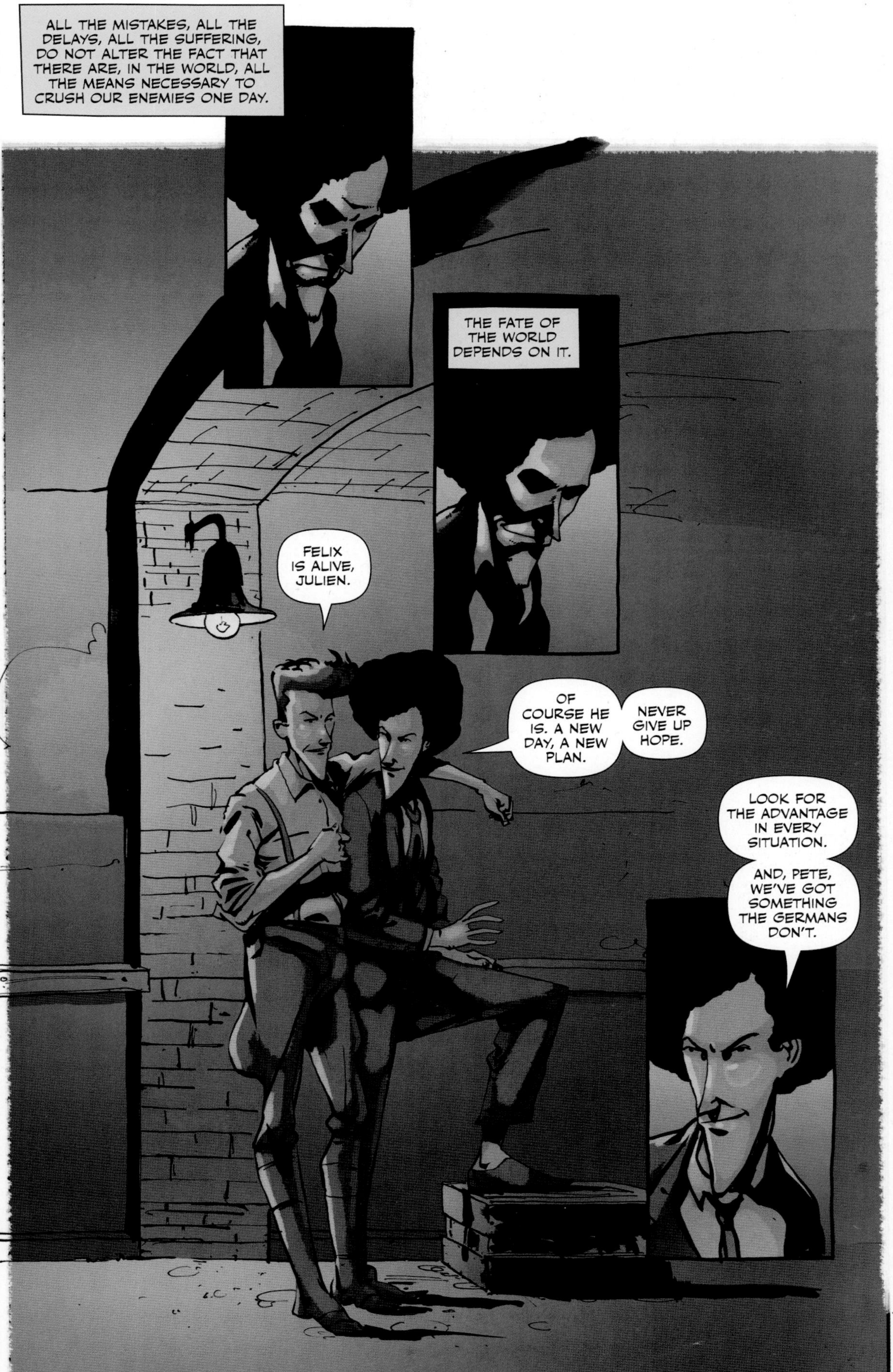
ALL THE MISTAKES, ALL THE DELAYS, ALL THE SUFFERING, DO NOT ALTER THE FACT THAT THERE ARE, IN THE WORLD, ALL THE MEANS NECESSARY TO CRUSH OUR ENEMIES ONE DAY.
THE FATE OF THE WORLD DEPENDS ON IT.
FELIX IS ALIVE, JULIEN.
OF COURSE HE IS. A NEW DAY, A NEW PLAN.
NEVER GIVE UP HOPE.
LOOK FOR THE ADVANTAGE IN EVERY SITUATION.
AND, PETE, WE'VE GOT SOMETHING THE GERMANS DON'T.

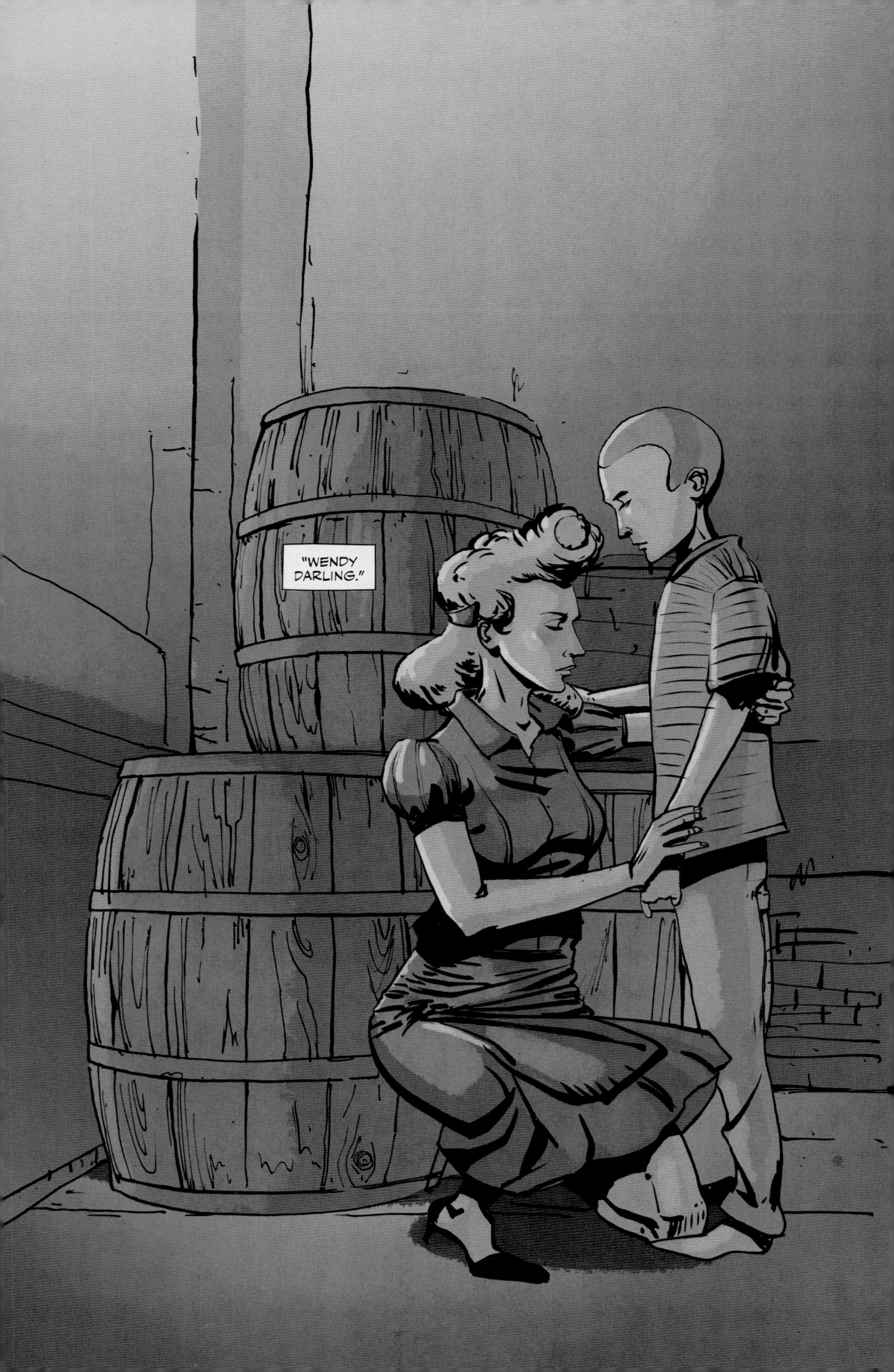
"WENDY DARLING."

CHAPTER EIGHT

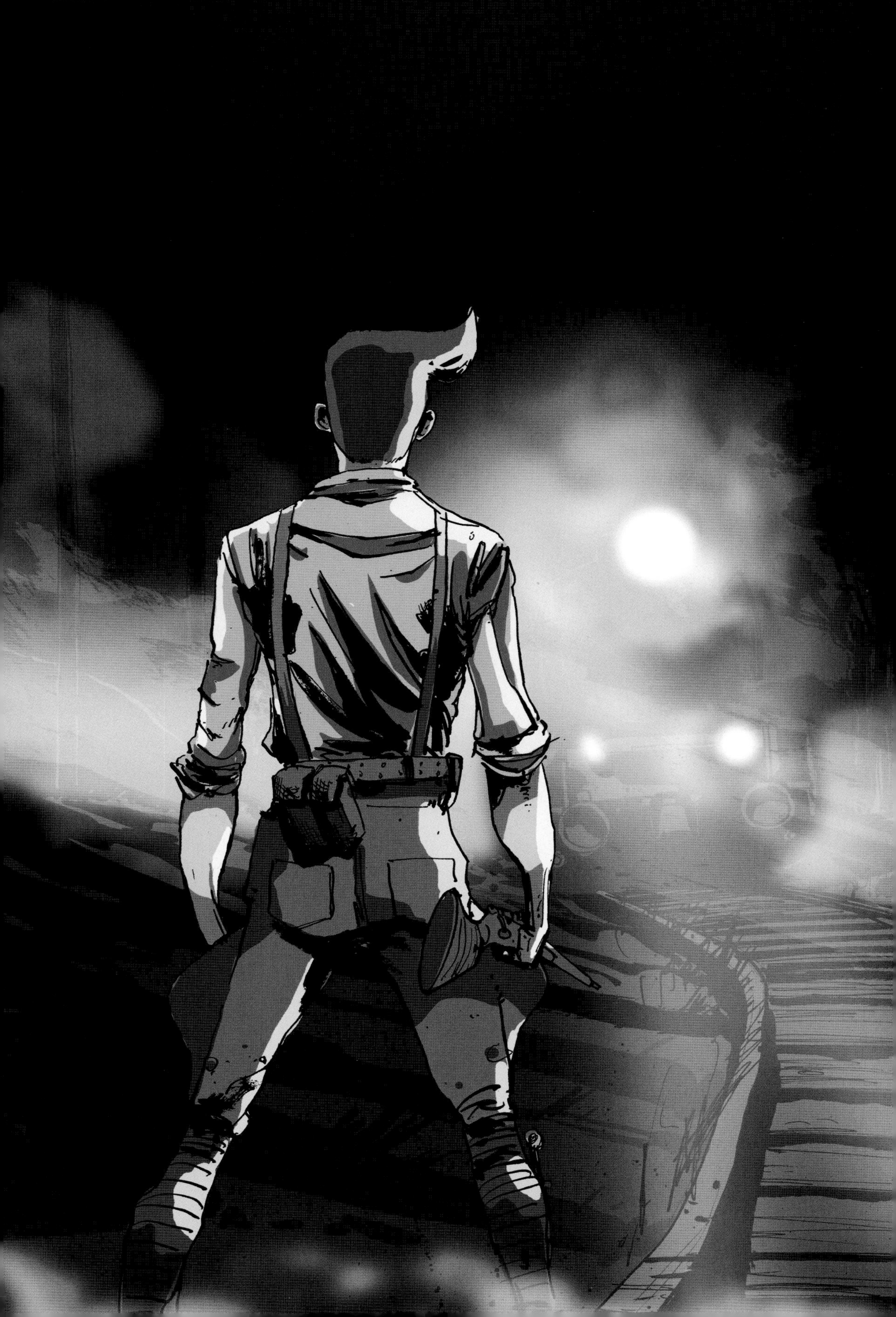

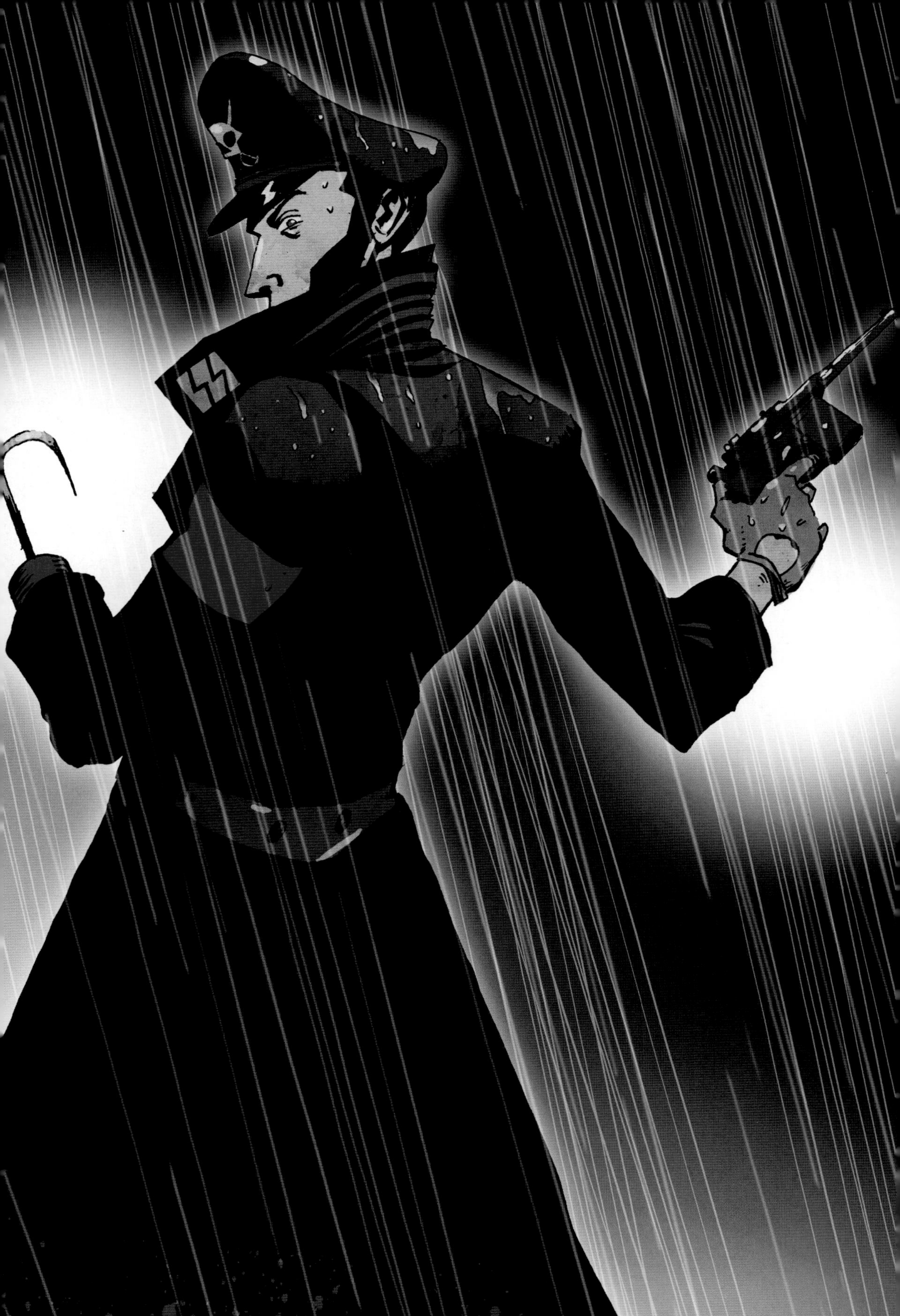

ISSUE EIGHT COVER B

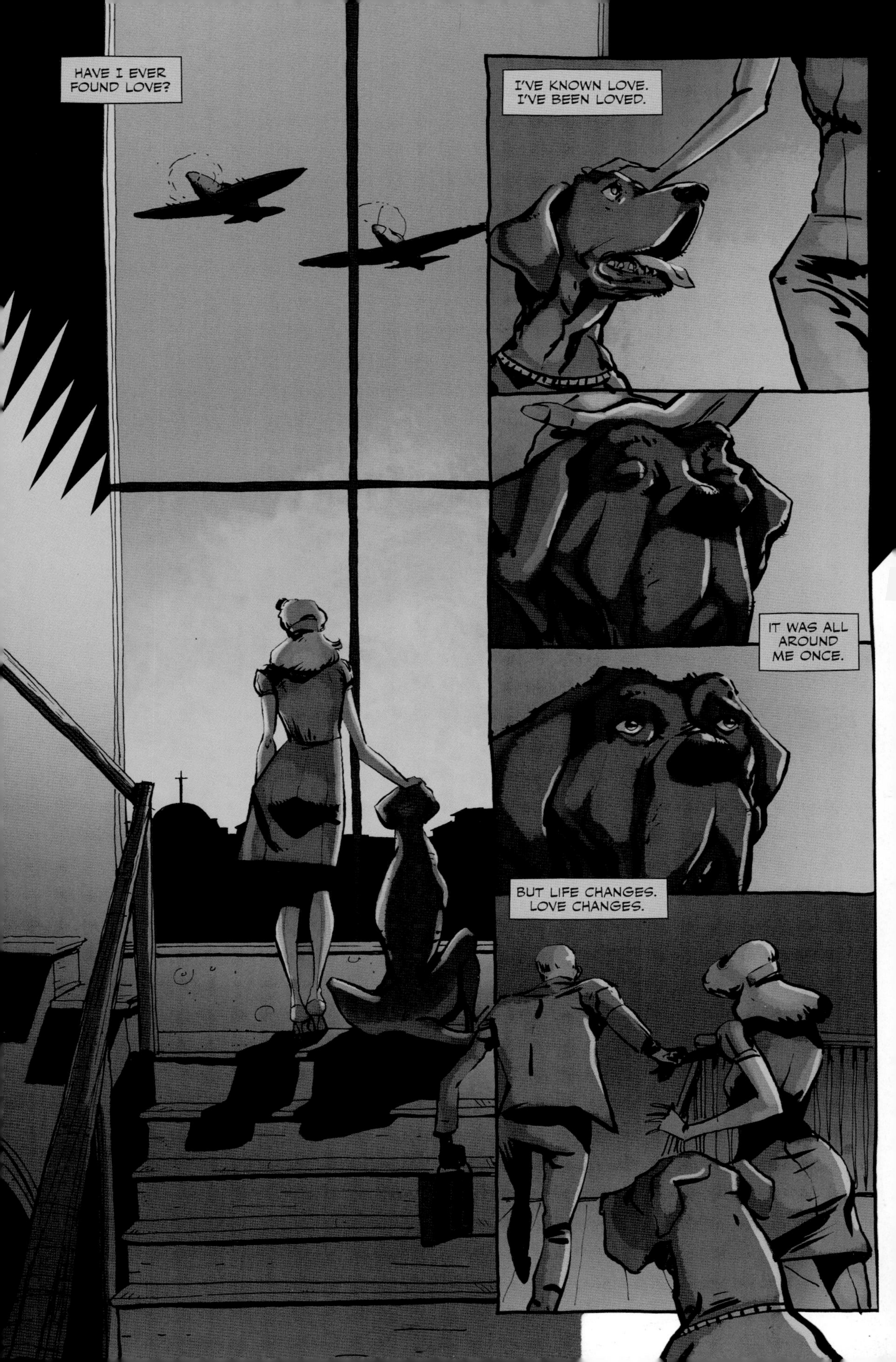
HAVE I EVER FOUND LOVE?
I'VE KNOWN LOVE. I'VE BEEN LOVED.
IT WAS ALL AROUND ME ONCE.
BUT LIFE CHANGES. LOVE CHANGES.

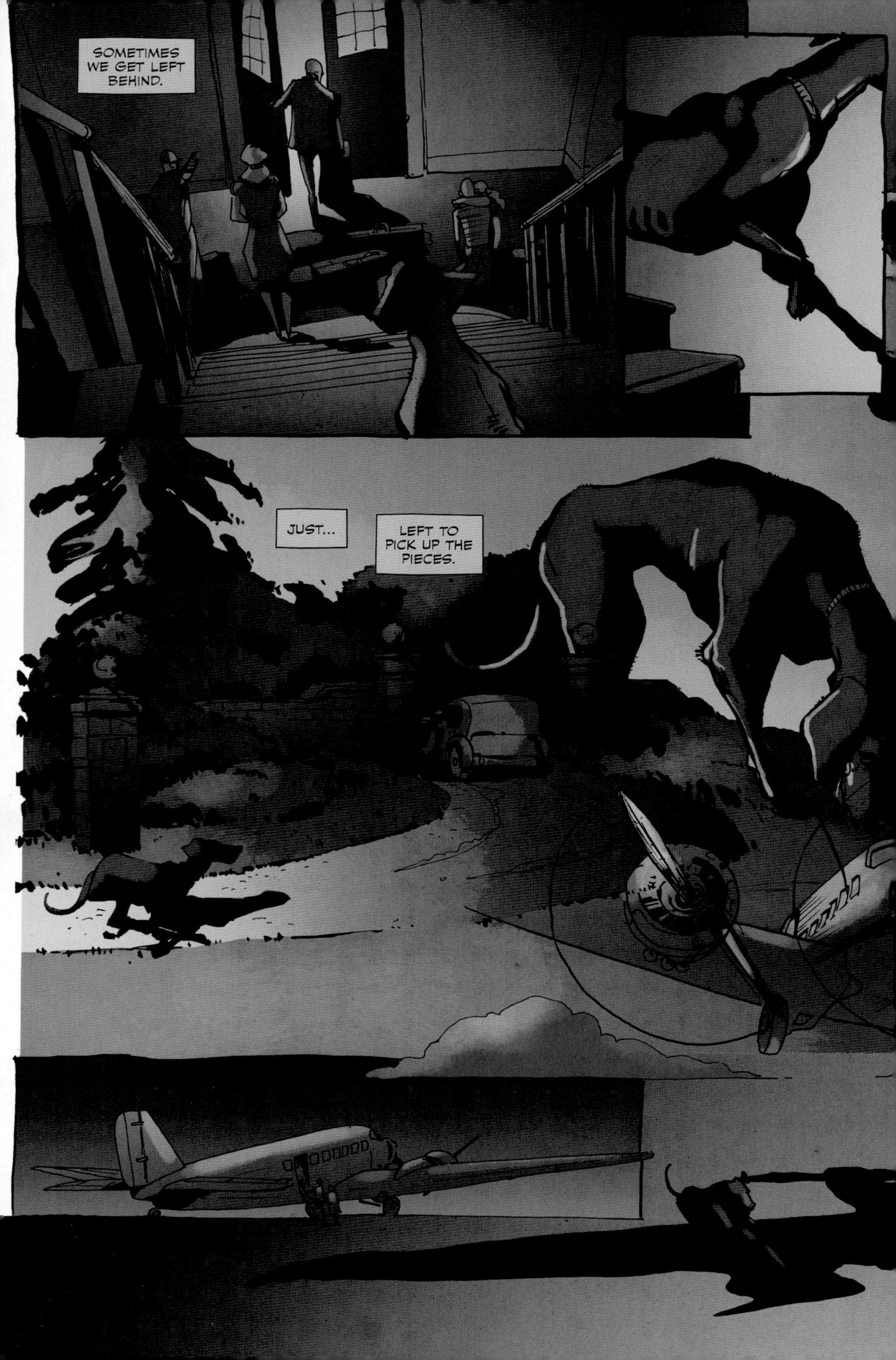
SOMETIMES WE GET LEFT BEHIND.
JUST...
LEFT TO PICK UP THE PIECES.

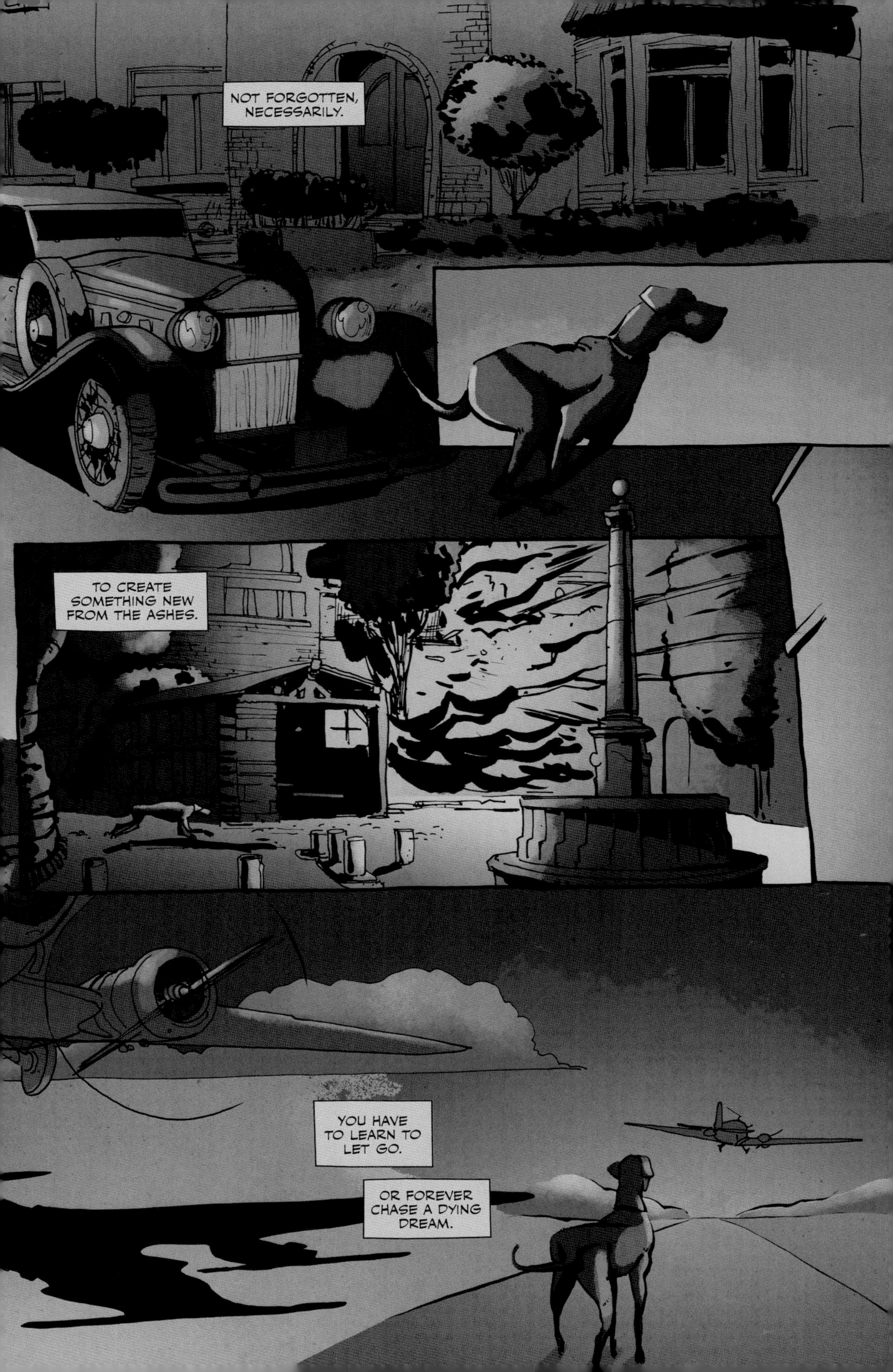
NOT FORGOTTEN, NECESSARILY.
TO CREATE SOMETHING NEW FROM THE ASHES.
YOU HAVE TO LEARN TO LET GO.
OR FOREVER CHASE A DYING DREAM.

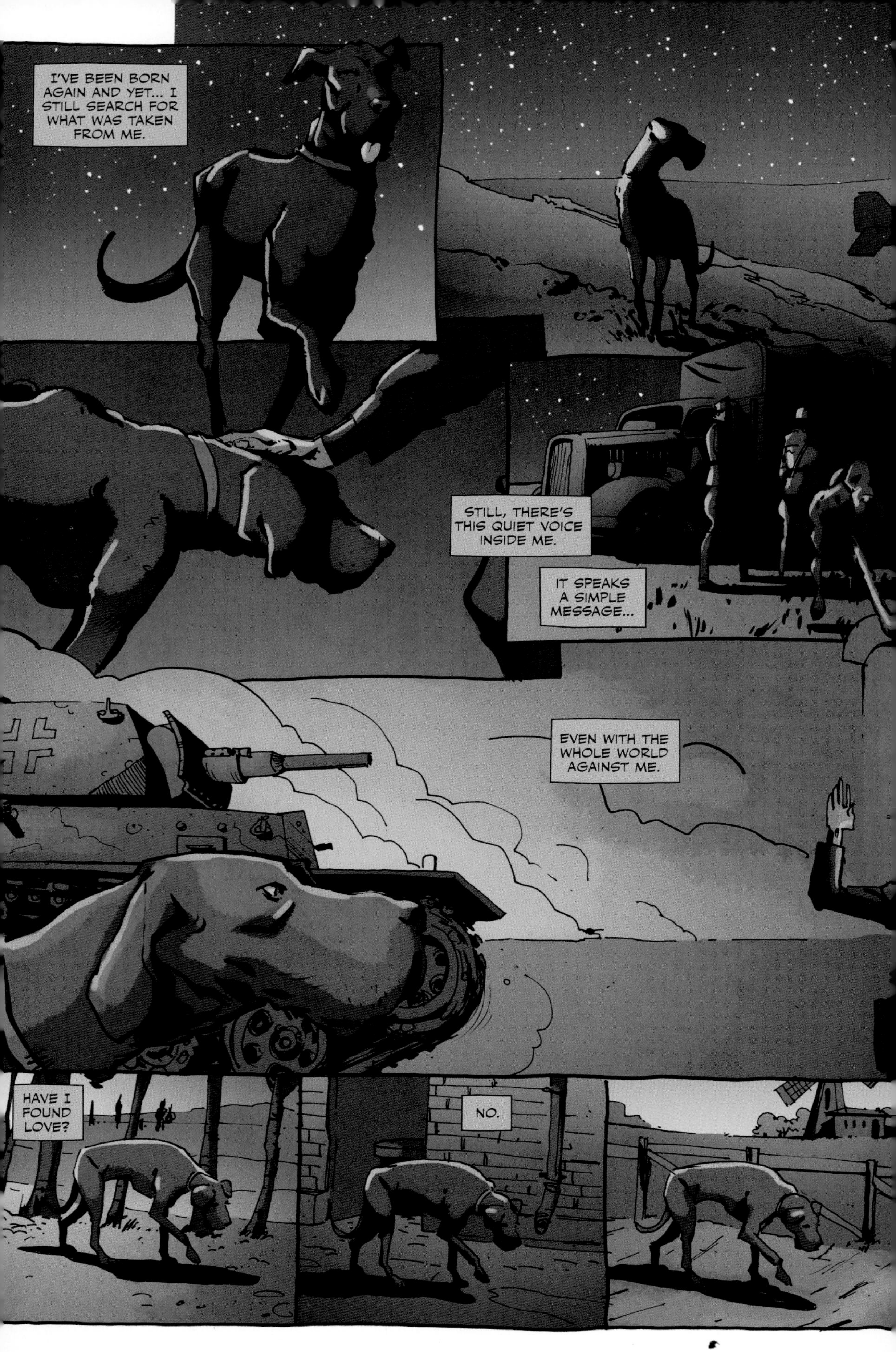
I'VE BEEN BORN AGAIN AND YET... I STILL SEARCH FOR WHAT WAS TAKEN FROM ME.
STILL, THERE'S THIS QUIET VOICE INSIDE ME.
IT SPEAKS A SIMPLE MESSAGE...
EVEN WITH THE WHOLE WORLD AGAINST ME.
HAVE I FOUND LOVE?
NO.

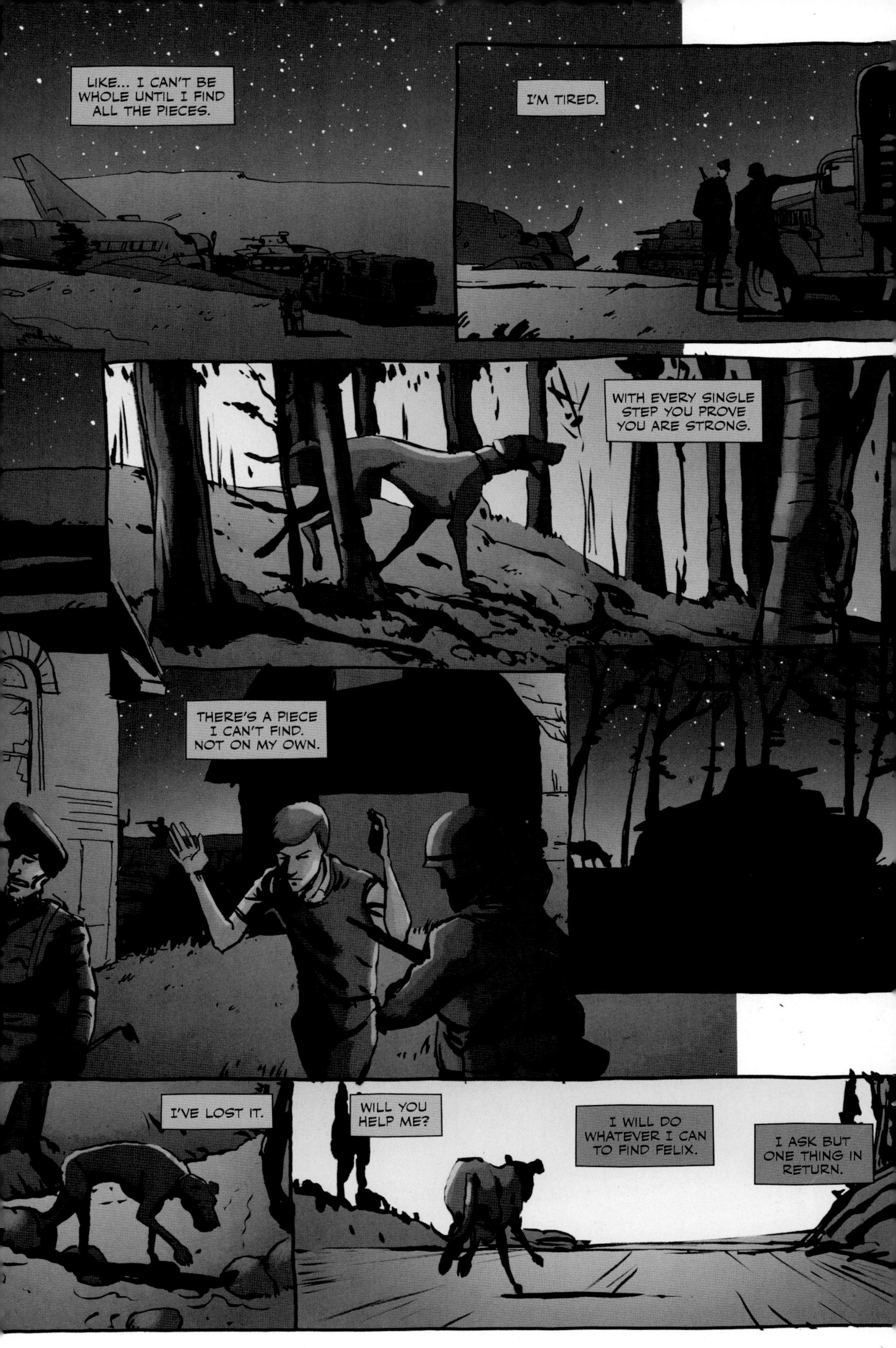
LIKE... I CAN'T BE WHOLE UNTIL I FIND ALL THE PIECES.
I'M TIRED.
WITH EVERY SINGLE STEP YOU PROVE YOU ARE STRONG.
THERE'S A PIECE I CAN'T FIND. NOT ON MY OWN.
I'VE LOST IT.
WILL YOU HELP ME?
I WILL DO WHATEVER I CAN TO FIND FELIX.
I ASK BUT ONE THING IN RETURN.

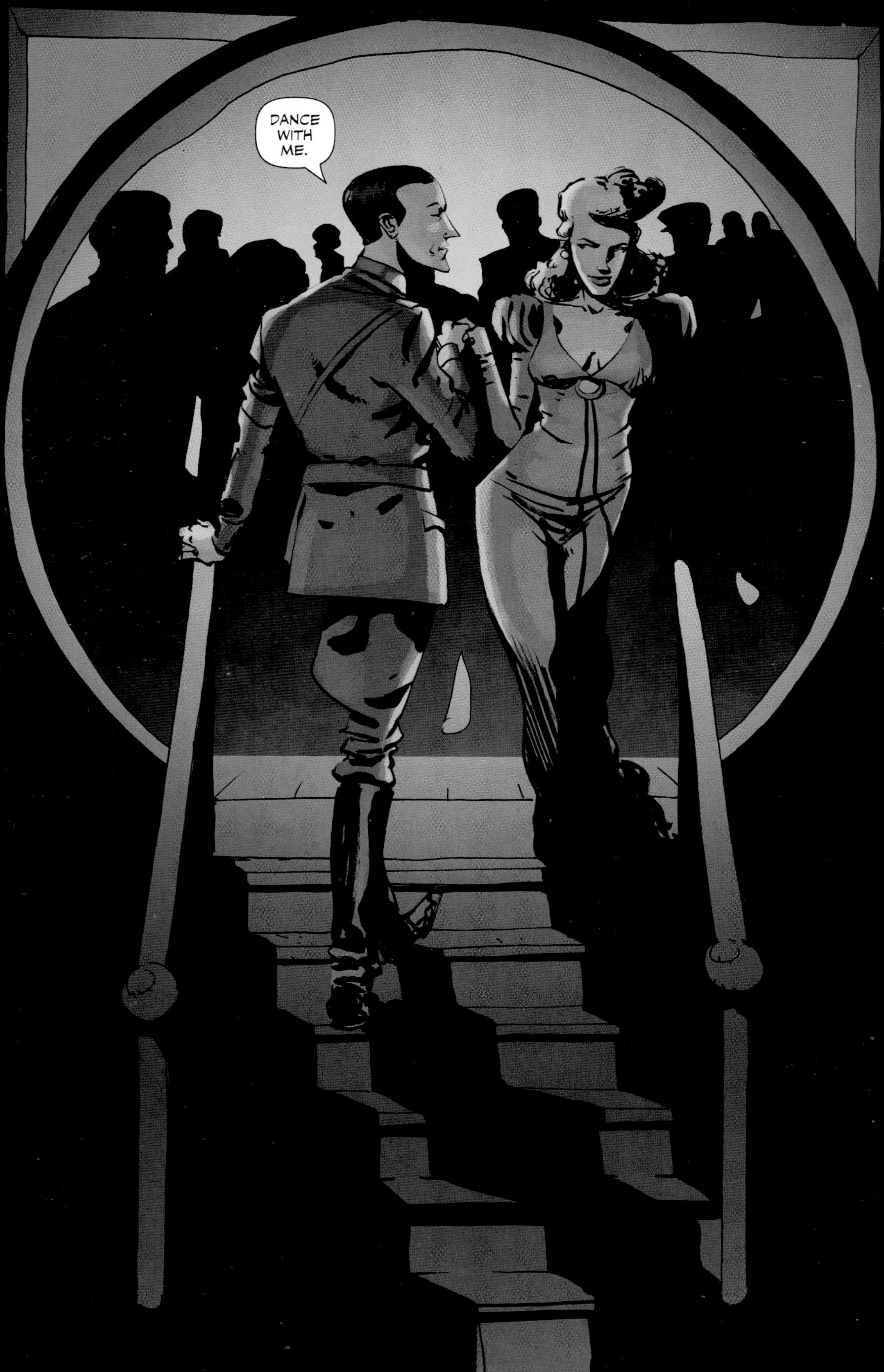
DANCE WITH ME.

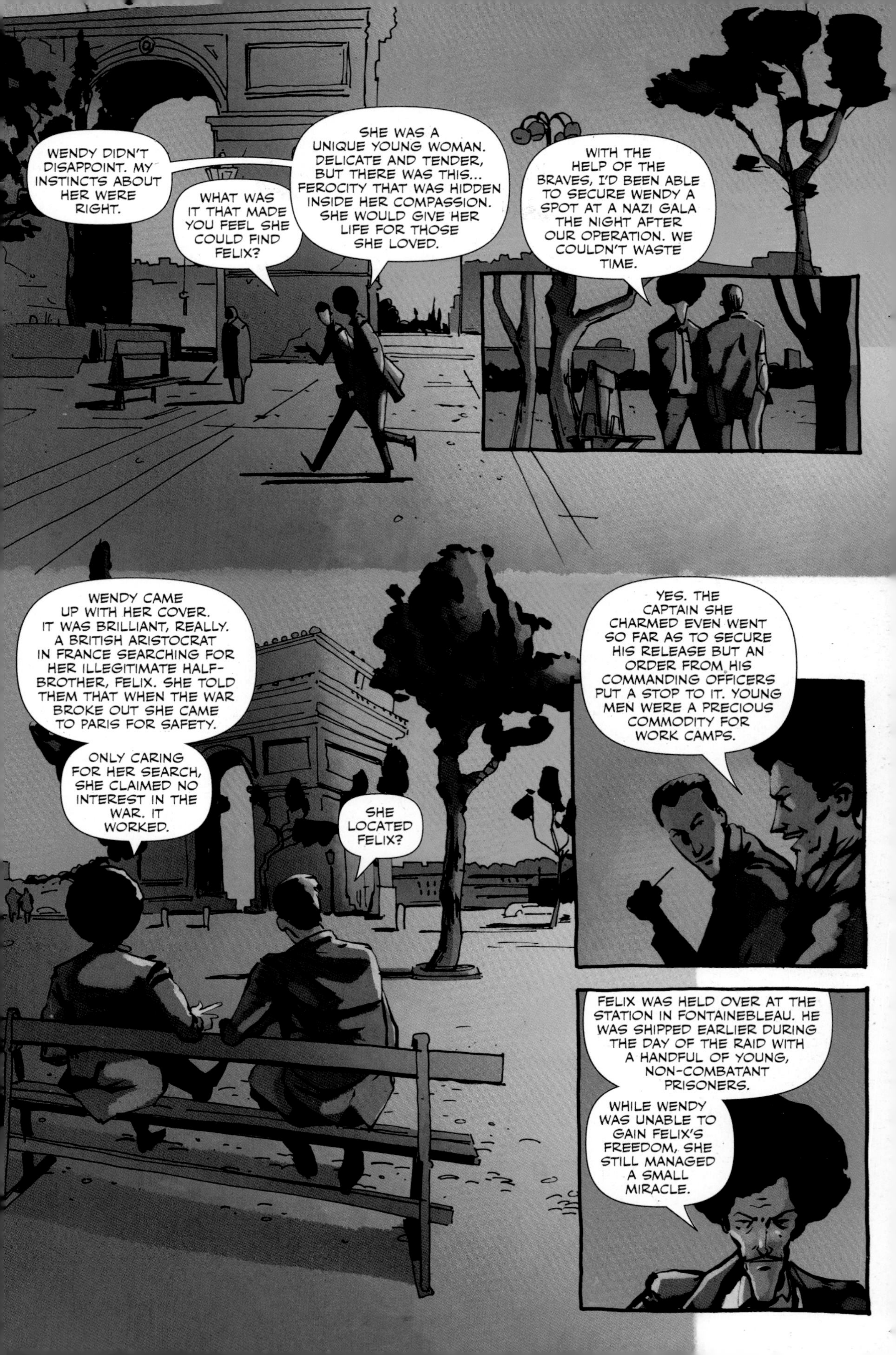
WENDY DIDN'T DISAPPOINT. MY INSTINCTS ABOUT HER WERE RIGHT.
WHAT WAS IT THAT MADE YOU FEEL SHE COULD FIND FELIX?
SHE WAS A UNIQUE YOUNG WOMAN. DELICATE AND TENDER, BUT THERE WAS THIS... FEROCITY THAT WAS HIDDEN INSIDE HER COMPASSION. SHE WOULD GIVE HER LIFE FOR THOSE SHE LOVED.
WITH THE HELP OF THE BRAVES, I'D BEEN ABLE TO SECURE WENDY A SPOT AT A NAZI GALA THE NIGHT AFTER OUR OPERATION. WE COULDN'T WASTE TIME.
WENDY CAME UP WITH HER COVER. IT WAS BRILLIANT, REALLY. A BRITISH ARISTOCRAT IN FRANCE SEARCHING FOR HER ILLEGITIMATE HALF-BROTHER, FELIX. SHE TOLD THEM THAT WHEN THE WAR BROKE OUT SHE CAME TO PARIS FOR SAFETY.
ONLY CARING FOR HER SEARCH, SHE CLAIMED NO INTEREST IN THE WAR. IT WORKED.
SHE LOCATED FELIX?
YES. THE CAPTAIN SHE CHARMED EVEN WENT SO FAR AS TO SECURE HIS RELEASE BUT AN ORDER FROM HIS COMMANDING OFFICERS PUT A STOP TO IT. YOUNG MEN WERE A PRECIOUS COMMODITY FOR WORK CAMPS.
FELIX WAS HELD OVER AT THE STATION IN FONTAINEBLEAU. HE WAS SHIPPED EARLIER DURING THE DAY OF THE RAID WITH A HANDFUL OF YOUNG, NON-COMBATANT PRISONERS.
WHILE WENDY WAS UNABLE TO GAIN FELIX'S FREEDOM, SHE STILL MANAGED A SMALL MIRACLE.

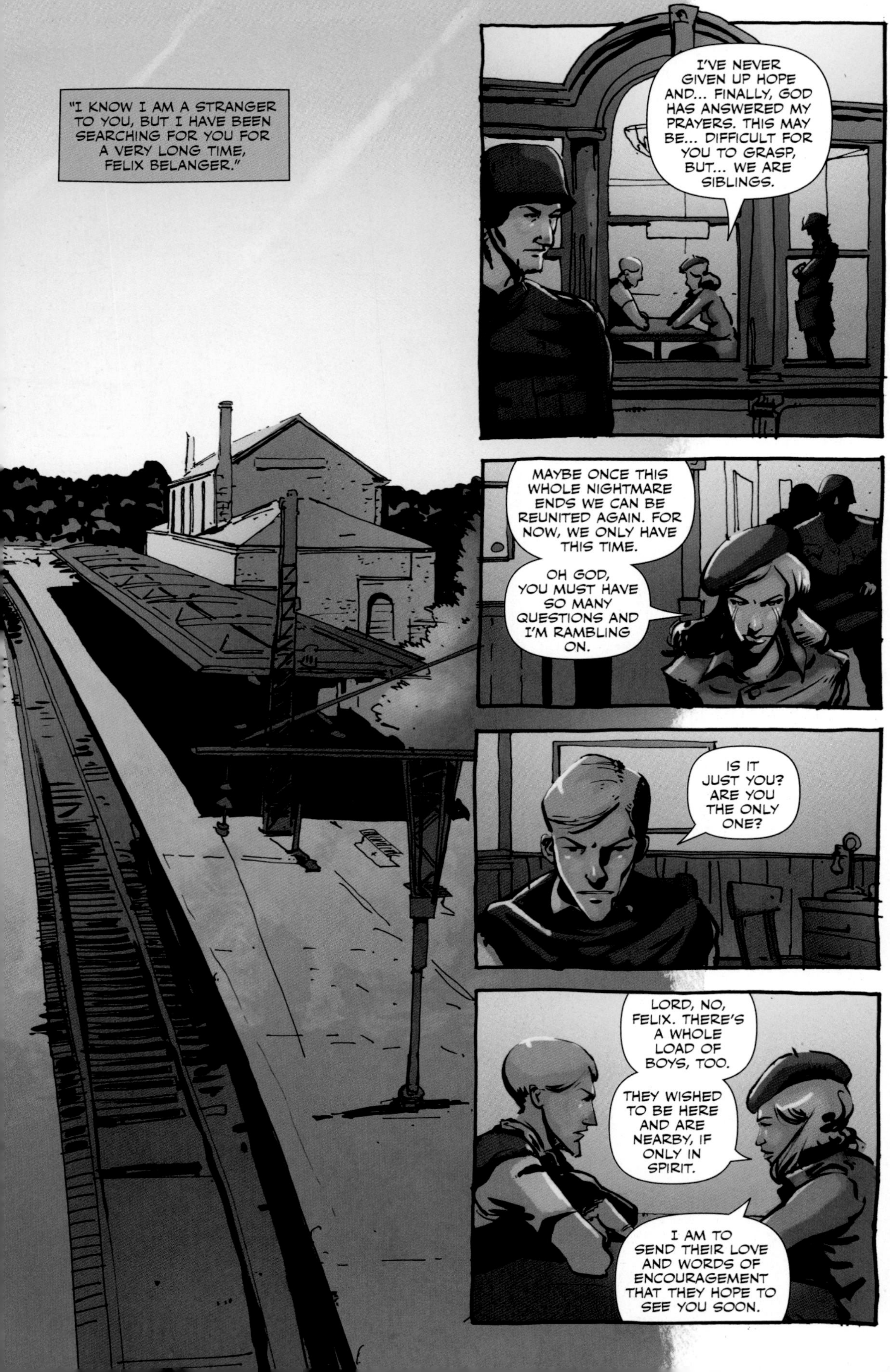
"I KNOW I AM A STRANGER TO YOU, BUT I HAVE BEEN SEARCHING FOR YOU FOR A VERY LONG TIME, FELIX BELANGER."
I'VE NEVER GIVEN UP HOPE AND... FINALLY, GOD HAS ANSWERED MY PRAYERS. THIS MAY BE... DIFFICULT FOR YOU TO GRASP, BUT... WE ARE SIBLINGS.
MAYBE ONCE THIS WHOLE NIGHTMARE ENDS WE CAN BE REUNITED AGAIN. FOR NOW, WE ONLY HAVE THIS TIME.
OH GOD, YOU MUST HAVE SO MANY QUESTIONS AND I'M RAMBLING ON.
IS IT JUST YOU? ARE YOU THE ONLY ONE?
LORD, NO, FELIX. THERE'S A WHOLE LOAD OF BOYS, TOO.
THEY WISHED TO BE HERE AND ARE NEARBY, IF ONLY IN SPIRIT.
I AM TO SEND THEIR LOVE AND WORDS OF ENCOURAGEMENT THAT THEY HOPE TO SEE YOU SOON.

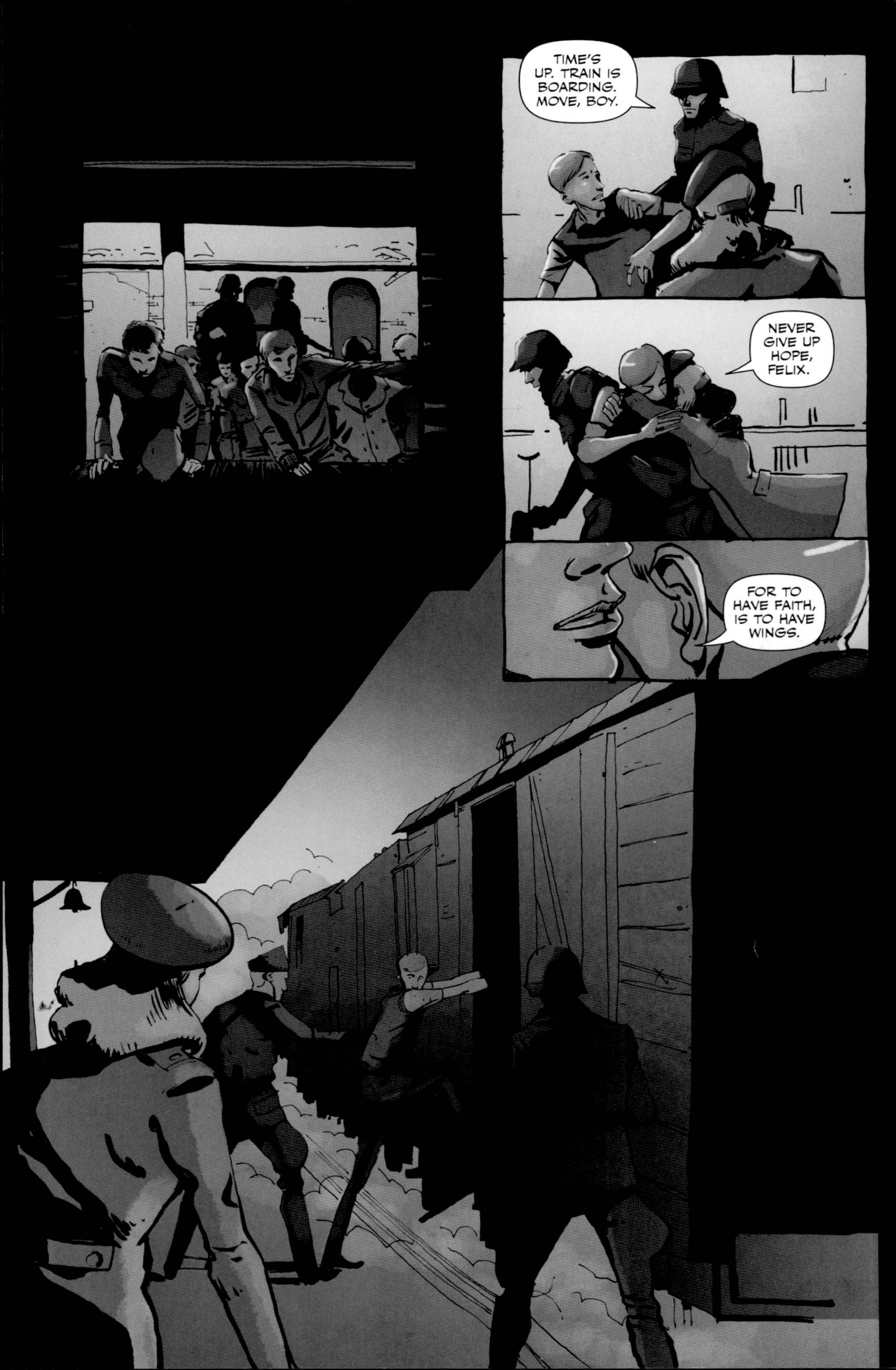
TIME'S UP. TRAIN IS BOARDING. MOVE, BOY.
NEVER GIVE UP HOPE, FELIX.
FOR TO HAVE FAITH, IS TO HAVE WINGS.

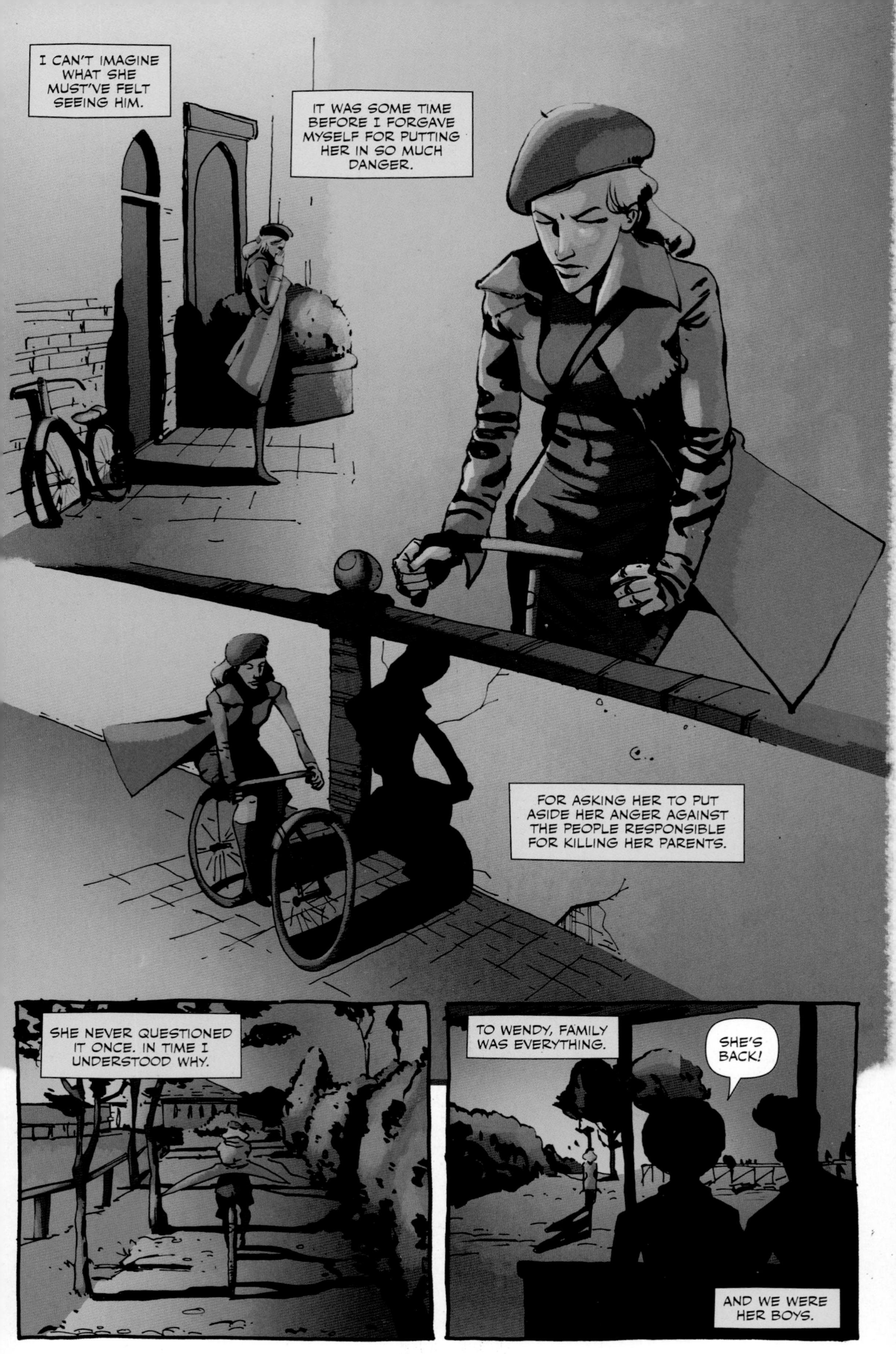
I CAN'T IMAGINE WHAT SHE MUST'VE FELT SEEING HIM.
IT WAS SOME TIME BEFORE I FORGAVE MYSELF FOR PUTTING HER IN SO MUCH DANGER.
FOR ASKING HER TO PUT ASIDE HER ANGER AGAINST THE PEOPLE RESPONSIBLE FOR KILLING HER PARENTS.
SHE NEVER QUESTIONED IT ONCE. IN TIME I UNDERSTOOD WHY.
TO WENDY, FAMILY WAS EVERYTHING.
SHE'S BACK!
AND WE WERE HER BOYS.

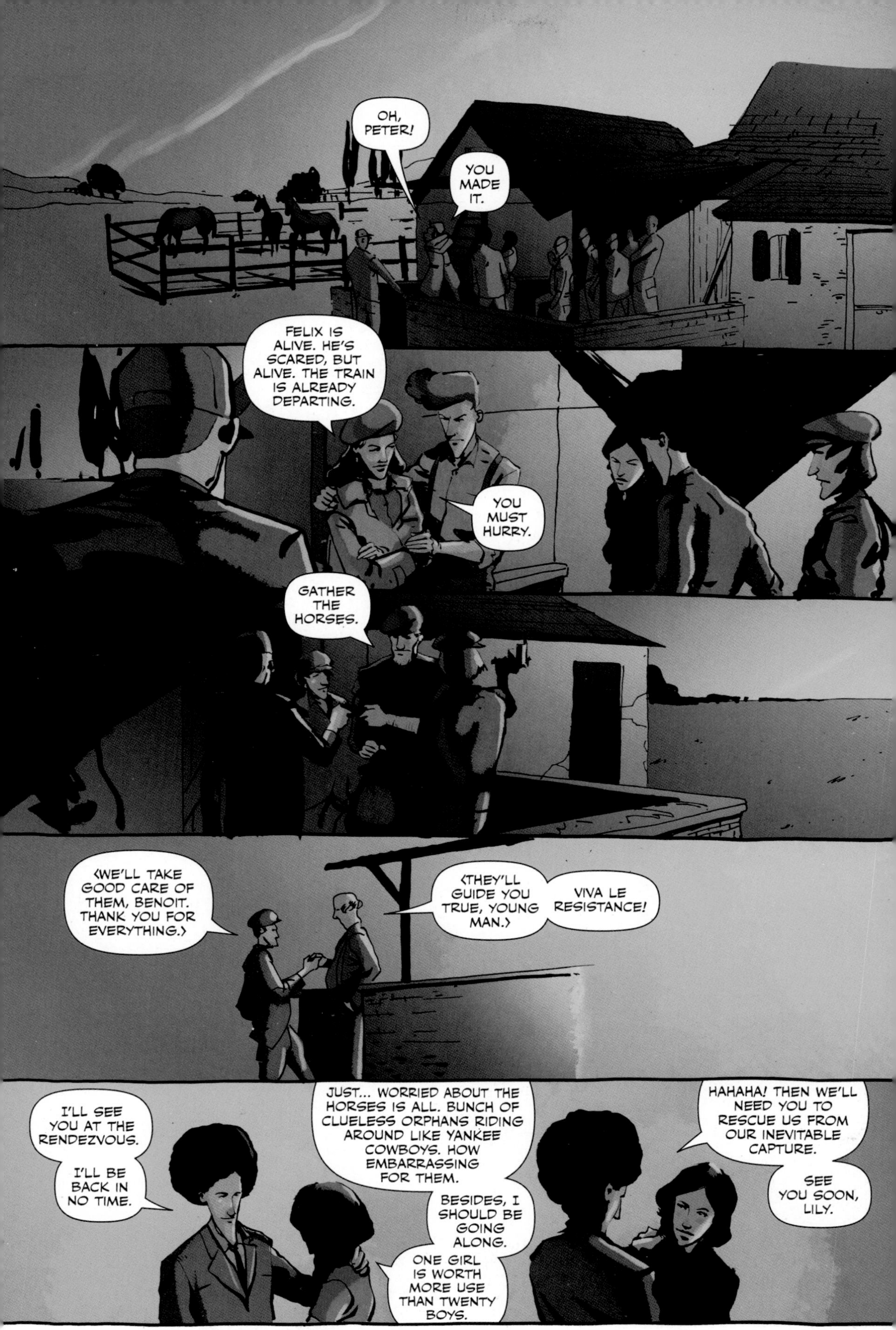
OH, PETER!
YOU MADE IT.
FELIX IS ALIVE. HE'S SCARED, BUT ALIVE. THE TRAIN IS ALREADY DEPARTING.
YOU MUST HURRY.
GATHER THE HORSES.
<WE'LL TAKE GOOD CARE OF THEM, BENOIT. THANK YOU FOR EVERYTHING.>
<THEY'LL GUIDE YOU TRUE, YOUNG MAN.>
VIVA LE RESISTANCE!
I'LL SEE YOU AT THE RENDEZVOUS.
I'LL BE BACK IN NO TIME.
JUST... WORRIED ABOUT THE HORSES IS ALL. BUNCH OF CLUELESS ORPHANS RIDING AROUND LIKE YANKEE COWBOYS. HOW EMBARRASSING FOR THEM.
BESIDES, I SHOULD BE GOING ALONG.
ONE GIRL IS WORTH MORE USE THAN TWENTY BOYS.
HAHAHA! THEN WE'LL NEED YOU TO RESCUE US FROM OUR INEVITABLE CAPTURE.
SEE YOU SOON, LILY.

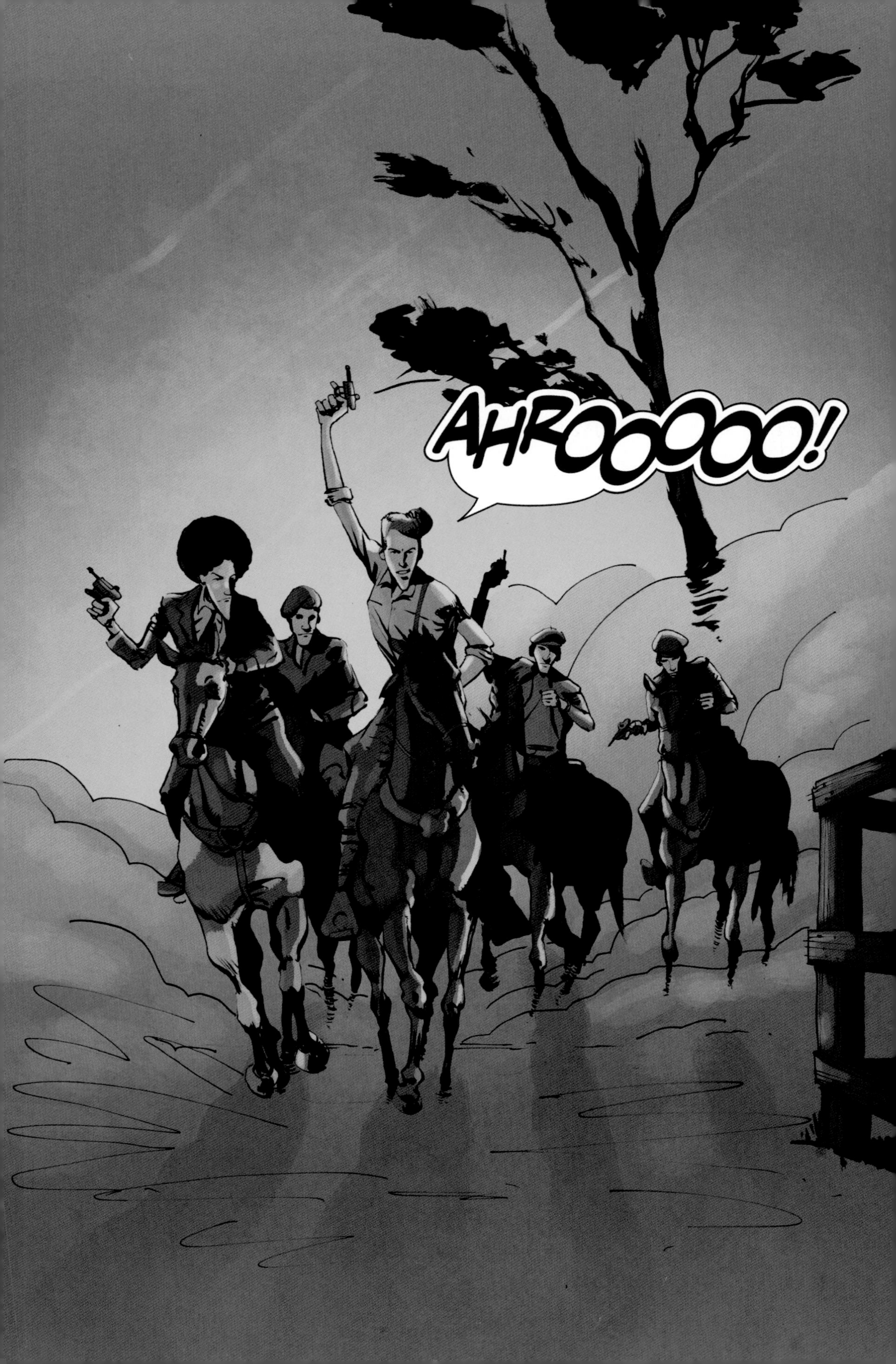
AHROOOOOO!

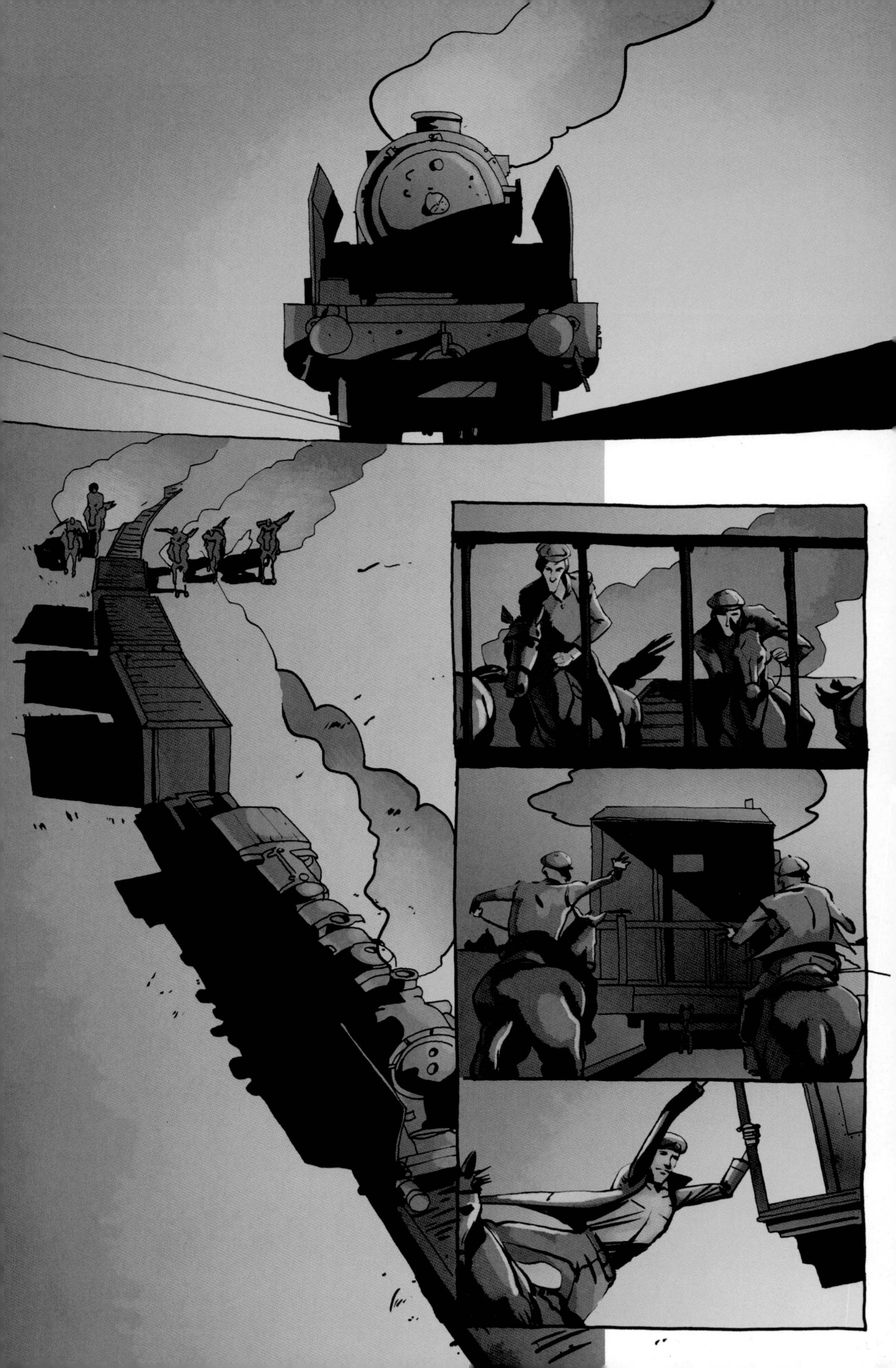

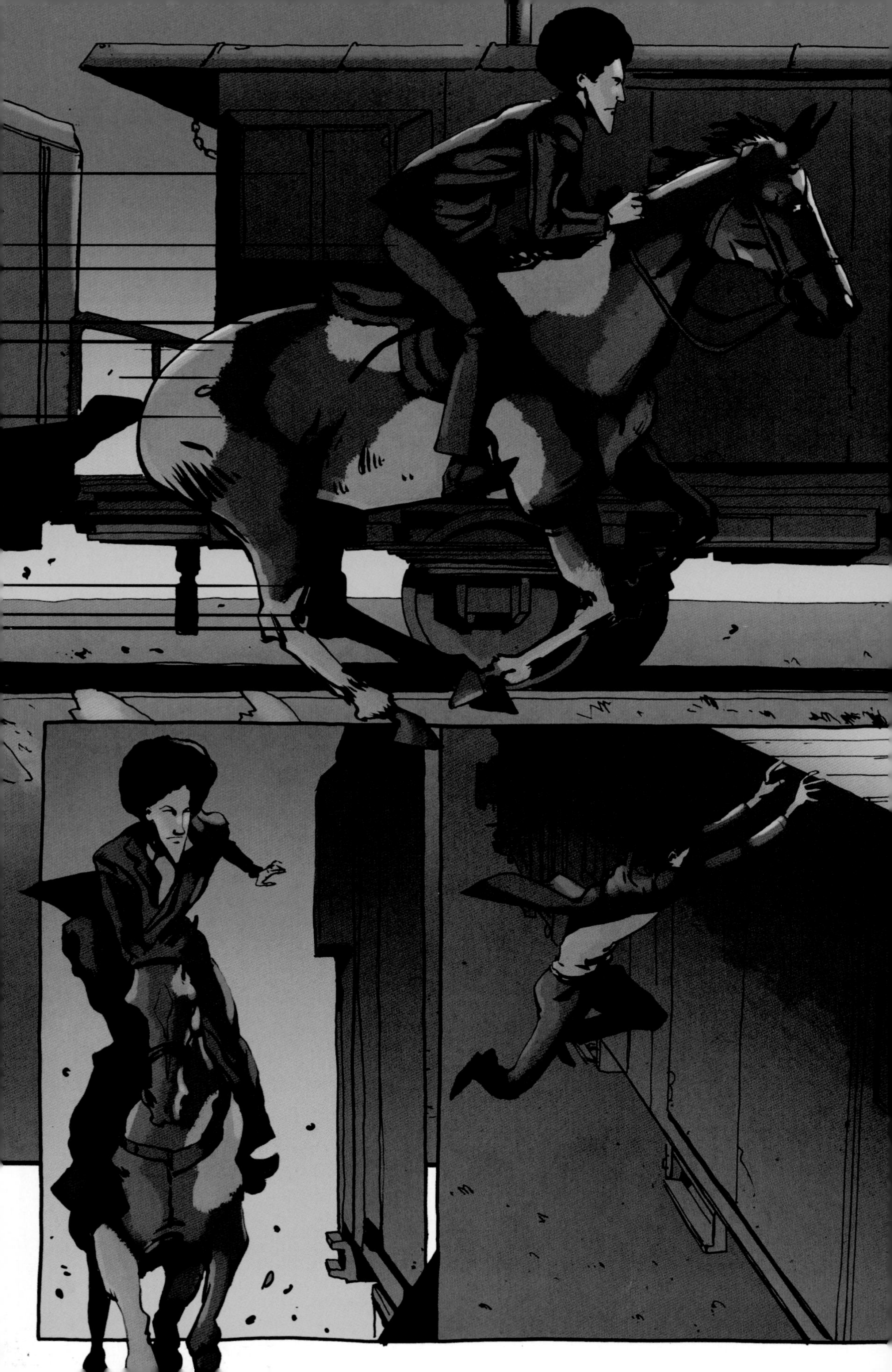

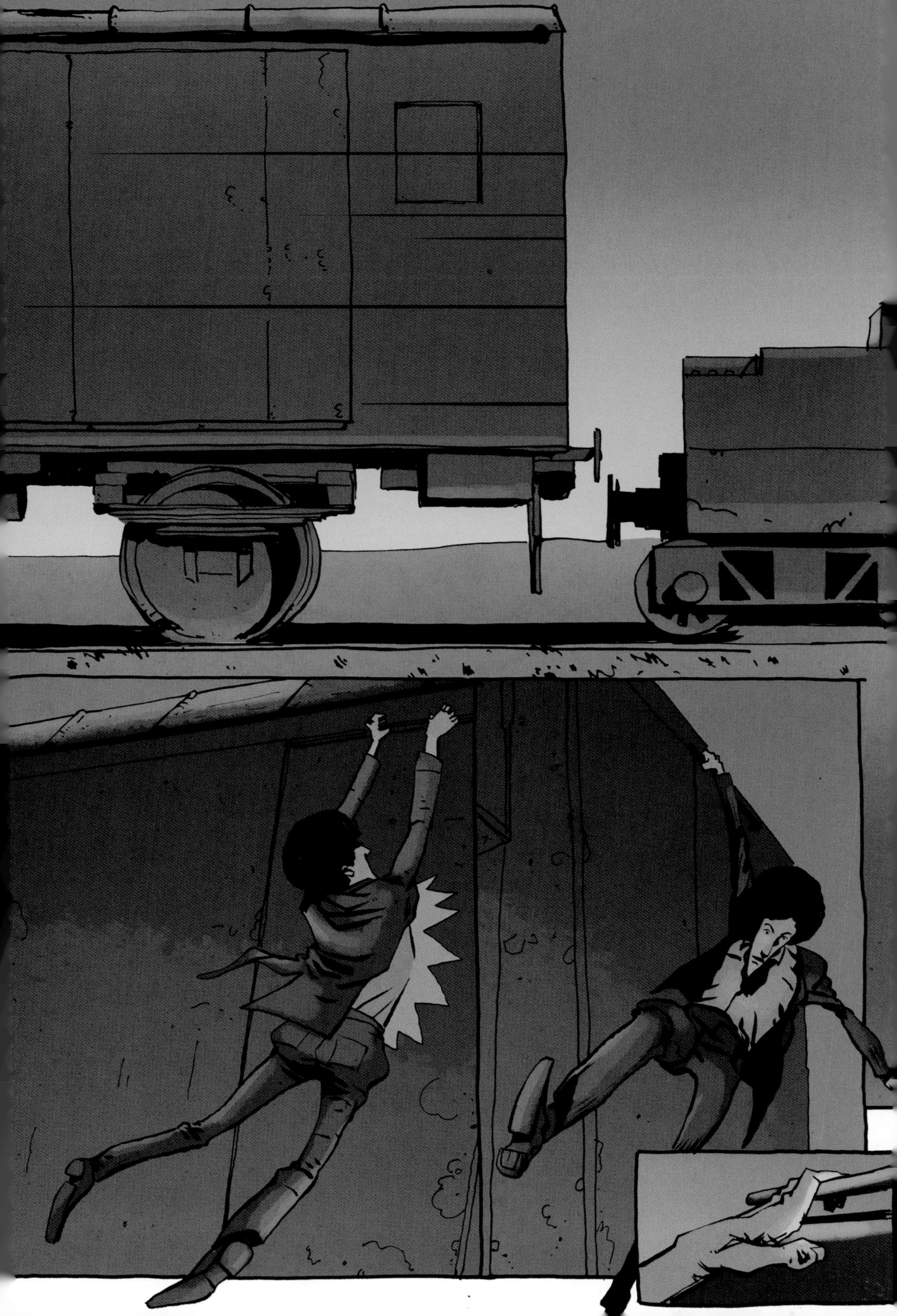

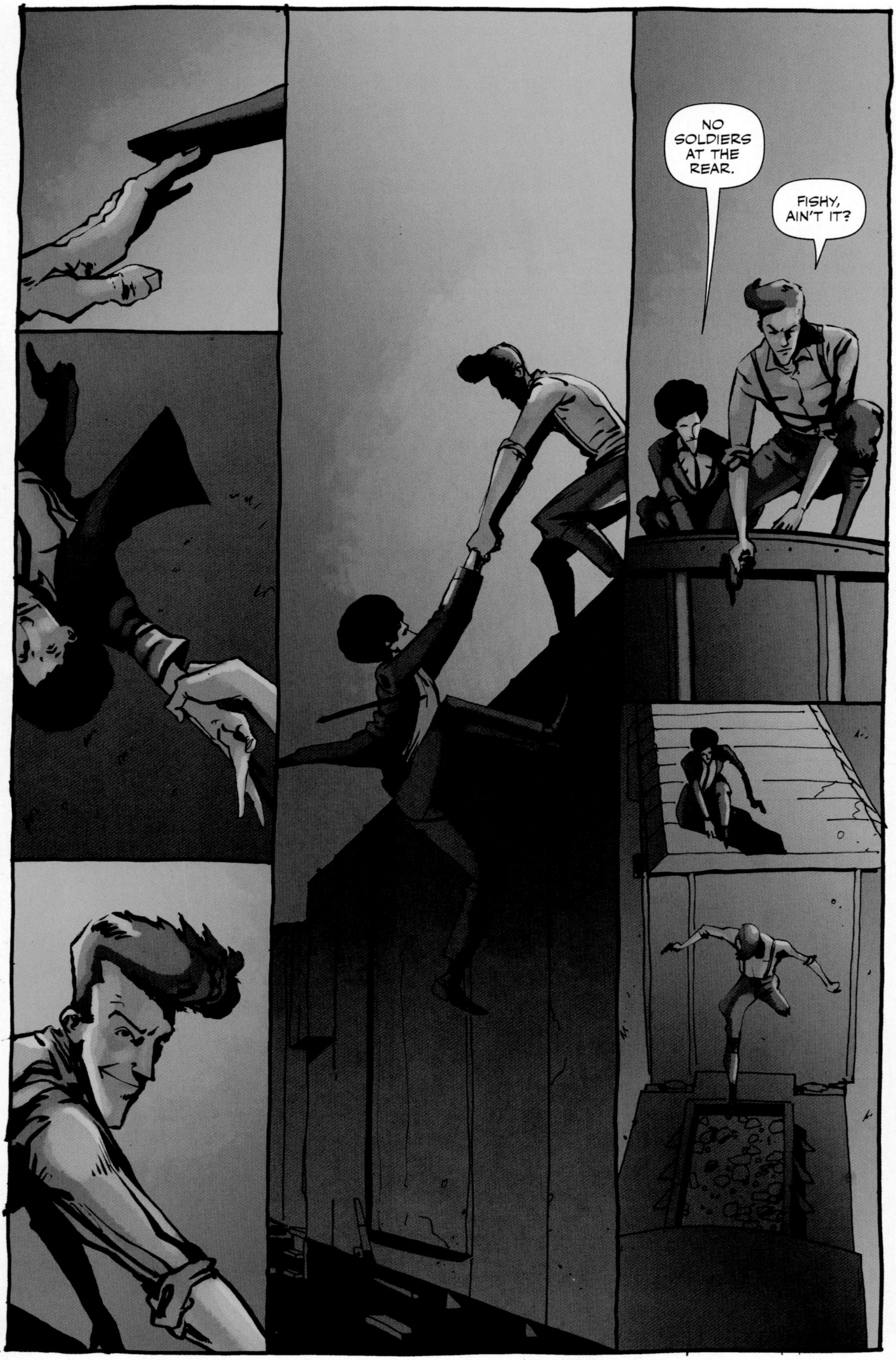

NO SOLDIERS AT THE REAR.
FISHY, AIN'T IT?

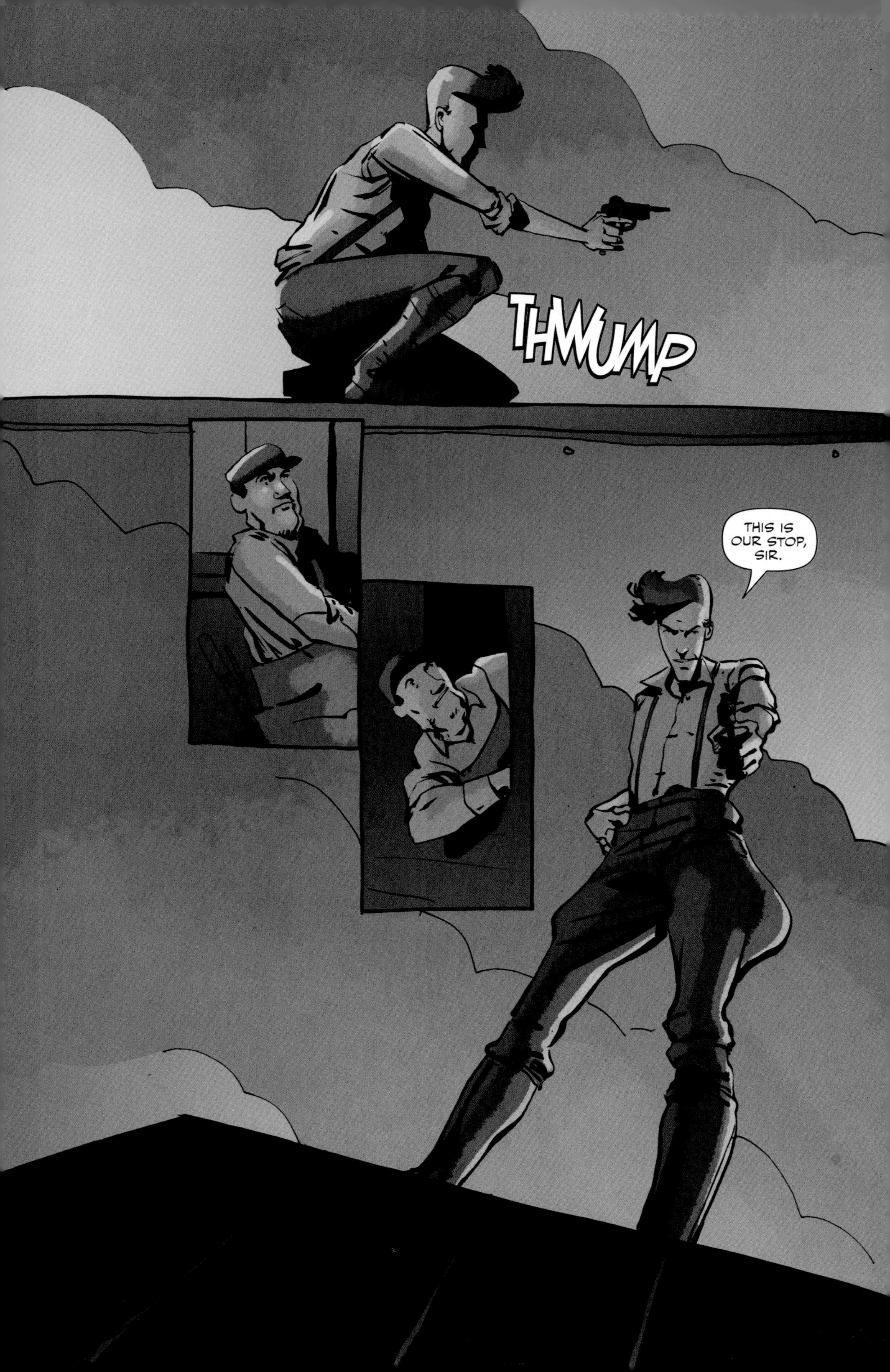
THMUMP
THIS IS OUR STOP, SIR.

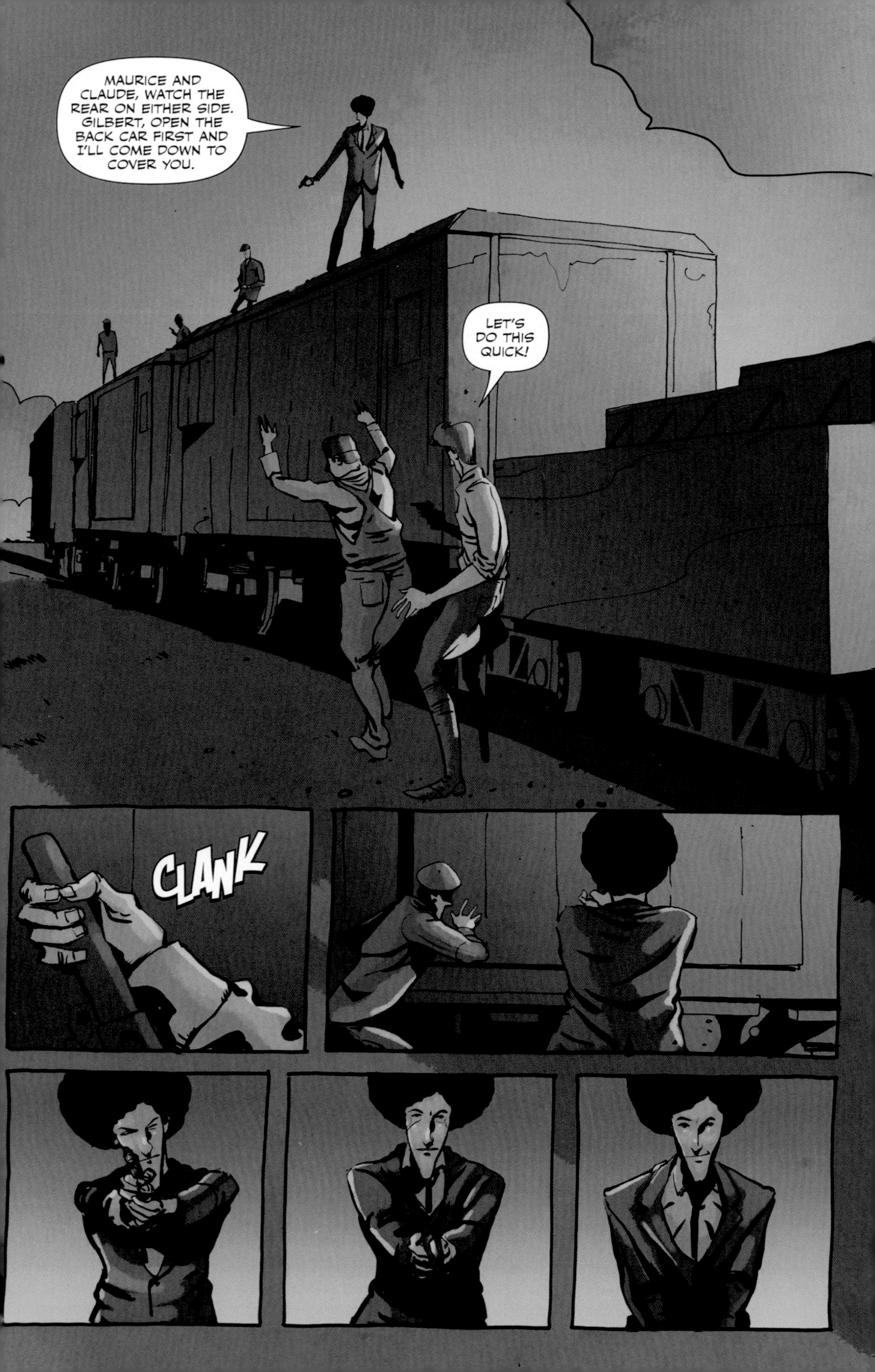
MAURICE AND CLAUDE, WATCH THE REAR ON EITHER SIDE. GILBERT, OPEN THE BACK CAR FIRST AND I'LL COME DOWN TO COVER YOU.
LET'S DO THIS QUICK!
CLANK

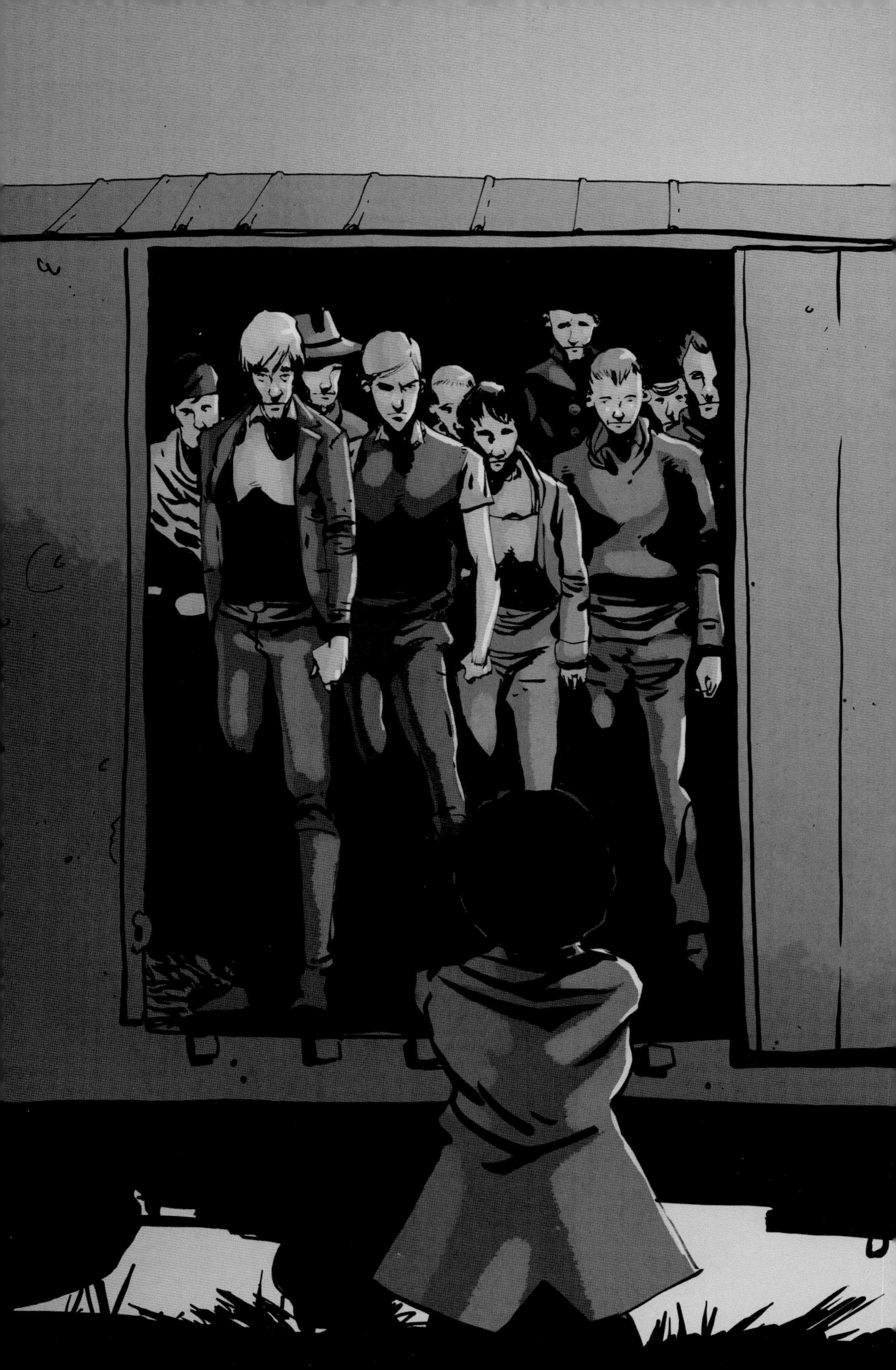

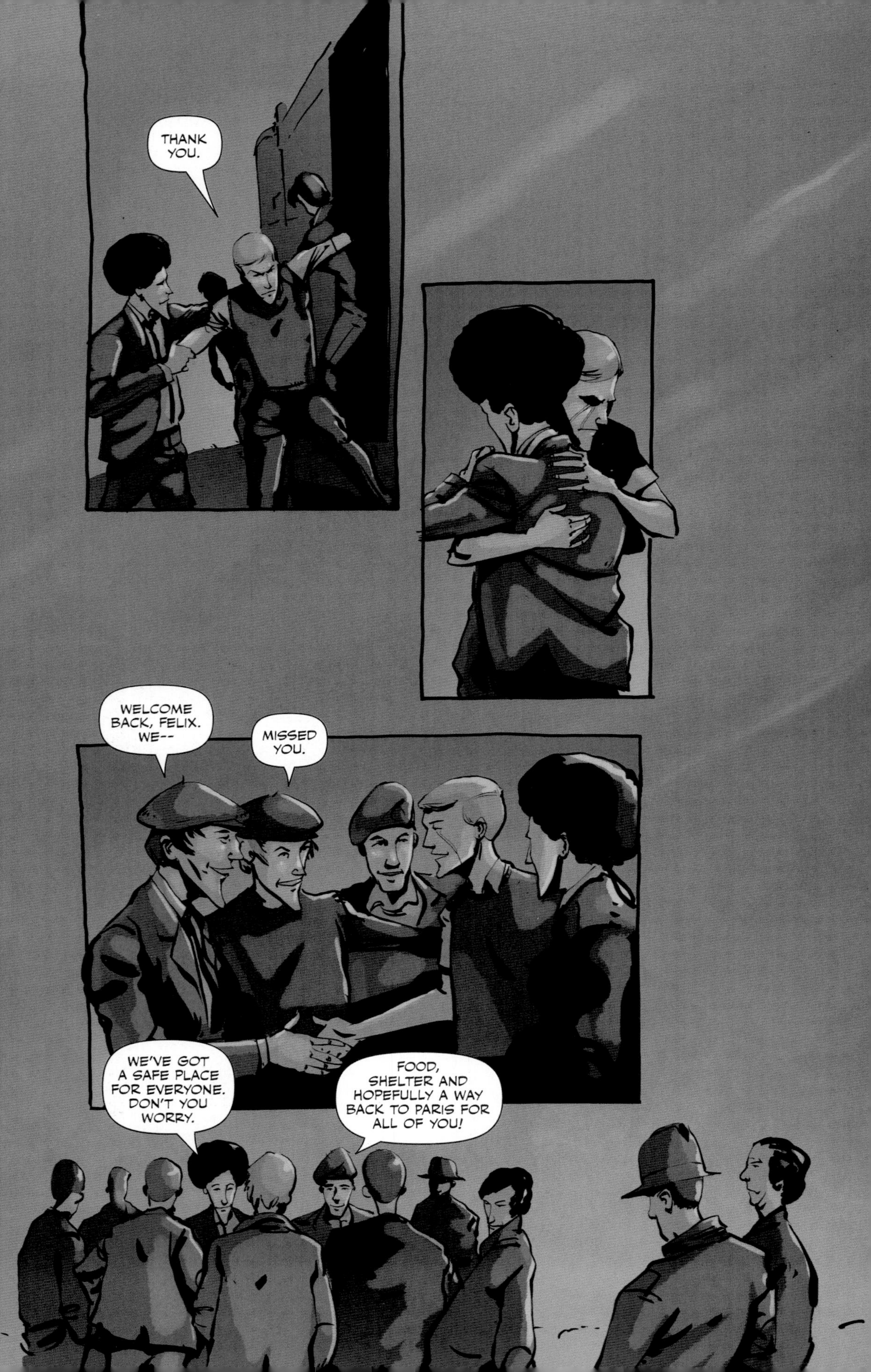
THANK YOU.
WELCOME BACK, FELIX. WE--
MISSED YOU.
WE'VE GOT A SAFE PLACE FOR EVERYONE. DON'T YOU WORRY.
FOOD, SHELTER AND HOPEFULLY A WAY BACK TO PARIS FOR ALL OF YOU!

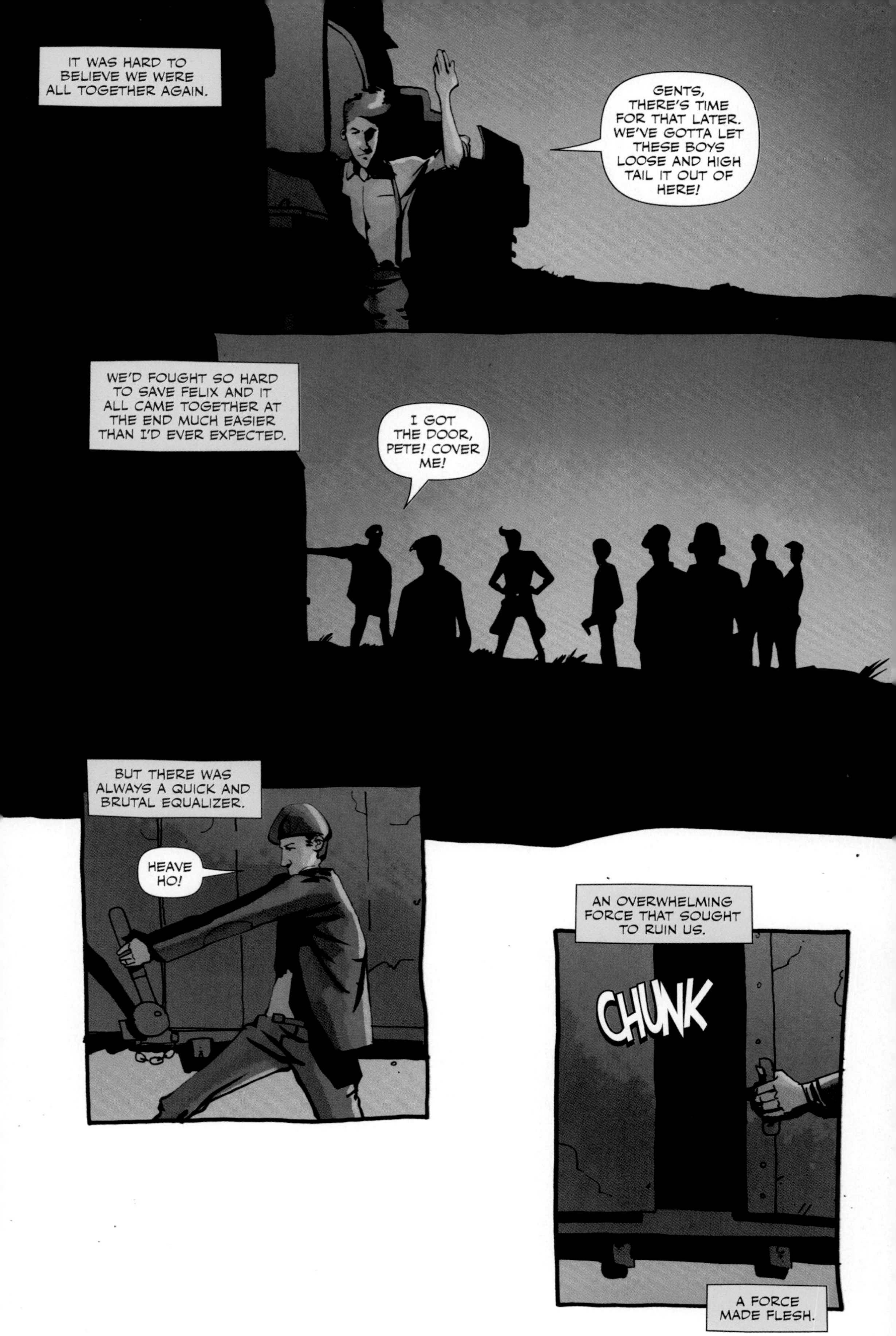
IT WAS HARD TO BELIEVE WE WERE ALL TOGETHER AGAIN.
GENTS, THERE'S TIME FOR THAT LATER. WE'VE GOTTA LET THESE BOYS LOOSE AND HIGH TAIL IT OUT OF HERE!
WE'D FOUGHT SO HARD TO SAVE FELIX AND IT ALL CAME TOGETHER AT THE END MUCH EASIER THAN I'D EVER EXPECTED.
I GOT THE DOOR, PETE! COVER ME!
BUT THERE WAS ALWAYS A QUICK AND BRUTAL EQUALIZER.
HEAVE HO!
AN OVERWHELMING FORCE THAT SOUGHT TO RUIN US.
CHUNK
A FORCE MADE FLESH.

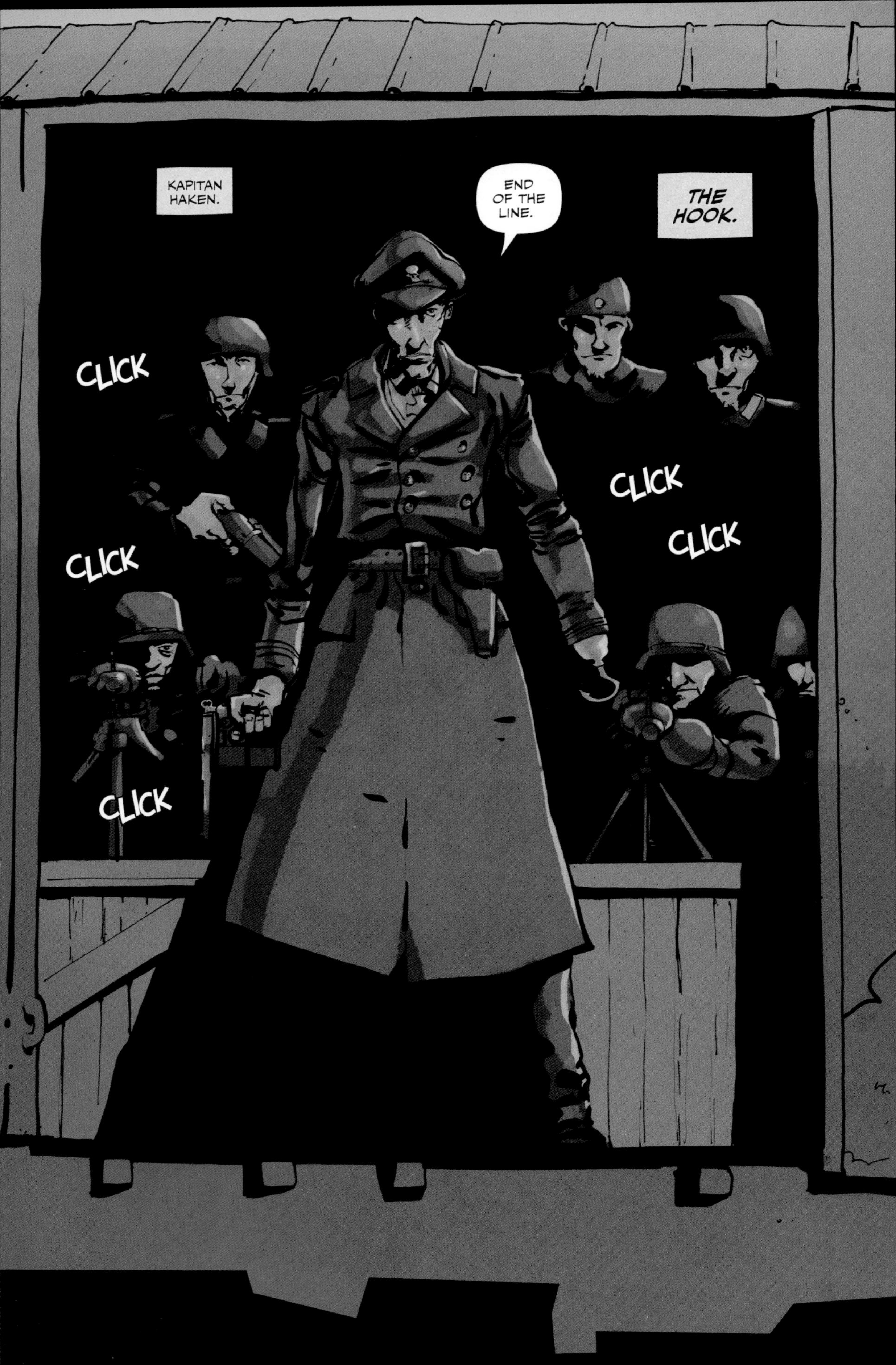
KAPITAN HAKEN.
END OF THE LINE.
THE HOOK.
CLICK
CLICK
CLICK
CLICK
CLICK
CLICK

CHAPTER NINE

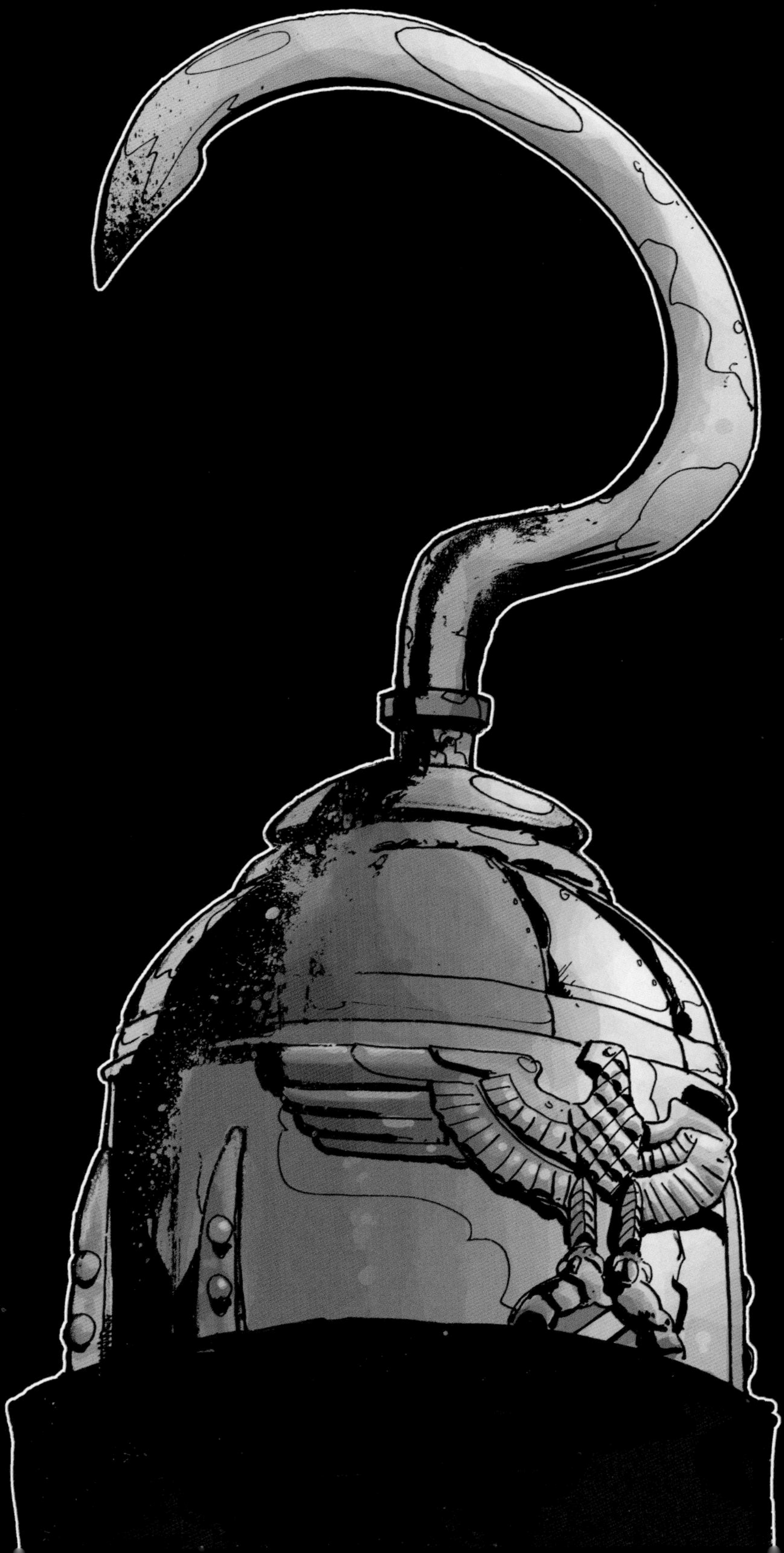

ISSUE NINE COVER B

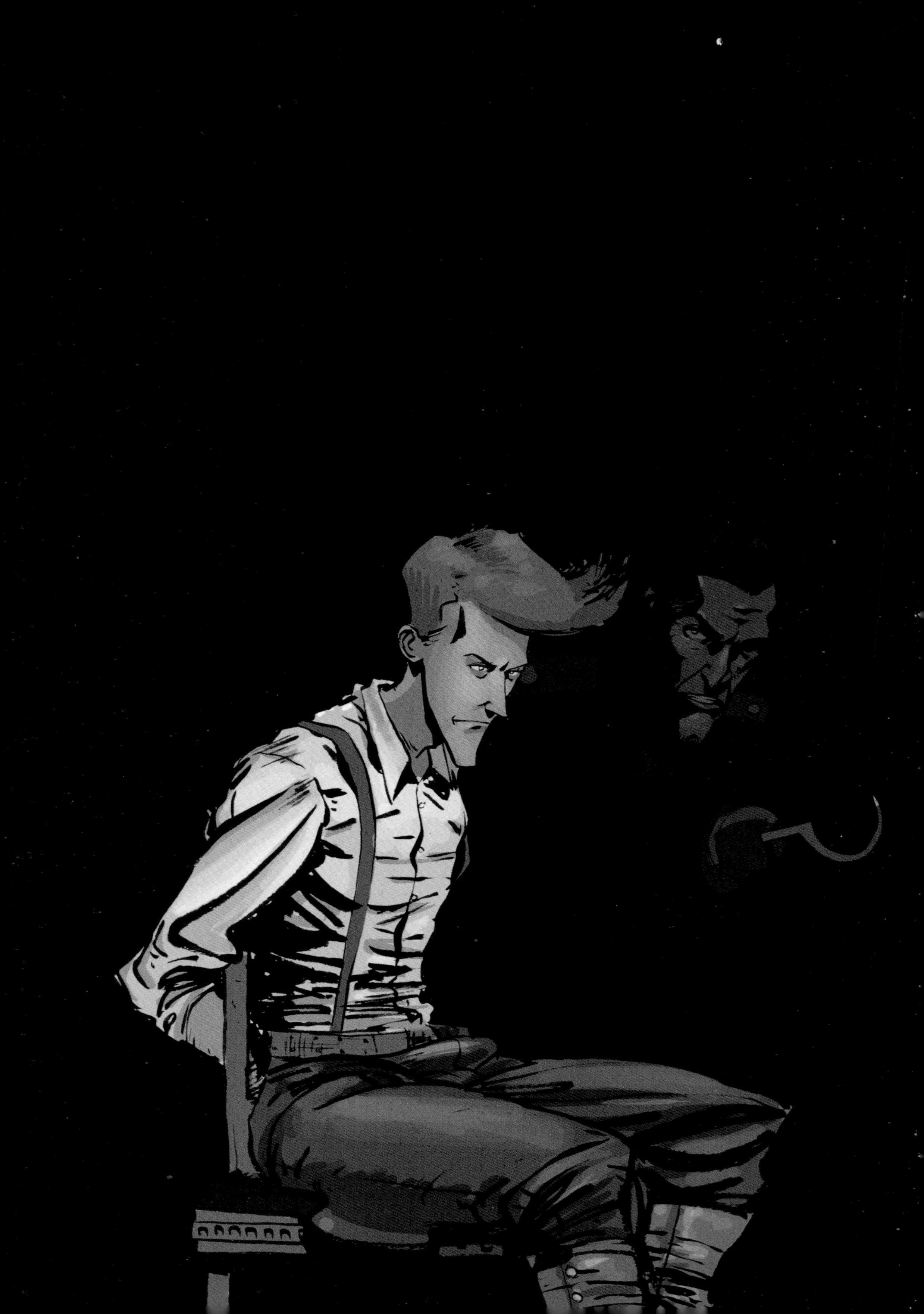

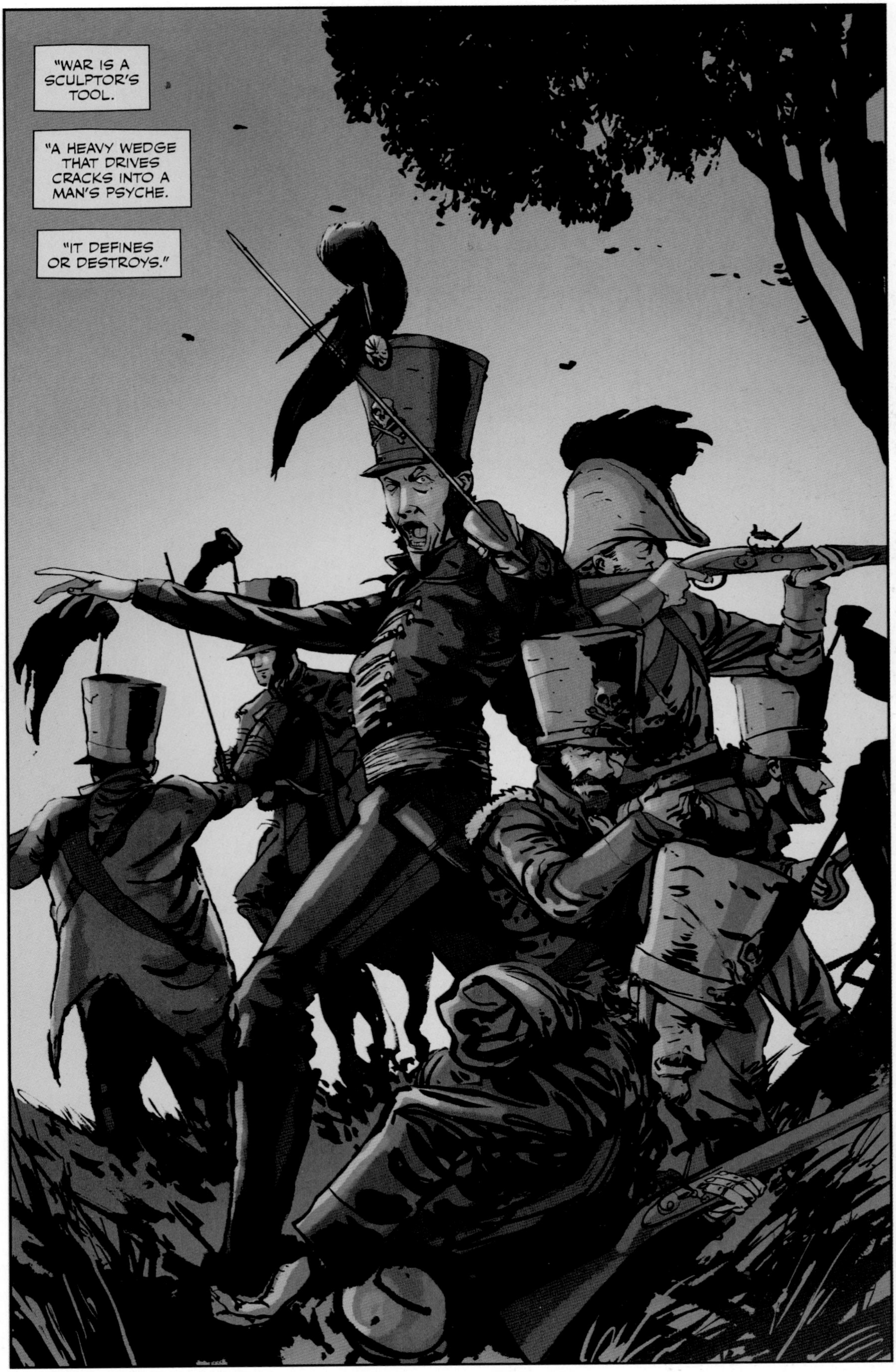
"WAR IS A SCULPTOR'S TOOL.
"A HEAVY WEDGE THAT DRIVES CRACKS INTO A MAN'S PSYCHE.
"IT DEFINES OR DESTROYS."

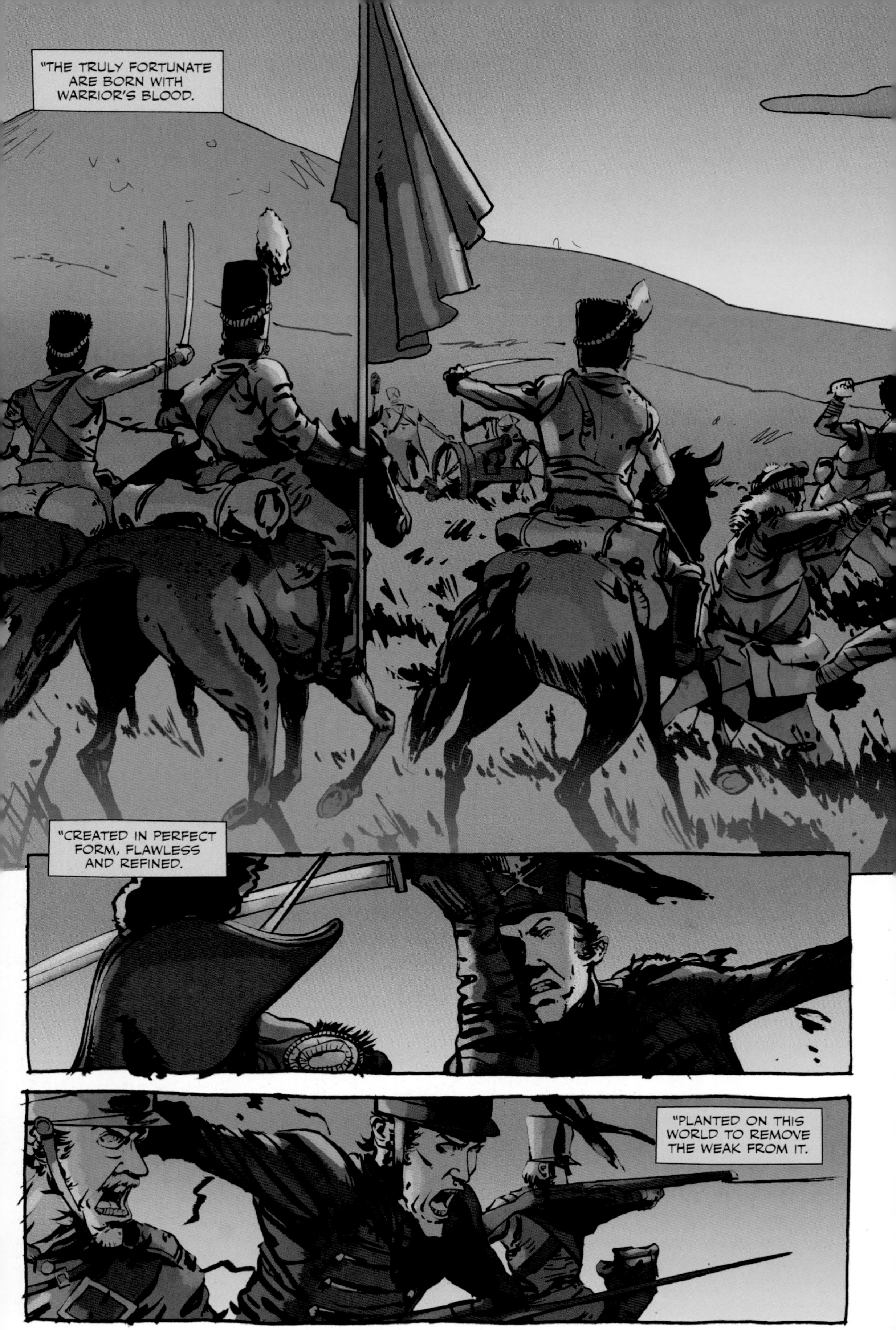
"THE TRULY FORTUNATE ARE BORN WITH WARRIOR'S BLOOD.
"CREATED IN PERFECT FORM, FLAWLESS AND REFINED.
"PLANTED ON THIS WORLD TO REMOVE THE WEAK FROM IT.

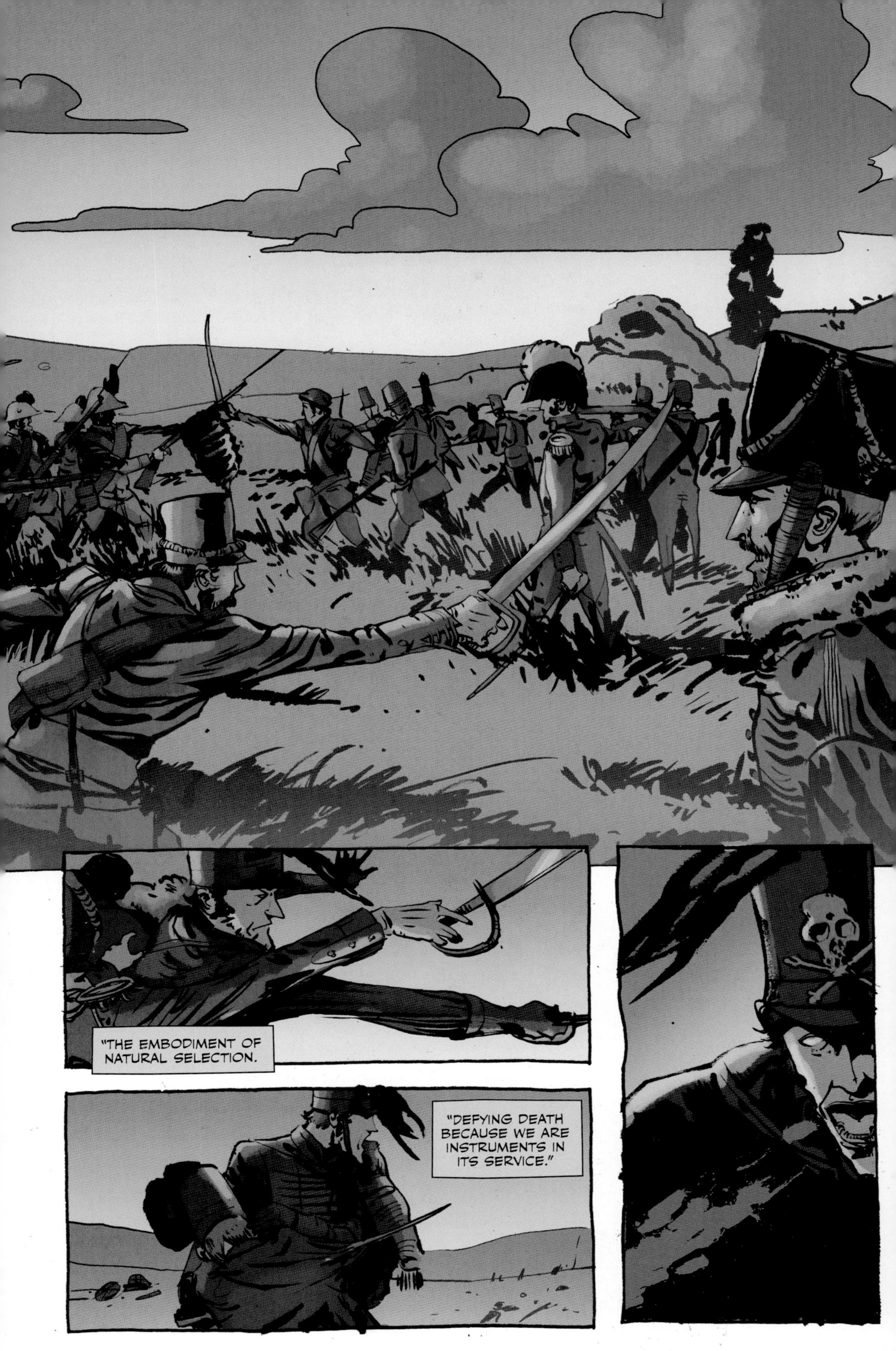
"THE EMBODIMENT OF NATURAL SELECTION.
"DEFYING DEATH BECAUSE WE ARE INSTRUMENTS IN ITS SERVICE."

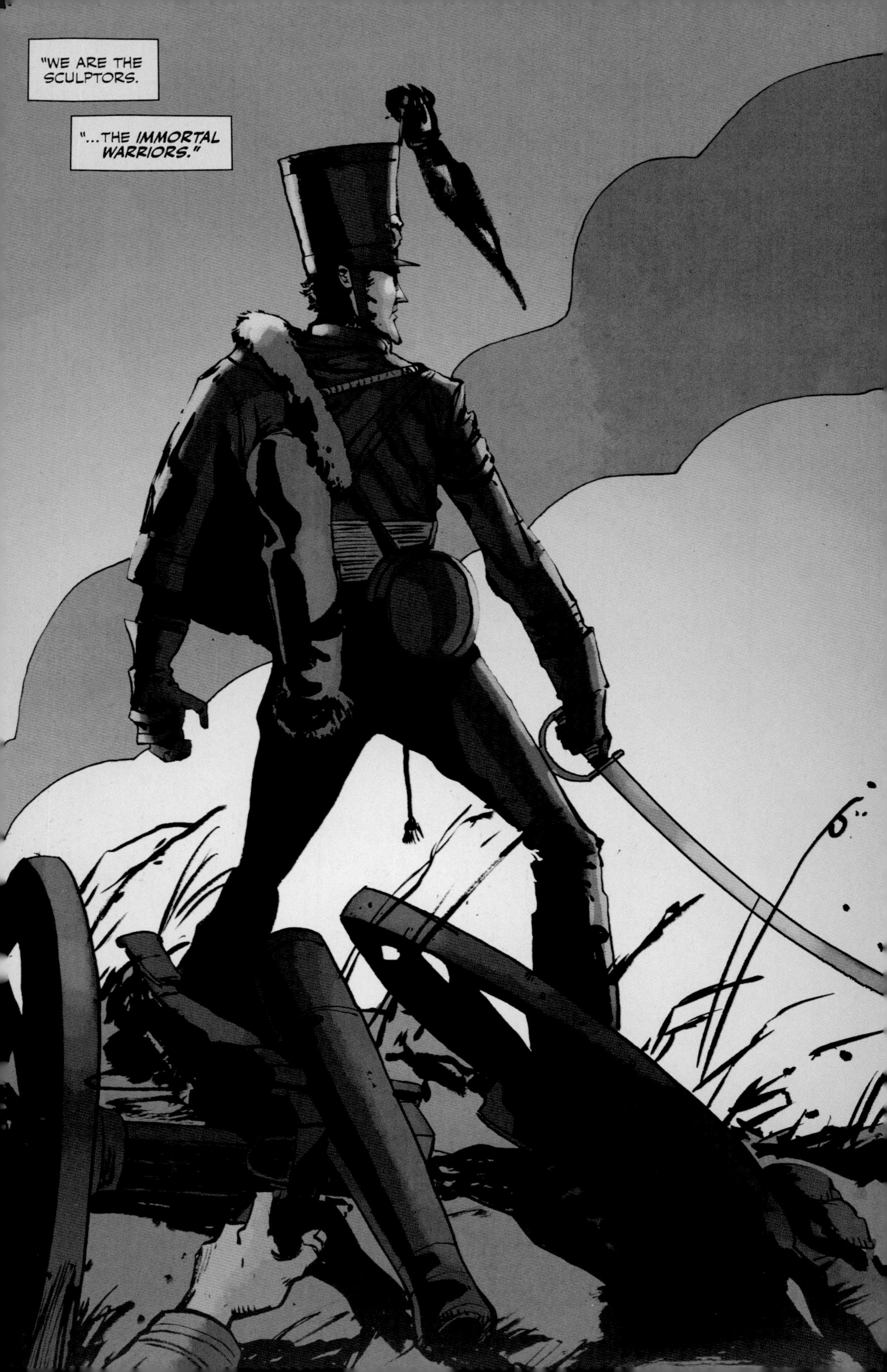
"WE ARE THE SCULPTORS.
"...THE *IMMORTAL WARRIORS.*"

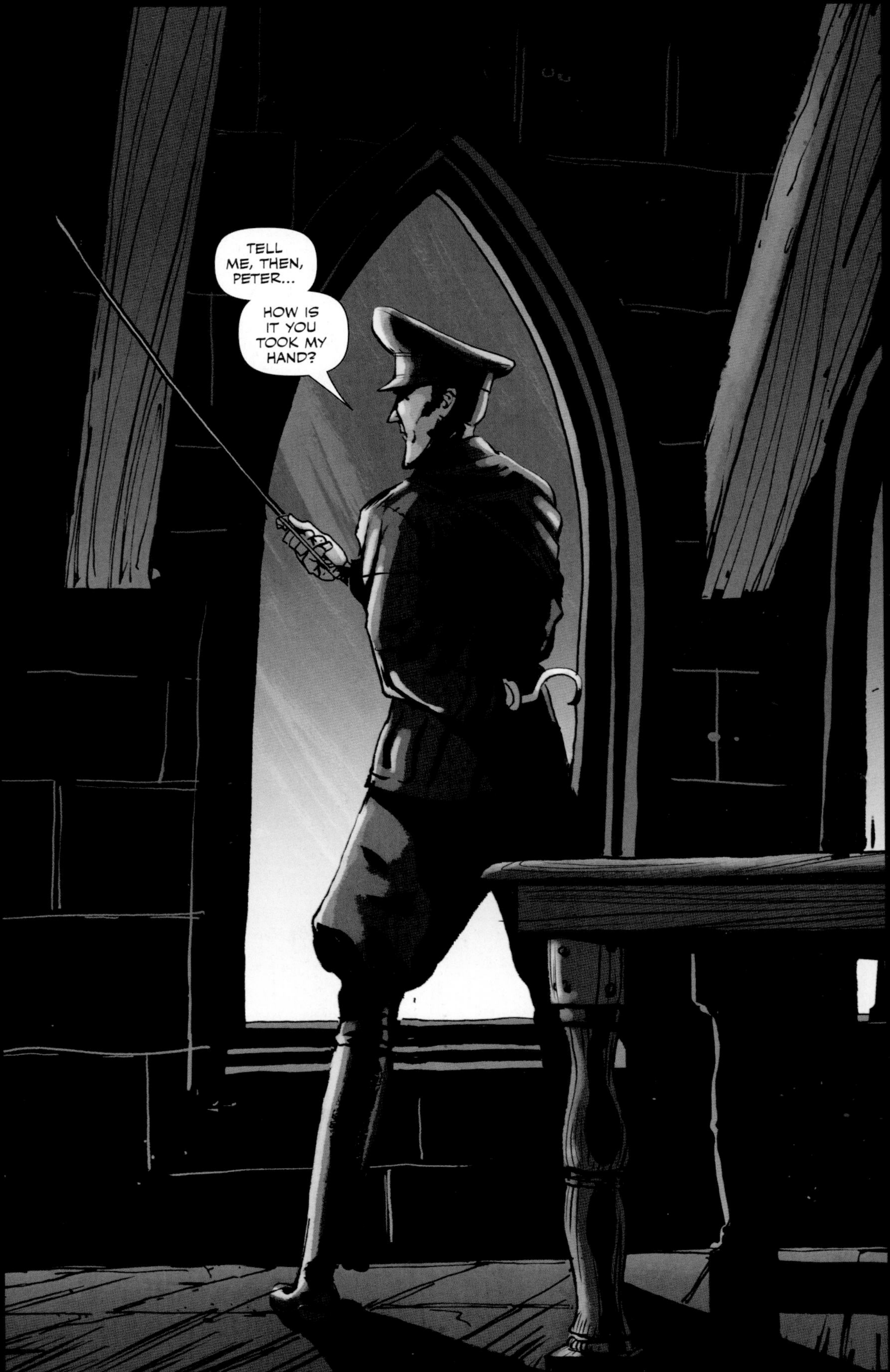
TELL ME, THEN, PETER...
HOW IS IT YOU TOOK MY HAND?

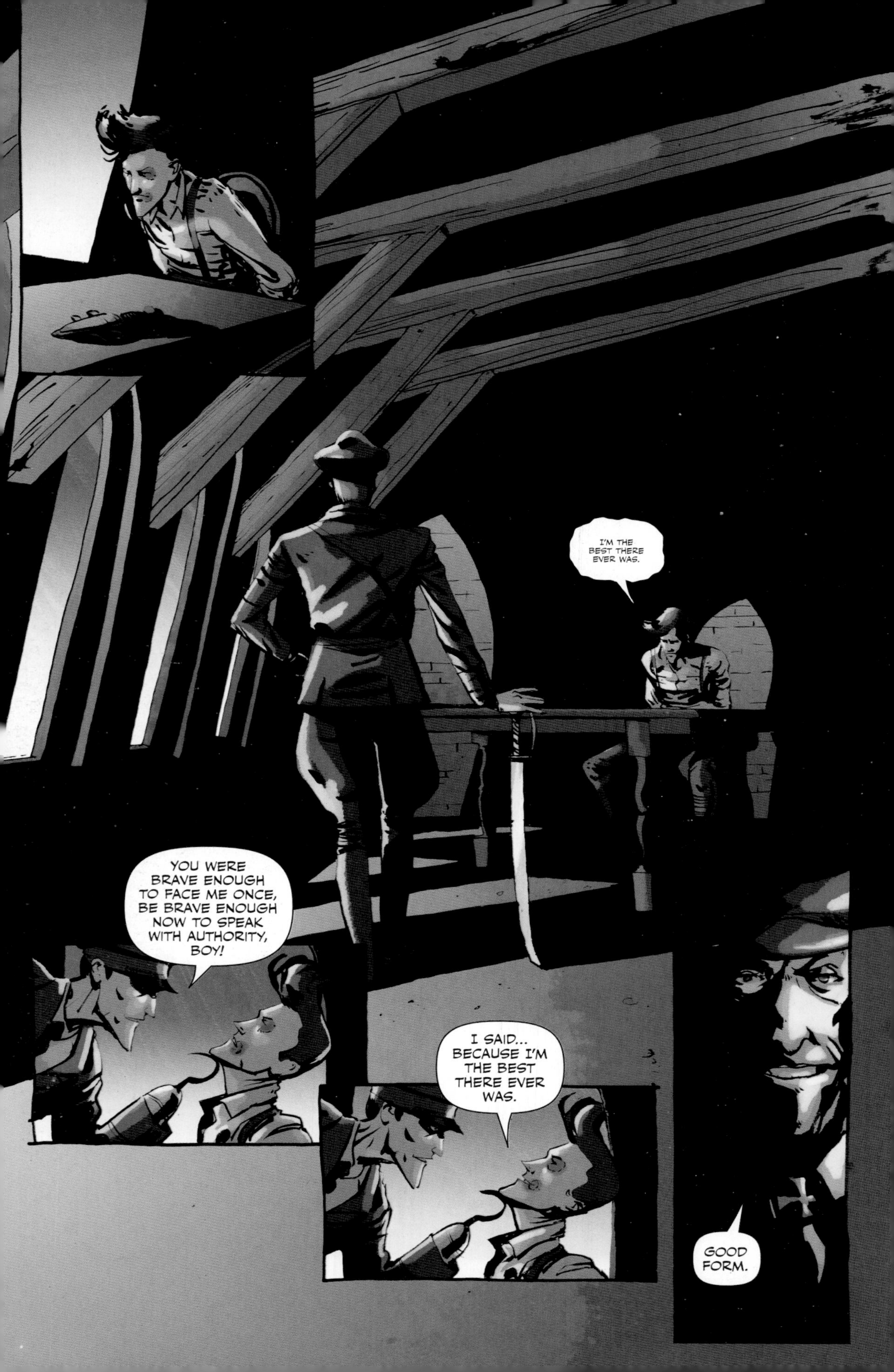
I'M THE BEST THERE EVER WAS.
YOU WERE BRAVE ENOUGH TO FACE ME ONCE, BE BRAVE ENOUGH NOW TO SPEAK WITH AUTHORITY, BOY!
I SAID... BECAUSE I'M THE BEST THERE EVER WAS.
GOOD FORM.

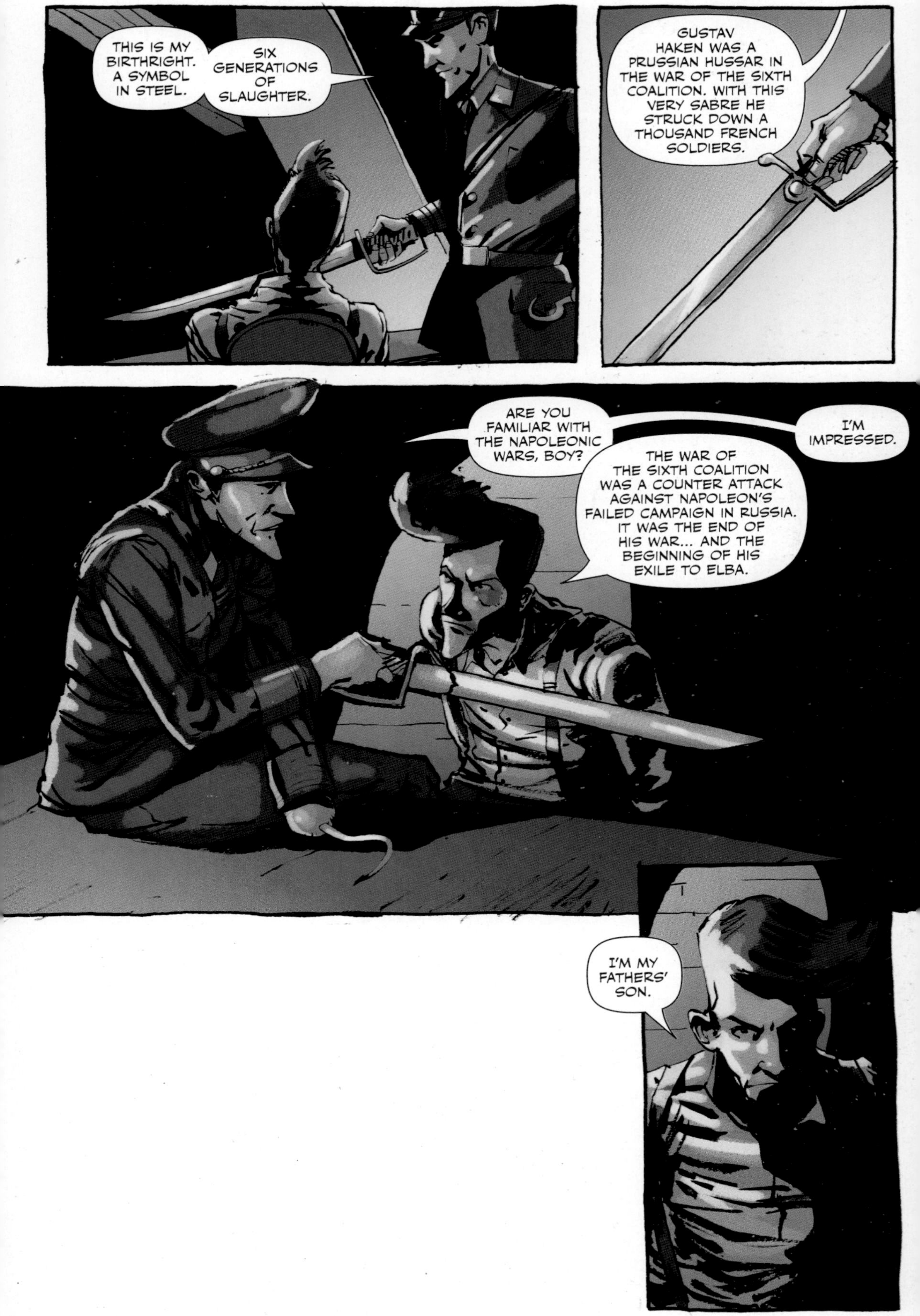
THIS IS MY BIRTHRIGHT. A SYMBOL IN STEEL.
SIX GENERATIONS OF SLAUGHTER.
GUSTAV HAKEN WAS A PRUSSIAN HUSSAR IN THE WAR OF THE SIXTH COALITION. WITH THIS VERY SABRE HE STRUCK DOWN A THOUSAND FRENCH SOLDIERS.
ARE YOU FAMILIAR WITH THE NAPOLEONIC WARS, BOY?
THE WAR OF THE SIXTH COALITION WAS A COUNTER ATTACK AGAINST NAPOLEON'S FAILED CAMPAIGN IN RUSSIA. IT WAS THE END OF HIS WAR... AND THE BEGINNING OF HIS EXILE TO ELBA.
I'M IMPRESSED.
I'M MY FATHERS' SON.

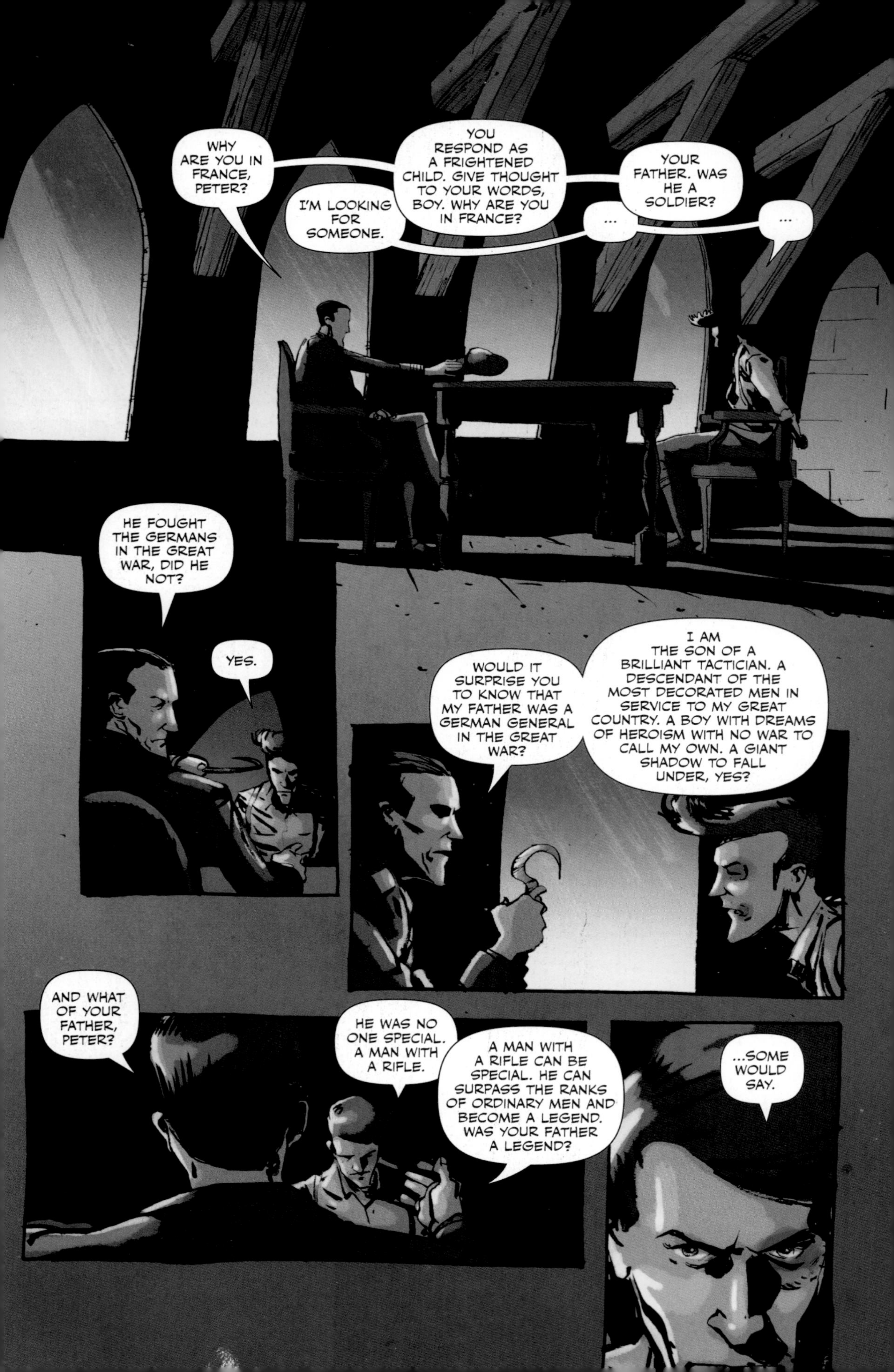
WHY ARE YOU IN FRANCE, PETER?
I'M LOOKING FOR SOMEONE.
YOU RESPOND AS A FRIGHTENED CHILD. GIVE THOUGHT TO YOUR WORDS, BOY. WHY ARE YOU IN FRANCE?
...
YOUR FATHER. WAS HE A SOLDIER?
...
HE FOUGHT THE GERMANS IN THE GREAT WAR, DID HE NOT?
YES.
WOULD IT SURPRISE YOU TO KNOW THAT MY FATHER WAS A GERMAN GENERAL IN THE GREAT WAR?
I AM THE SON OF A BRILLIANT TACTICIAN. A DESCENDANT OF THE MOST DECORATED MEN IN SERVICE TO MY GREAT COUNTRY. A BOY WITH DREAMS OF HEROISM WITH NO WAR TO CALL MY OWN. A GIANT SHADOW TO FALL UNDER, YES?
AND WHAT OF YOUR FATHER, PETER?
HE WAS NO ONE SPECIAL. A MAN WITH A RIFLE.
A MAN WITH A RIFLE CAN BE SPECIAL. HE CAN SURPASS THE RANKS OF ORDINARY MEN AND BECOME A LEGEND. WAS YOUR FATHER A LEGEND?
...SOME WOULD SAY.

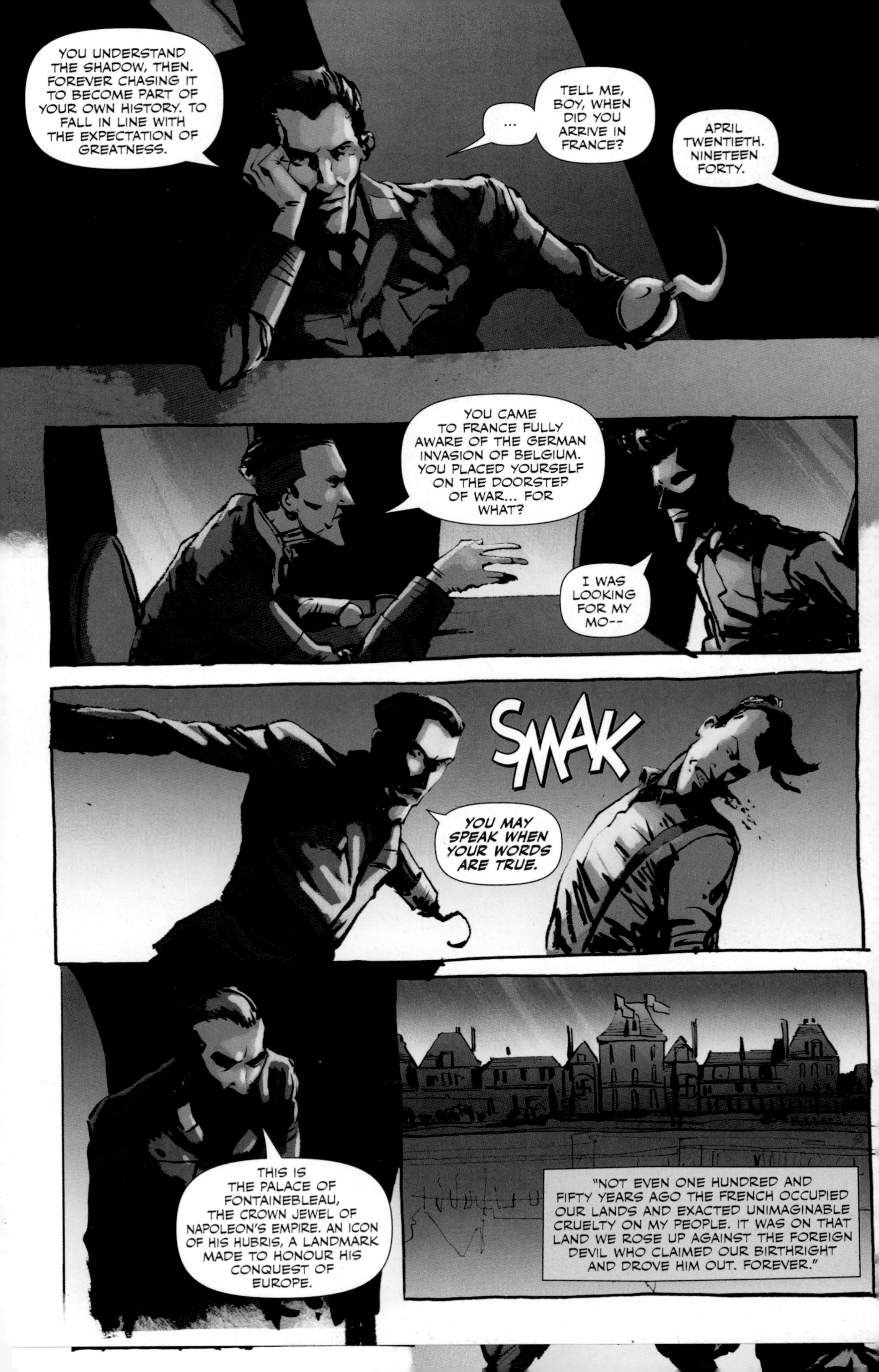

YOU UNDERSTAND THE SHADOW, THEN. FOREVER CHASING IT TO BECOME PART OF YOUR OWN HISTORY. TO FALL IN LINE WITH THE EXPECTATION OF GREATNESS.
...
TELL ME, BOY, WHEN DID YOU ARRIVE IN FRANCE?
APRIL TWENTIETH. NINETEEN FORTY.
YOU CAME TO FRANCE FULLY AWARE OF THE GERMAN INVASION OF BELGIUM. YOU PLACED YOURSELF ON THE DOORSTEP OF WAR... FOR WHAT?
I WAS LOOKING FOR MY MO--
SMAK
YOU MAY SPEAK WHEN YOUR WORDS ARE TRUE.
THIS IS THE PALACE OF FONTAINEBLEAU, THE CROWN JEWEL OF NAPOLEON'S EMPIRE. AN ICON OF HIS HUBRIS, A LANDMARK MADE TO HONOUR HIS CONQUEST OF EUROPE.
"NOT EVEN ONE HUNDRED AND FIFTY YEARS AGO THE FRENCH OCCUPIED OUR LANDS AND EXACTED UNIMAGINABLE CRUELTY ON MY PEOPLE. IT WAS ON THAT LAND WE ROSE UP AGAINST THE FOREIGN DEVIL WHO CLAIMED OUR BIRTHRIGHT AND DROVE HIM OUT. FOREVER."

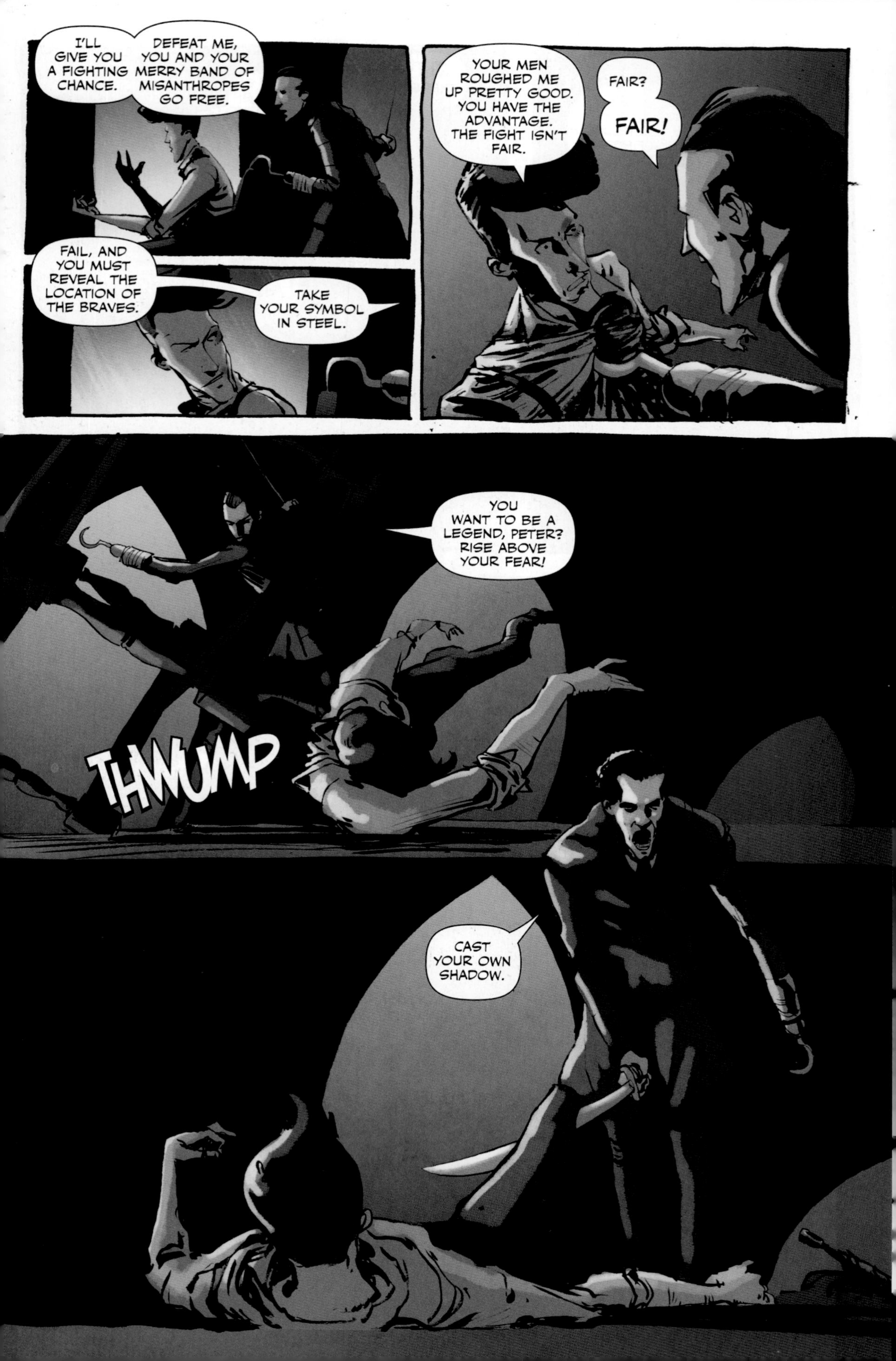
I'LL GIVE YOU A FIGHTING CHANCE.
DEFEAT ME, YOU AND YOUR MERRY BAND OF MISANTHROPES GO FREE.
FAIL, AND YOU MUST REVEAL THE LOCATION OF THE BRAVES.
TAKE YOUR SYMBOL IN STEEL.
YOUR MEN ROUGHED ME UP PRETTY GOOD. YOU HAVE THE ADVANTAGE. THE FIGHT ISN'T FAIR.
FAIR?
FAIR!
YOU WANT TO BE A LEGEND, PETER? RISE ABOVE YOUR FEAR!
THWUMP
CAST YOUR OWN SHADOW.

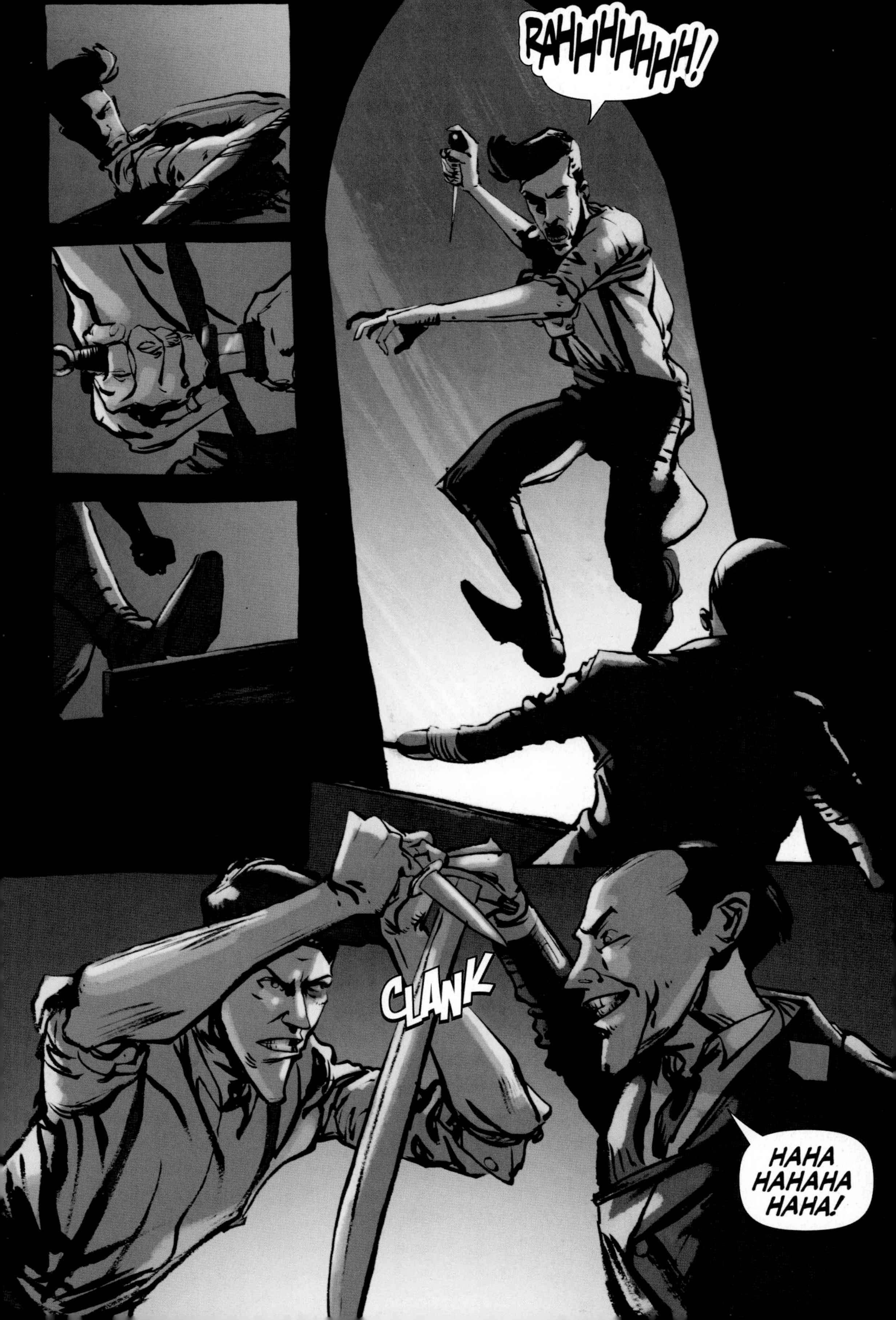
RAHHHHHHH!
CLANK
HAHA HAHAHA HAHA!

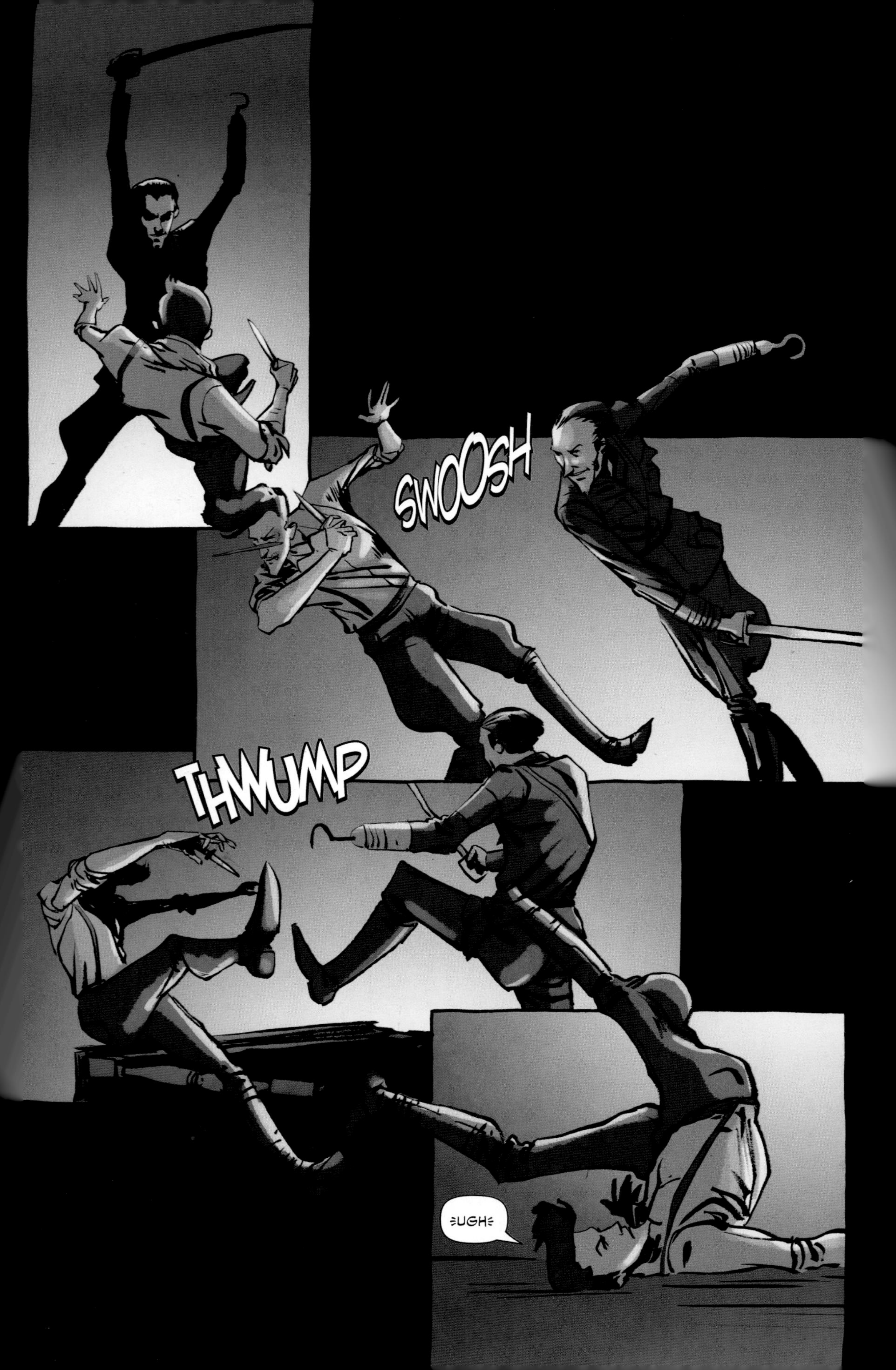
SWOOSH
THWUMP
UGH

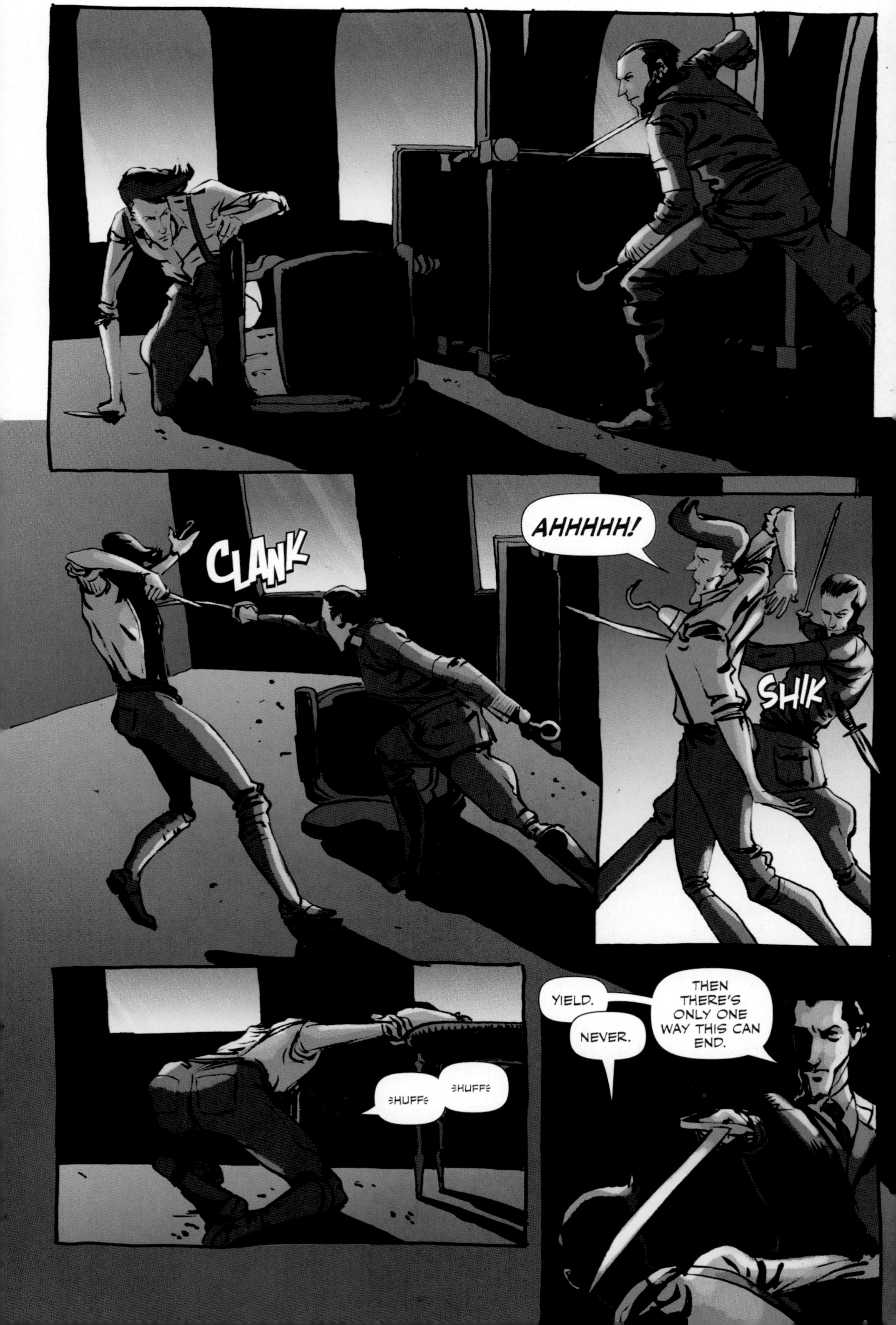
CLANK
AHHHHH!
SHIK
HUFF
HUFF
YIELD.
NEVER.
THEN THERE'S ONLY ONE WAY THIS CAN END.

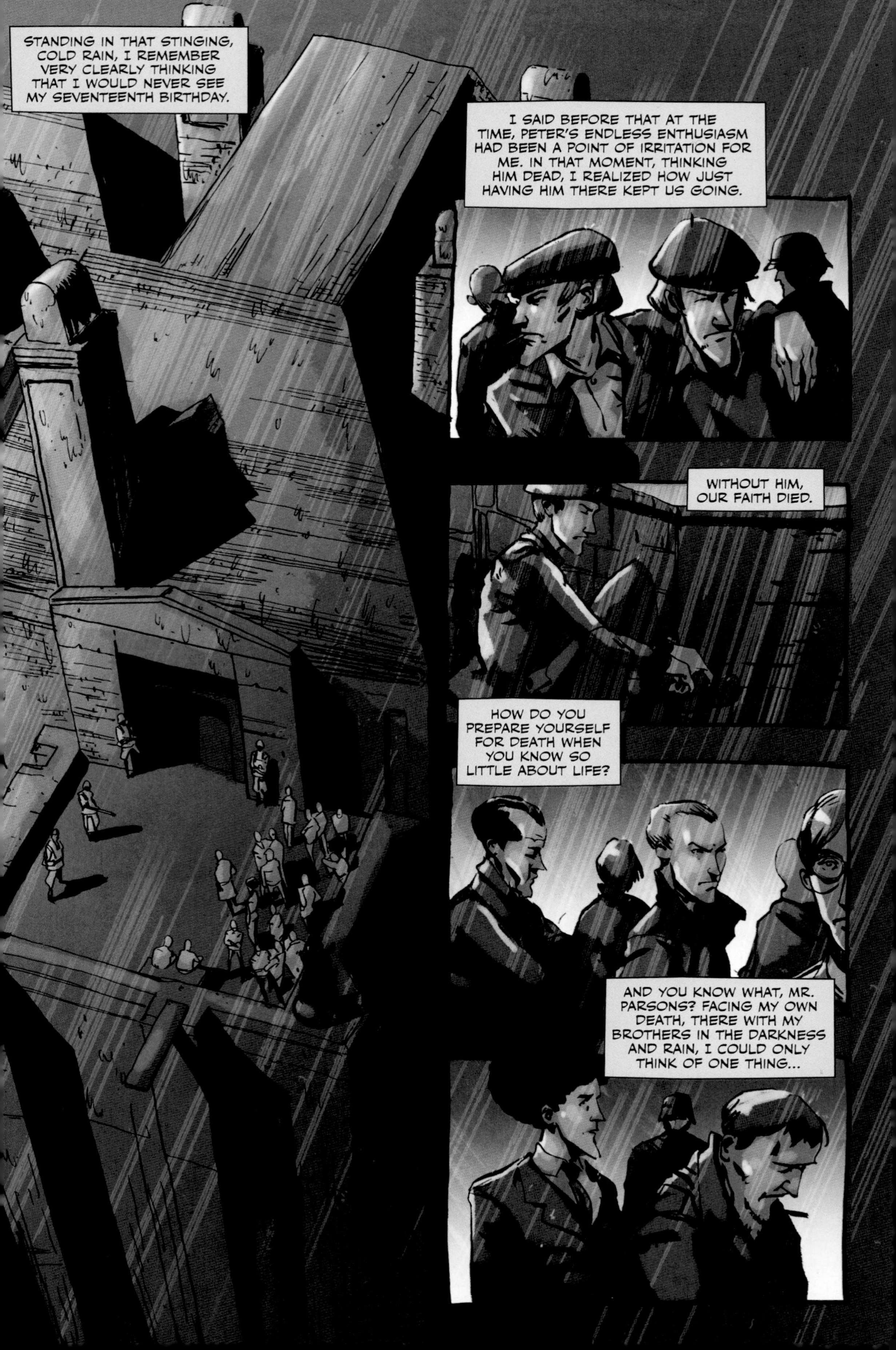
STANDING IN THAT STINGING, COLD RAIN, I REMEMBER VERY CLEARLY THINKING THAT I WOULD NEVER SEE MY SEVENTEENTH BIRTHDAY.
I SAID BEFORE THAT AT THE TIME, PETER'S ENDLESS ENTHUSIASM HAD BEEN A POINT OF IRRITATION FOR ME. IN THAT MOMENT, THINKING HIM DEAD, I REALIZED HOW JUST HAVING HIM THERE KEPT US GOING.
WITHOUT HIM, OUR FAITH DIED.
HOW DO YOU PREPARE YOURSELF FOR DEATH WHEN YOU KNOW SO LITTLE ABOUT LIFE?
AND YOU KNOW WHAT, MR. PARSONS? FACING MY OWN DEATH, THERE WITH MY BROTHERS IN THE DARKNESS AND RAIN, I COULD ONLY THINK OF ONE THING...

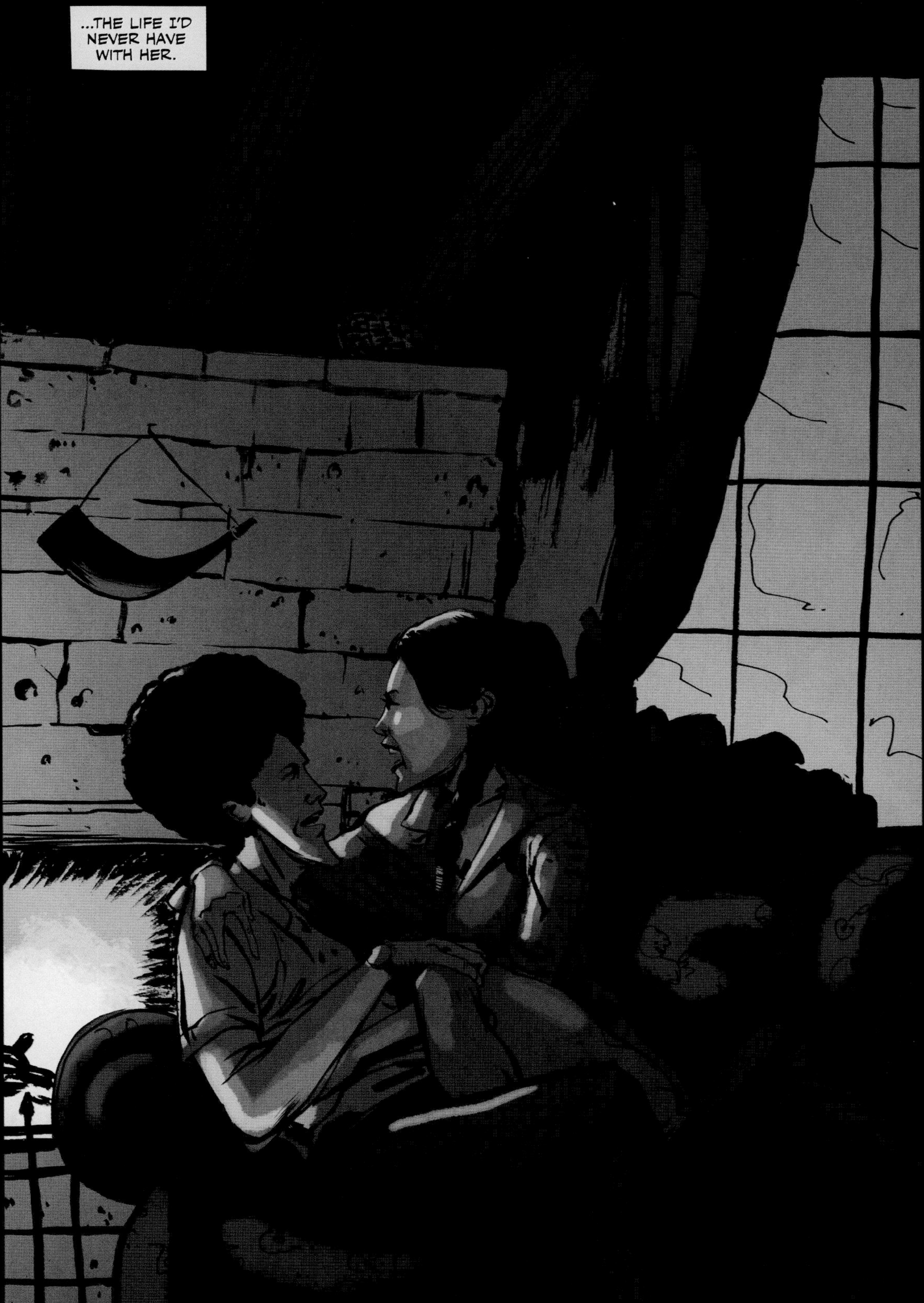
...THE LIFE I'D NEVER HAVE WITH HER.

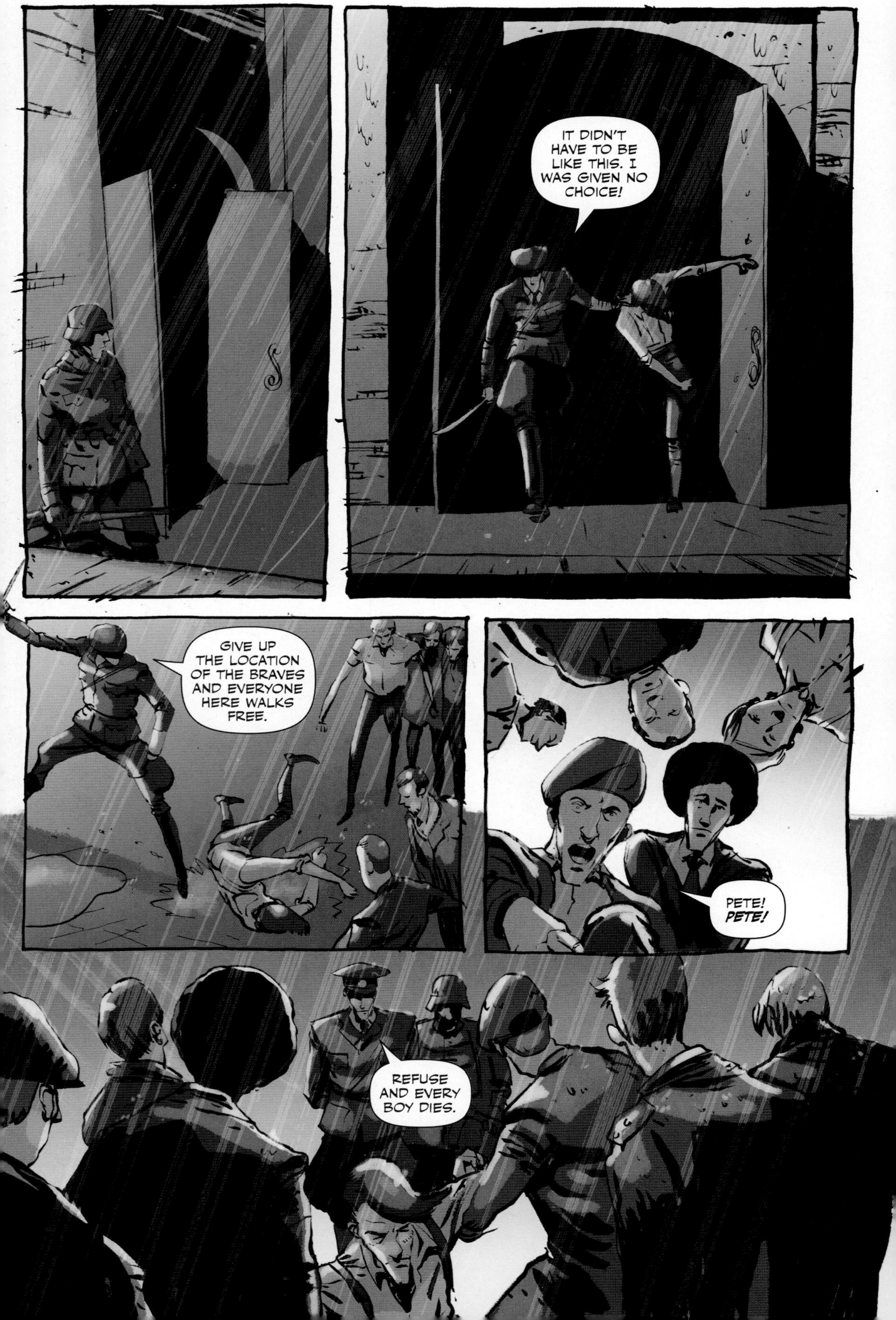
IT DIDN'T HAVE TO BE LIKE THIS. I WAS GIVEN NO CHOICE!
GIVE UP THE LOCATION OF THE BRAVES AND EVERYONE HERE WALKS FREE.
PETE! *PETE!*
REFUSE AND EVERY BOY DIES.

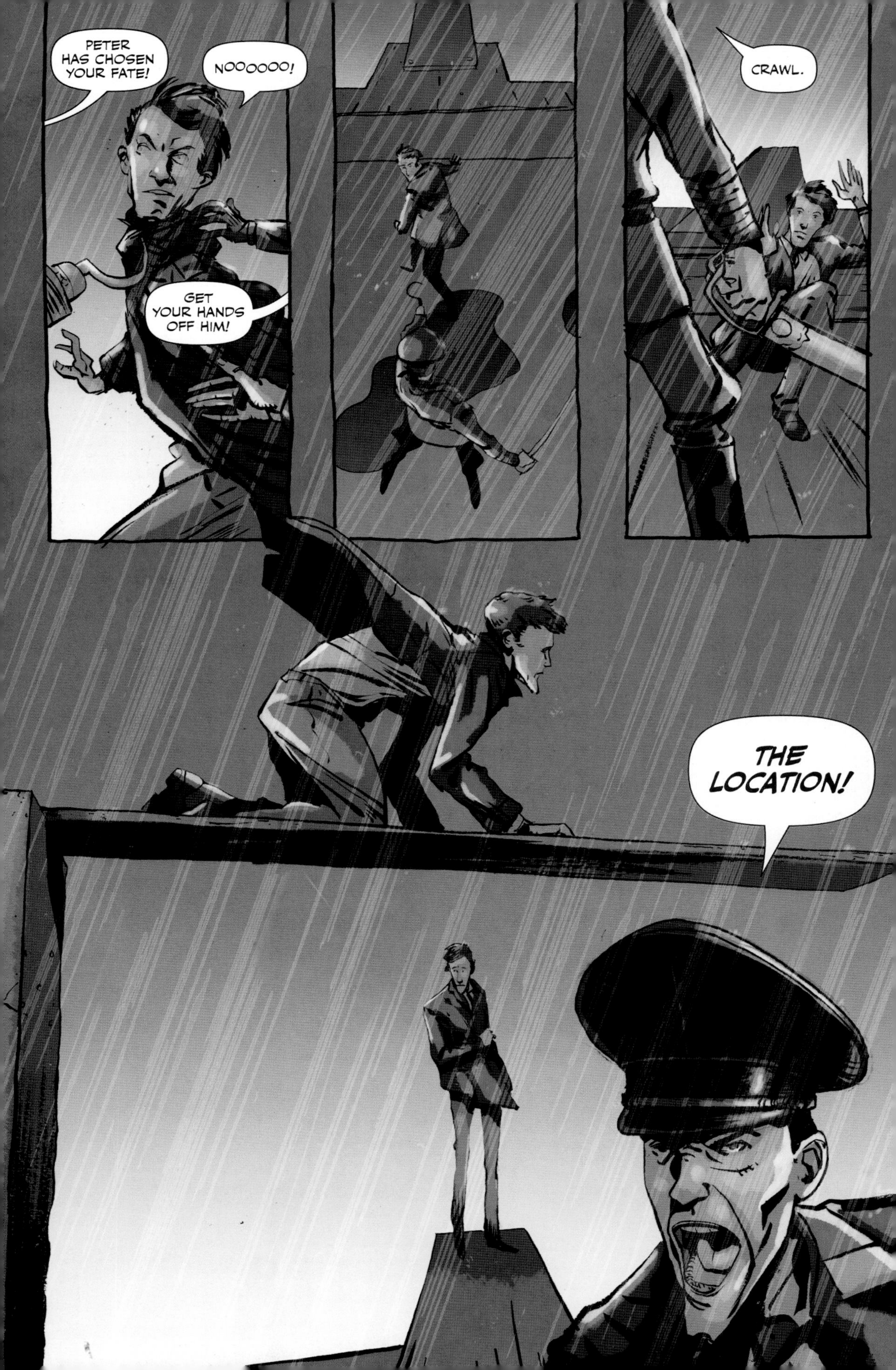
PETER HAS CHOSEN YOUR FATE!
NOOOOOO!
GET YOUR HANDS OFF HIM!
CRAWL.
THE LOCATION!

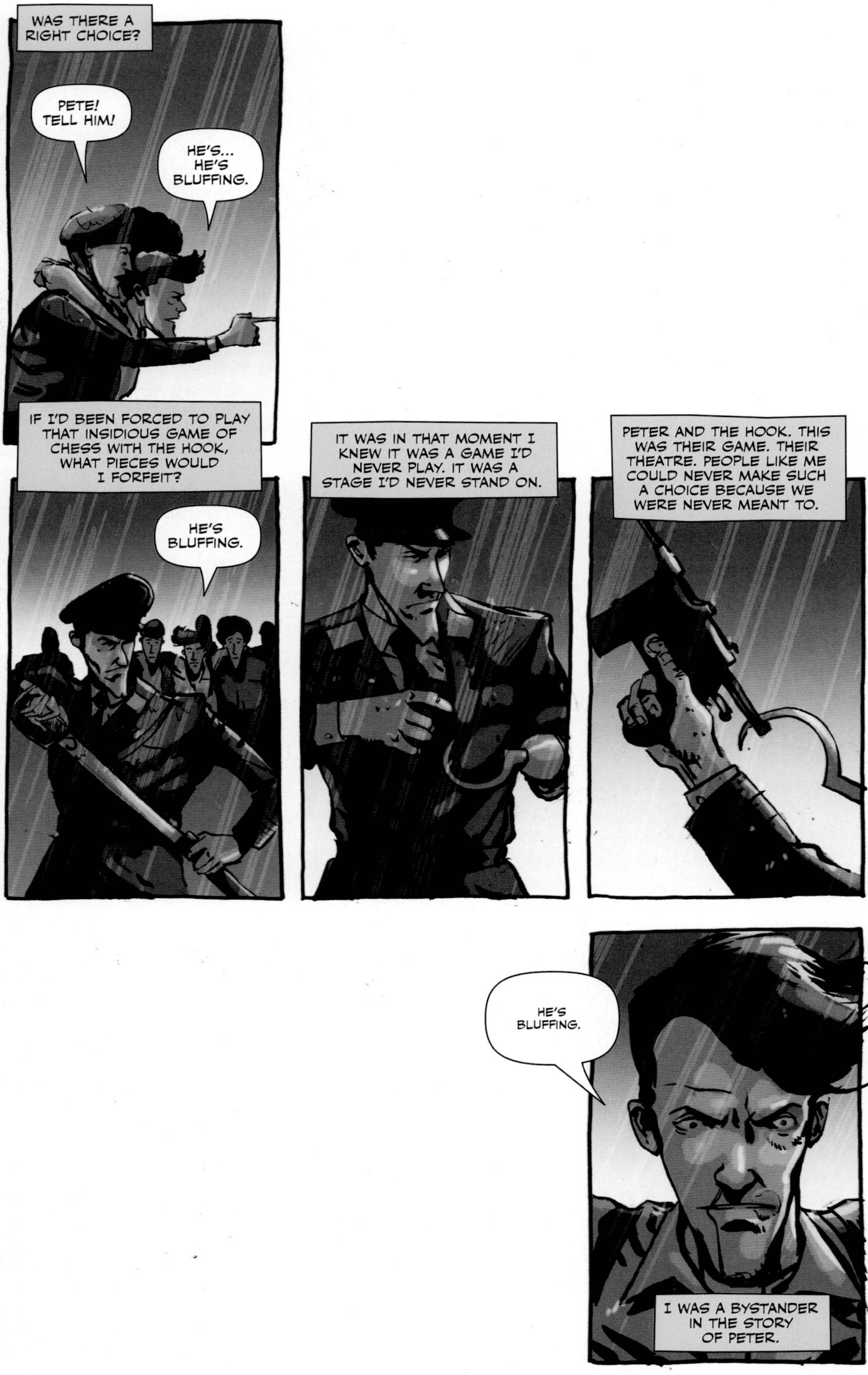
WAS THERE A RIGHT CHOICE?
PETE! TELL HIM!
HE'S... HE'S BLUFFING.
IF I'D BEEN FORCED TO PLAY THAT INSIDIOUS GAME OF CHESS WITH THE HOOK, WHAT PIECES WOULD I FORFEIT?
HE'S BLUFFING.
IT WAS IN THAT MOMENT I KNEW IT WAS A GAME I'D NEVER PLAY. IT WAS A STAGE I'D NEVER STAND ON.
PETER AND THE HOOK. THIS WAS THEIR GAME. THEIR THEATRE. PEOPLE LIKE ME COULD NEVER MAKE SUCH A CHOICE BECAUSE WE WERE NEVER MEANT TO.
HE'S BLUFFING.
I WAS A BYSTANDER IN THE STORY OF PETER.

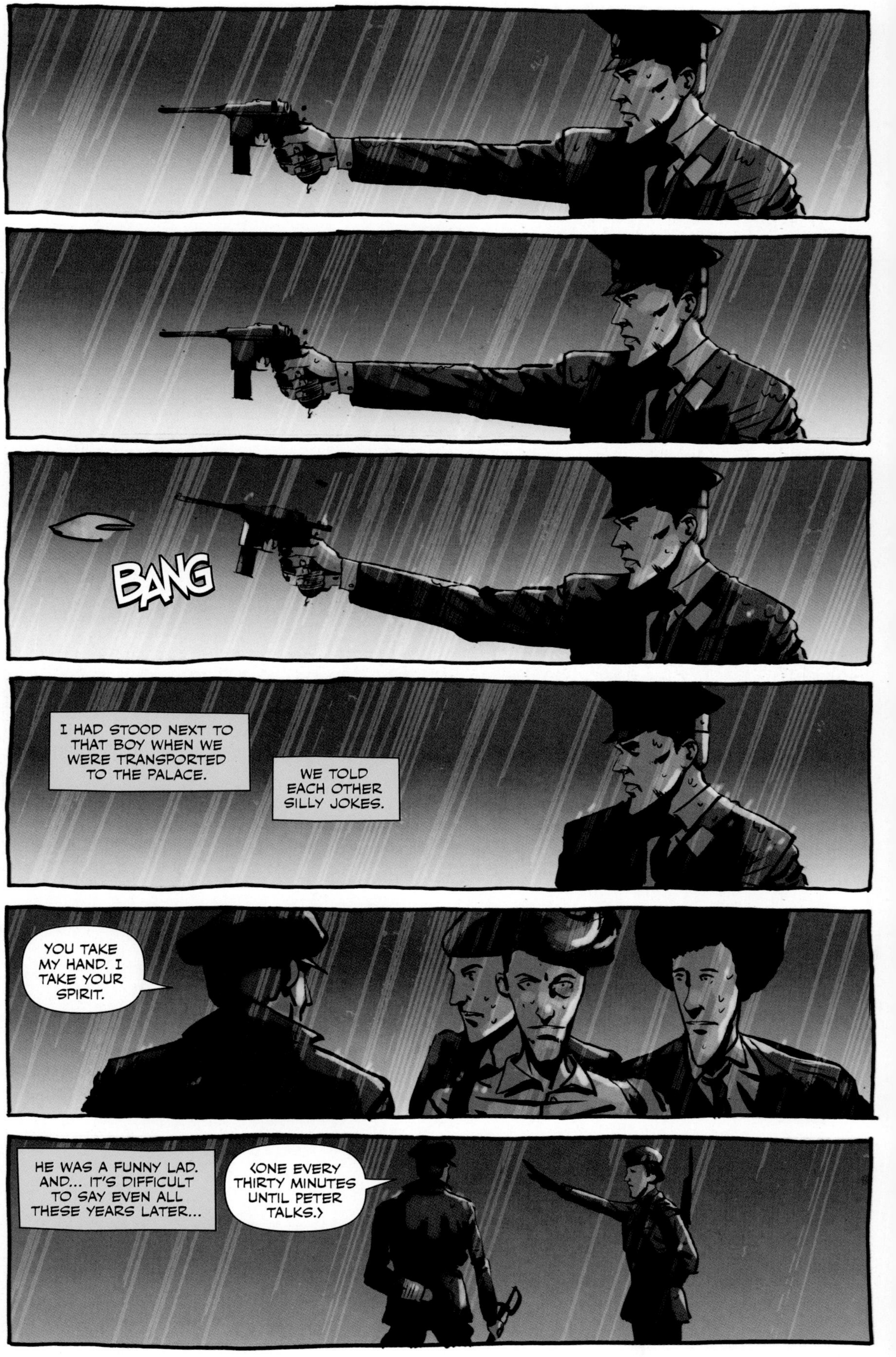
BANG
I HAD STOOD NEXT TO THAT BOY WHEN WE WERE TRANSPORTED TO THE PALACE.
WE TOLD EACH OTHER SILLY JOKES.
YOU TAKE MY HAND. I TAKE YOUR SPIRIT.
HE WAS A FUNNY LAD. AND... IT'S DIFFICULT TO SAY EVEN ALL THESE YEARS LATER...
<ONE EVERY THIRTY MINUTES UNTIL PETER TALKS.>

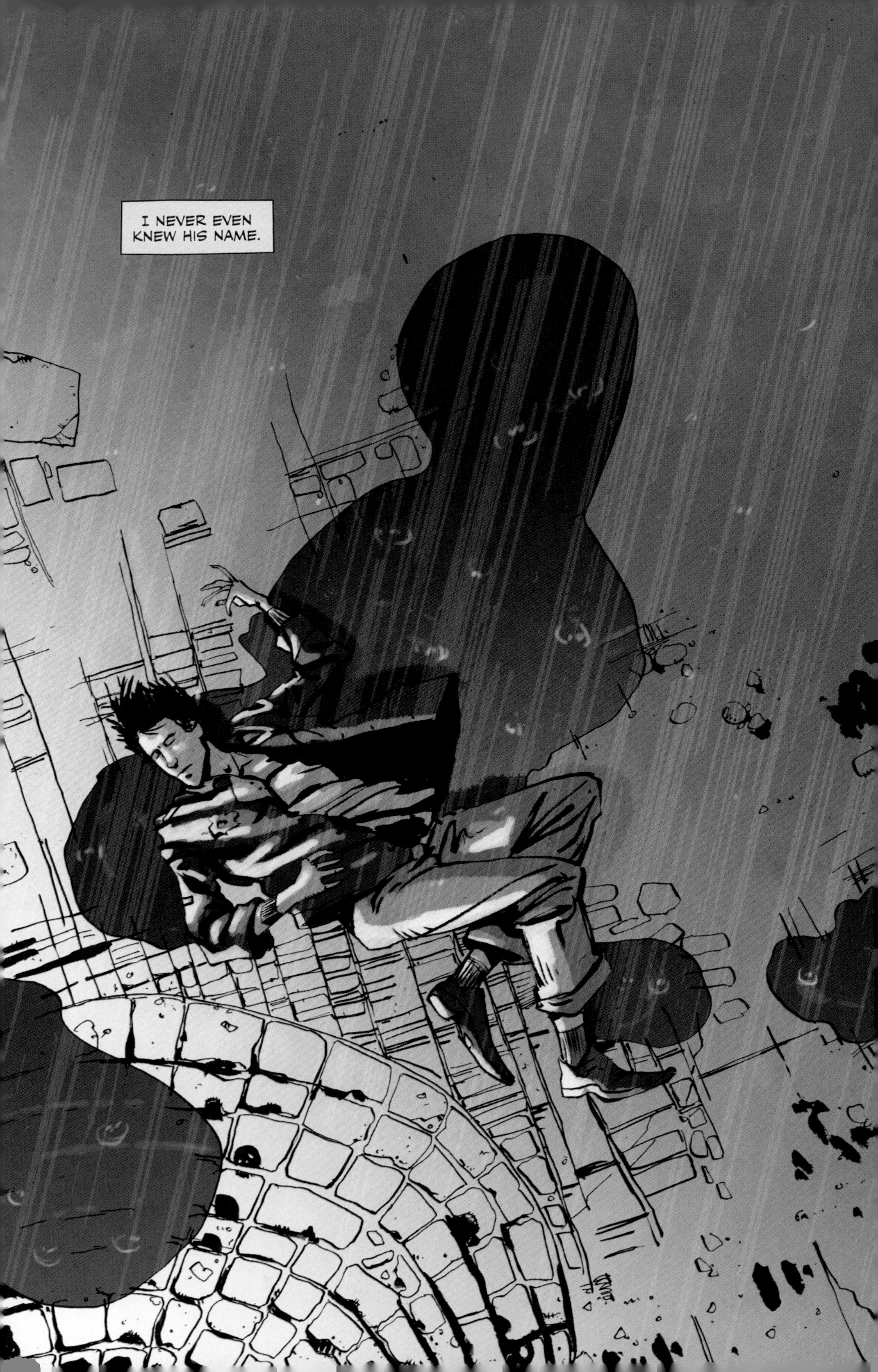
I NEVER EVEN KNEW HIS NAME.

CHAPTER TEN

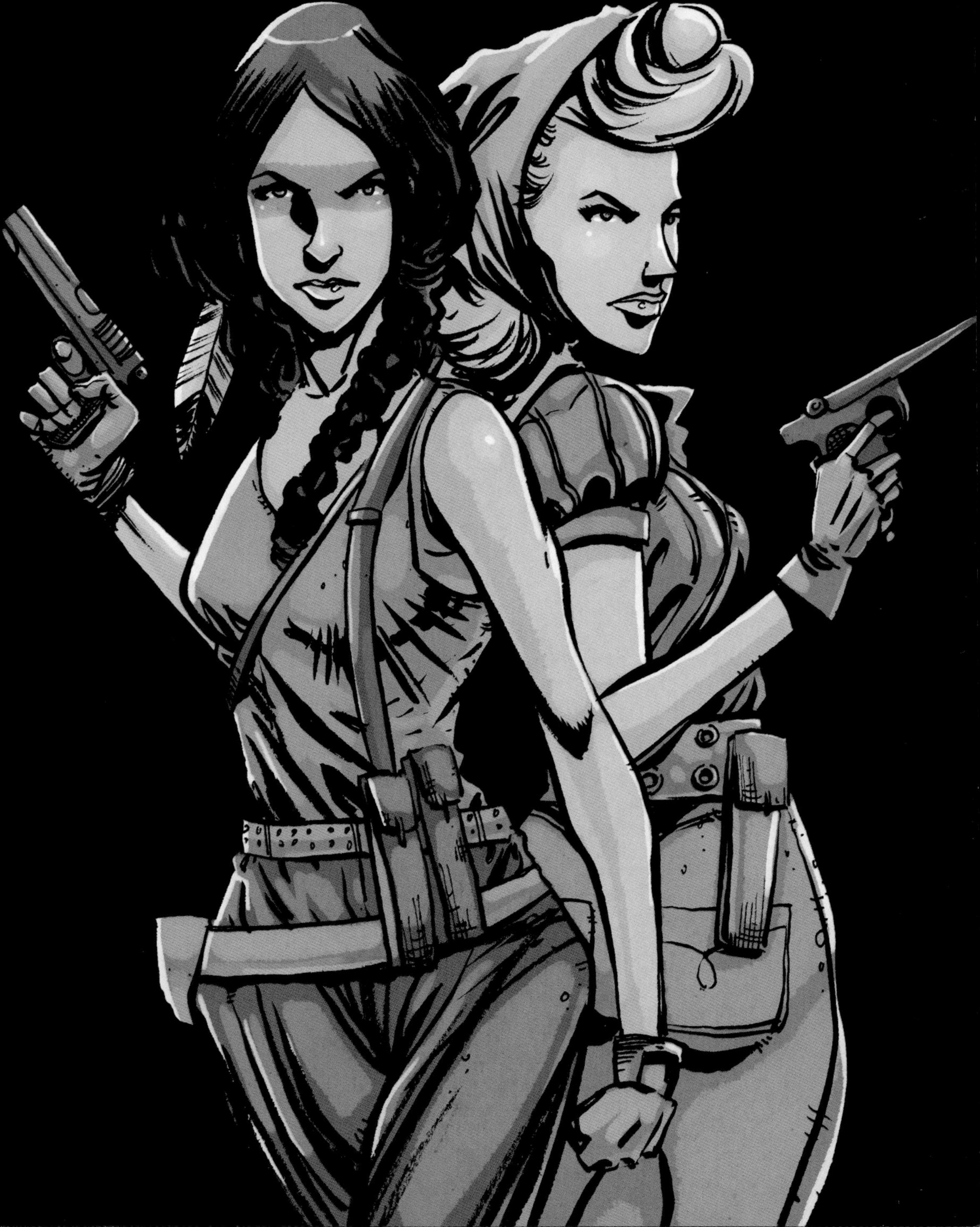

ISSUE TEN COVER B

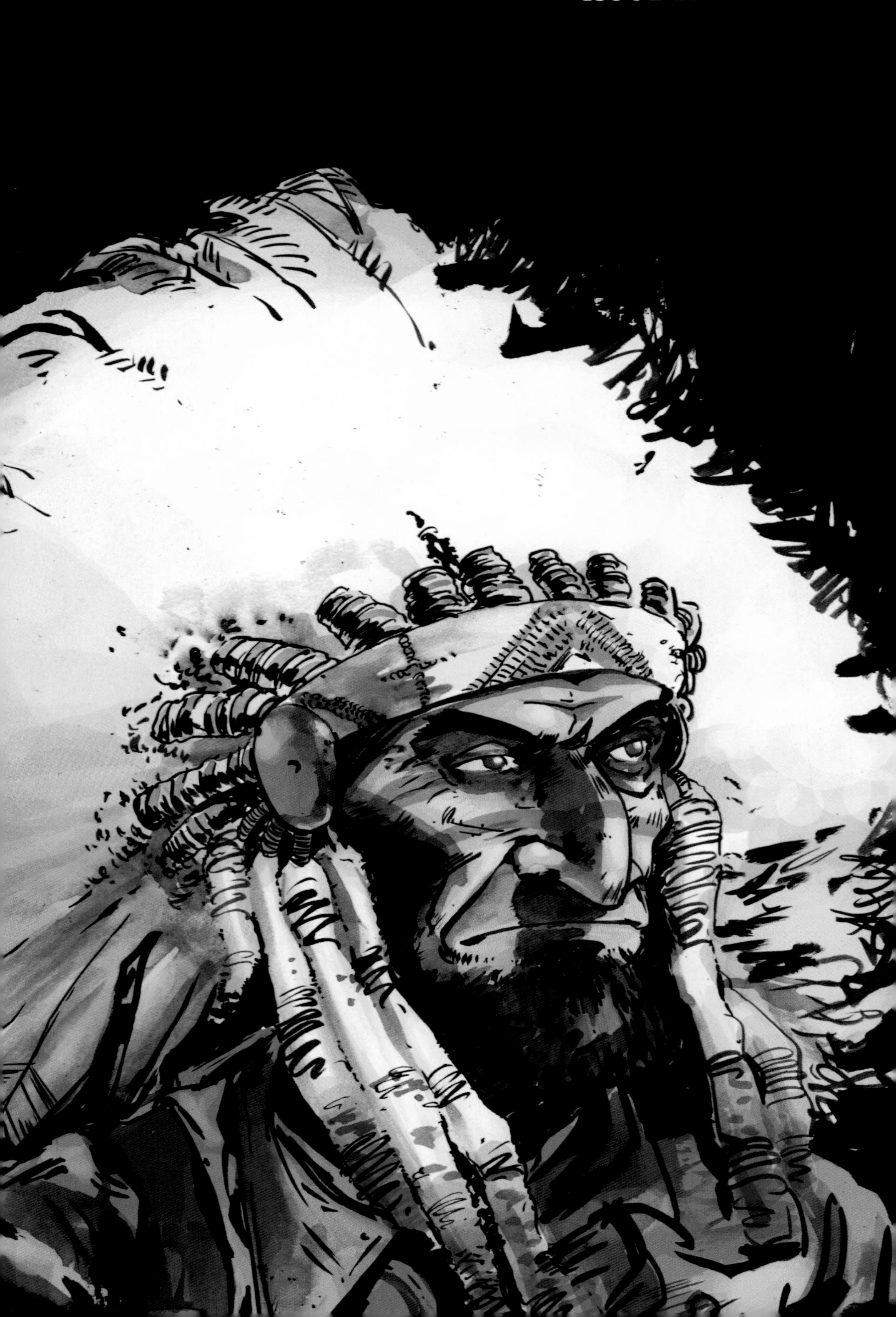

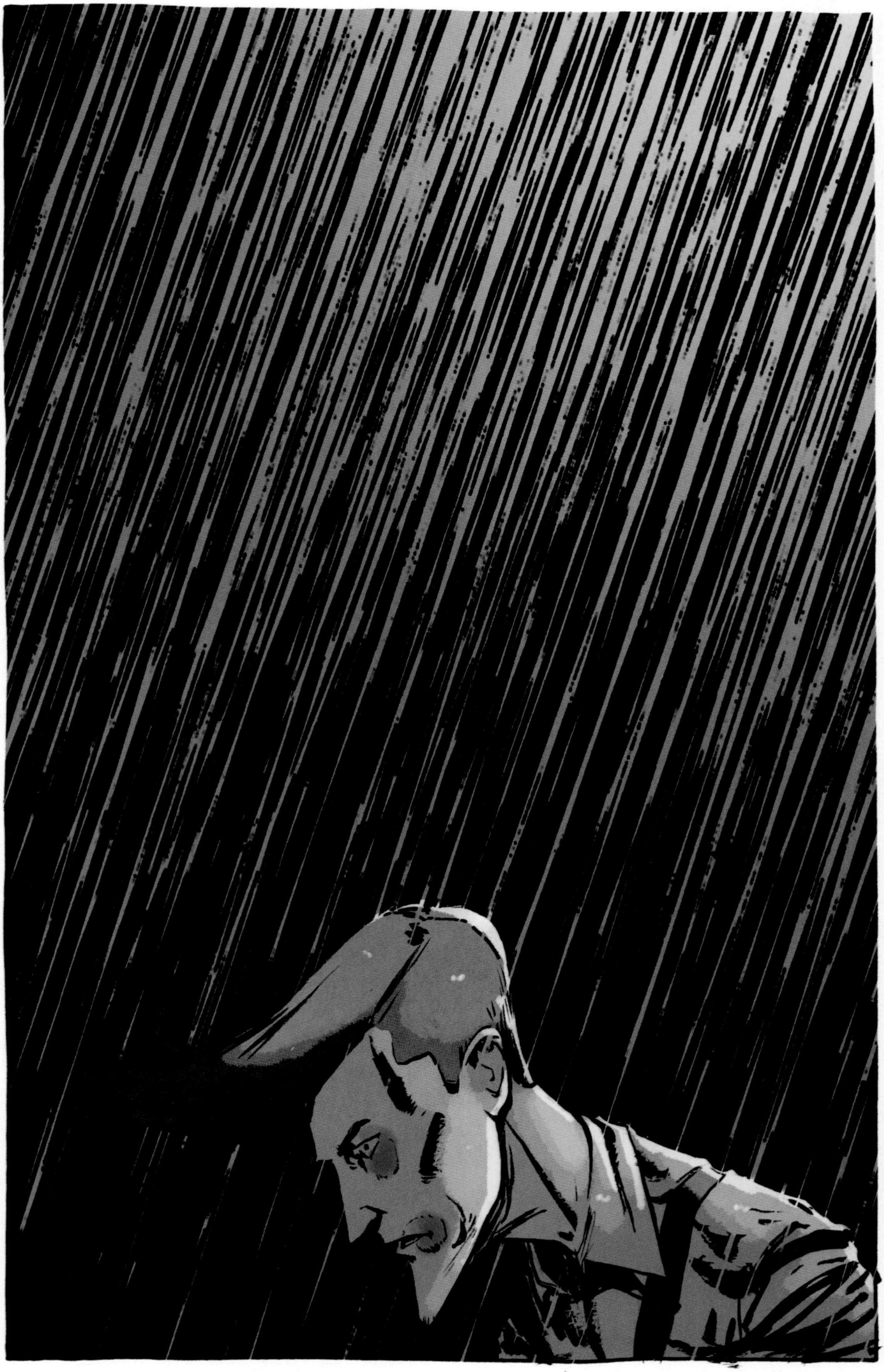

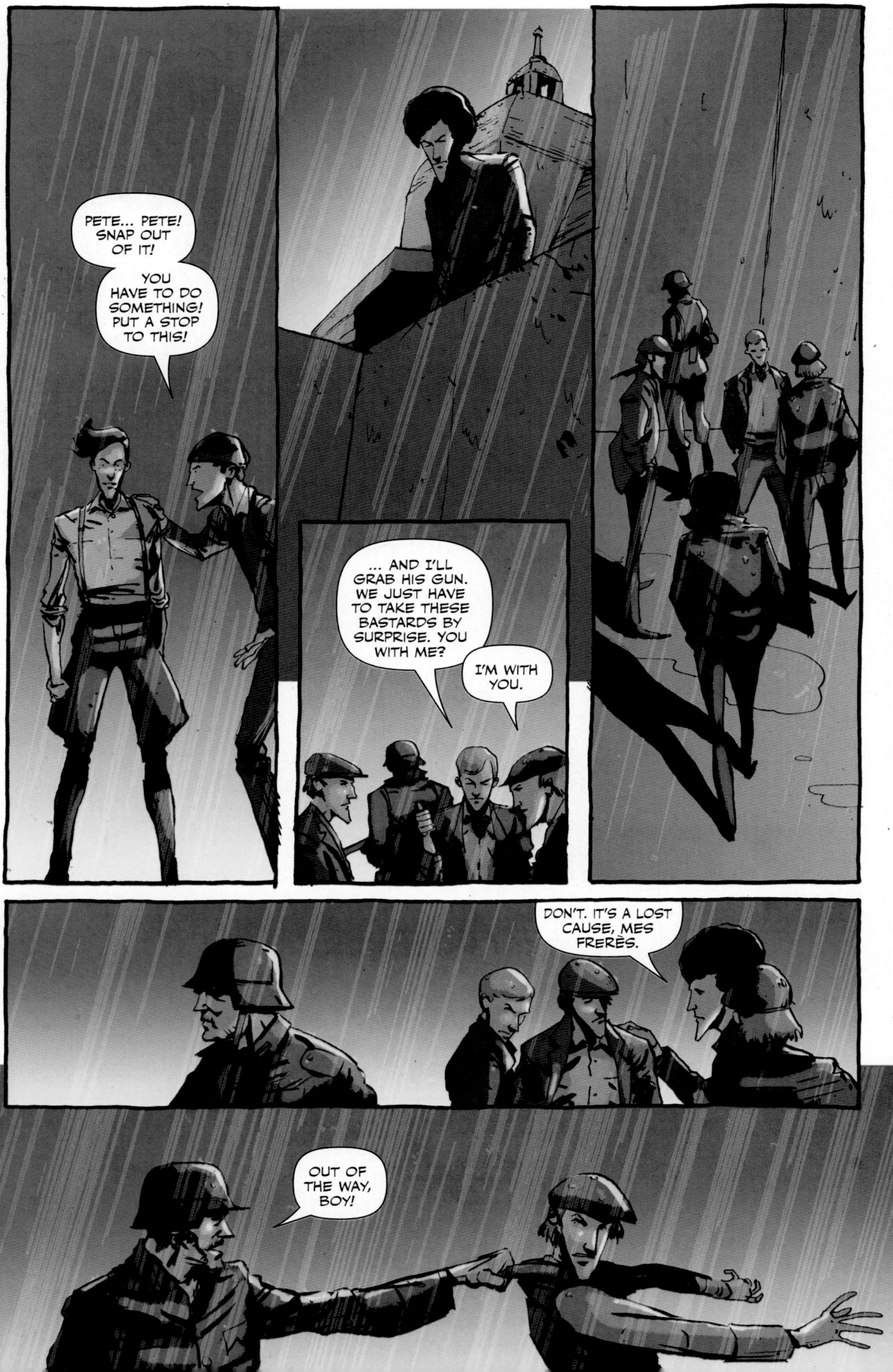
PETE... PETE! SNAP OUT OF IT!
YOU HAVE TO DO SOMETHING! PUT A STOP TO THIS!
... AND I'LL GRAB HIS GUN. WE JUST HAVE TO TAKE THESE BASTARDS BY SURPRISE. YOU WITH ME?
I'M WITH YOU.
DON'T. IT'S A LOST CAUSE, MES FRERÈS.
OUT OF THE WAY, BOY!

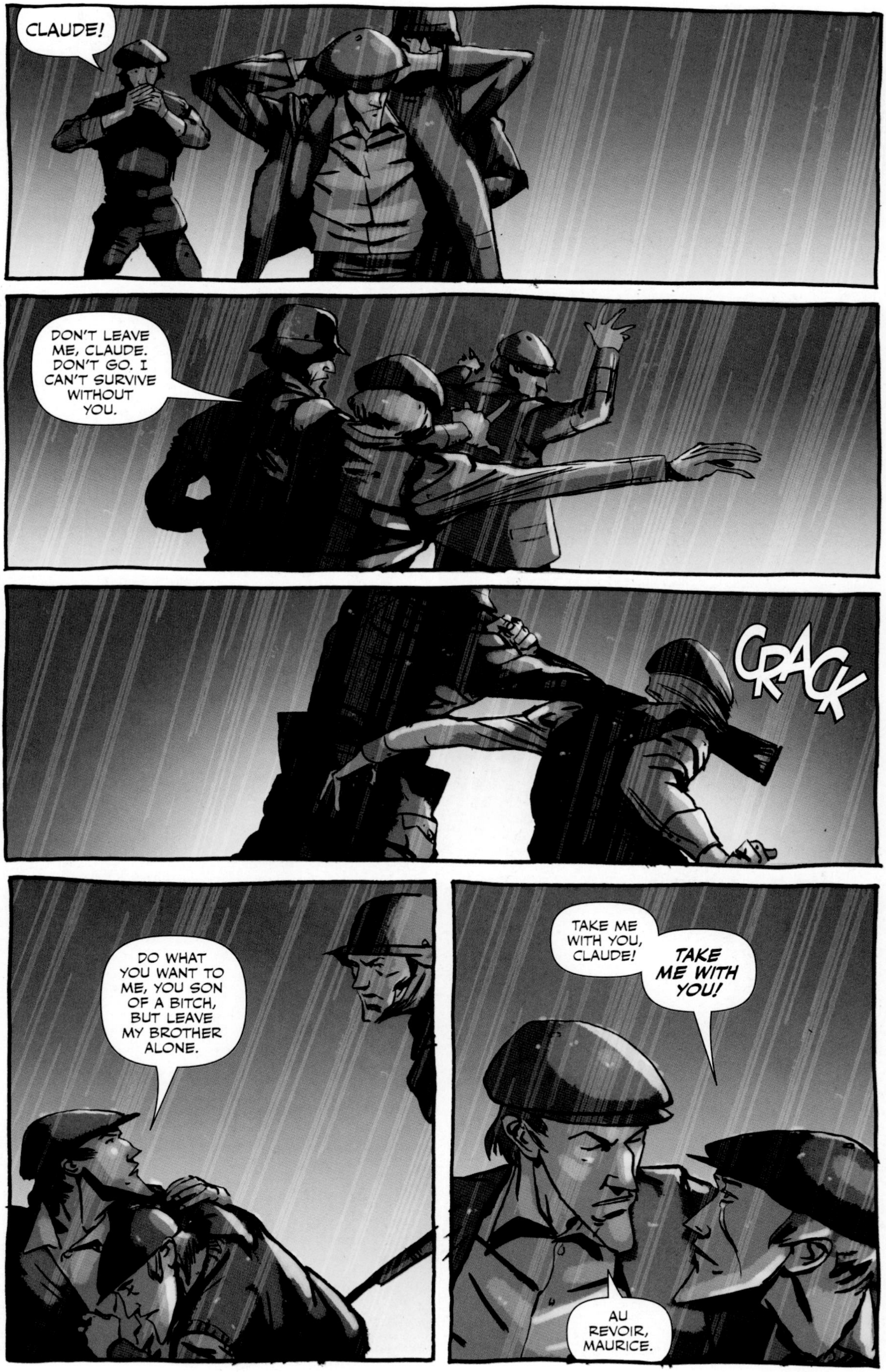
CLAUDE!
DON'T LEAVE ME, CLAUDE. DON'T GO. I CAN'T SURVIVE WITHOUT YOU.
CRACK
DO WHAT YOU WANT TO ME, YOU SON OF A BITCH, BUT LEAVE MY BROTHER ALONE.
TAKE ME WITH YOU, CLAUDE!
TAKE ME WITH YOU!
AU REVOIR, MAURICE.

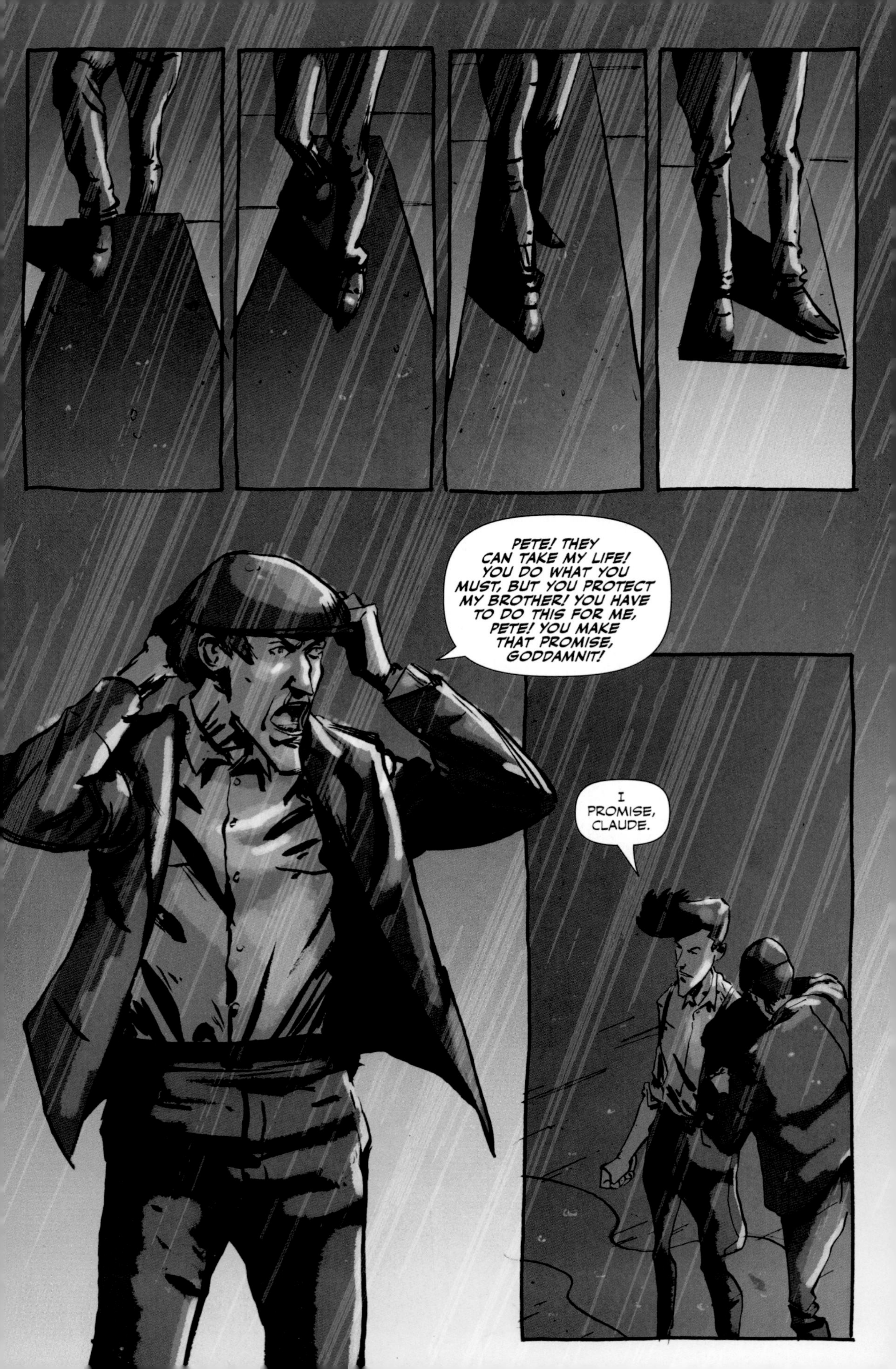
PETE! THEY CAN TAKE MY LIFE! YOU DO WHAT YOU MUST, BUT YOU PROTECT MY BROTHER! YOU HAVE TO DO THIS FOR ME, PETE! YOU MAKE THAT PROMISE, GODDAMNIT!
I PROMISE, CLAUDE.

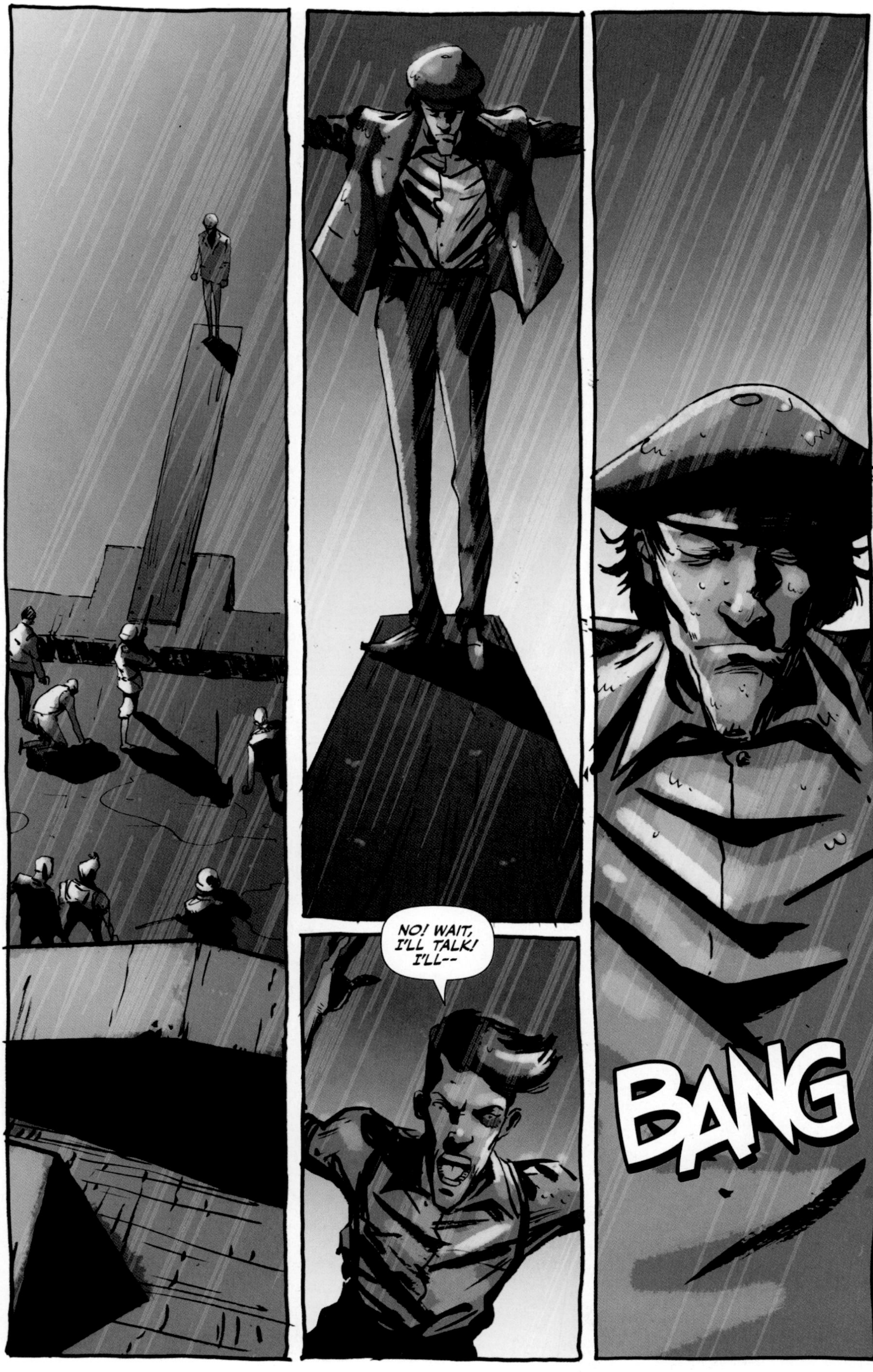
NO! WAIT, I'LL TALK! I'LL--
BANG

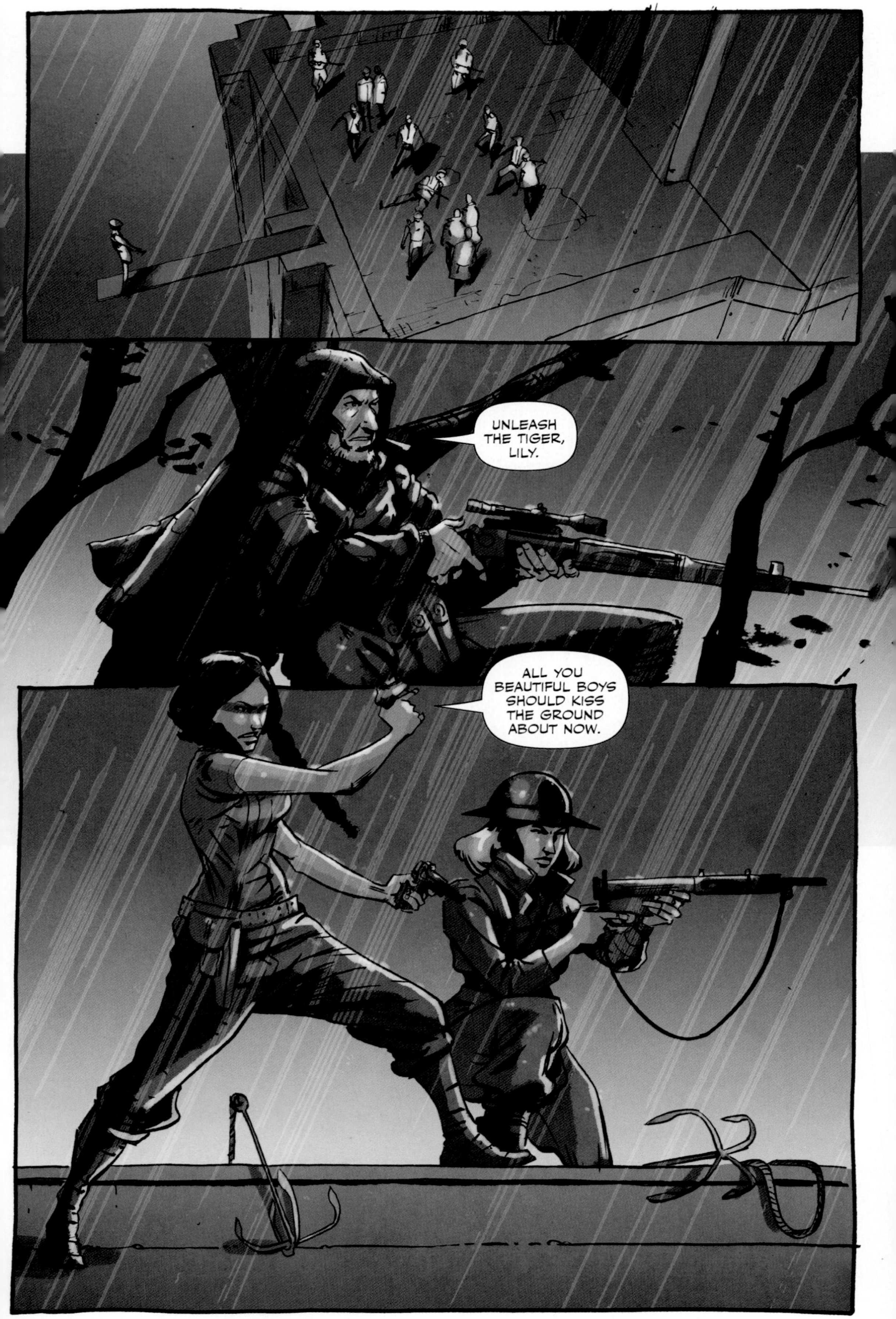
UNLEASH THE TIGER, LILY.
ALL YOU BEAUTIFUL BOYS SHOULD KISS THE GROUND ABOUT NOW.

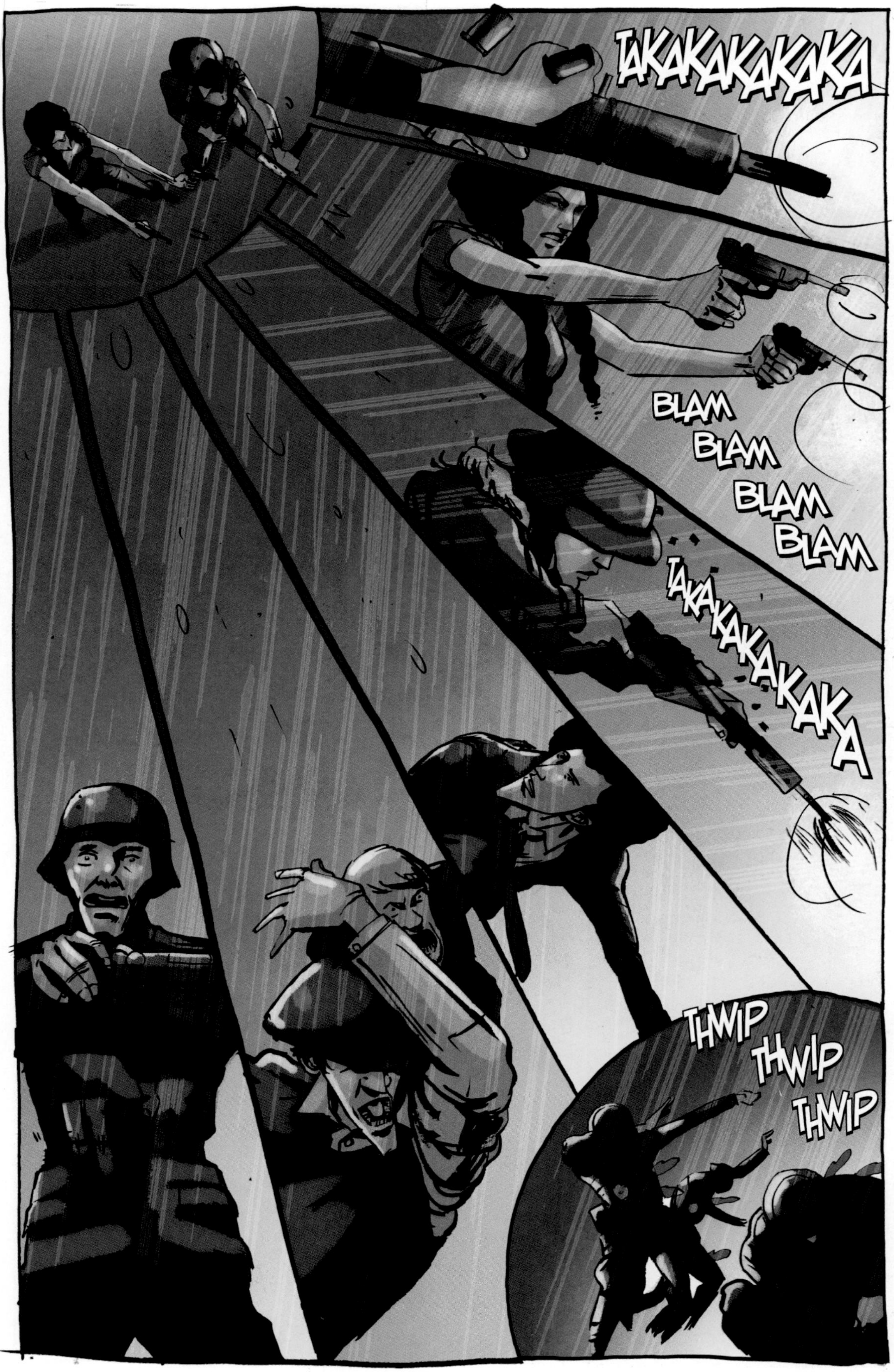
TAKAKAKAKAKAKA
BLAM
BLAM
BLAM
BLAM
TAKAKAKAKAKAKA
THWIP
THWIP
THWIP

SHE GUIDED US. UNFLINCHING. UNAFRAID.

THE BOYS TOLD ME LATER THAT SIRENS HAD SOUNDED THE MOMENT WE HIT THE GROUND. I CAN'T SAY I RECALL HEARING THEM, MR. PARSONS.

THEY ALSO SAID WE TOOK FIRE AS WE RAN ACROSS THE ENDLESS MUDDY FIELD.

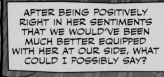

HAHAHA! I STILL LAUGH NOW, THE SILLIEST THOUGHTS RUNNING THROUGH MY MIND ABOUT HOW I COULD EVER THANK HER FOR SAVING US.

AFTER BEING POSITIVELY RIGHT IN HER SENTIMENTS THAT WE WOULD'VE BEEN MUCH BETTER EQUIPPED WITH HER AT OUR SIDE, WHAT COULD I POSSIBLY SAY?

WHEN I FINALLY FOUND THE COURAGE, I REALIZED VERY QUICKLY...

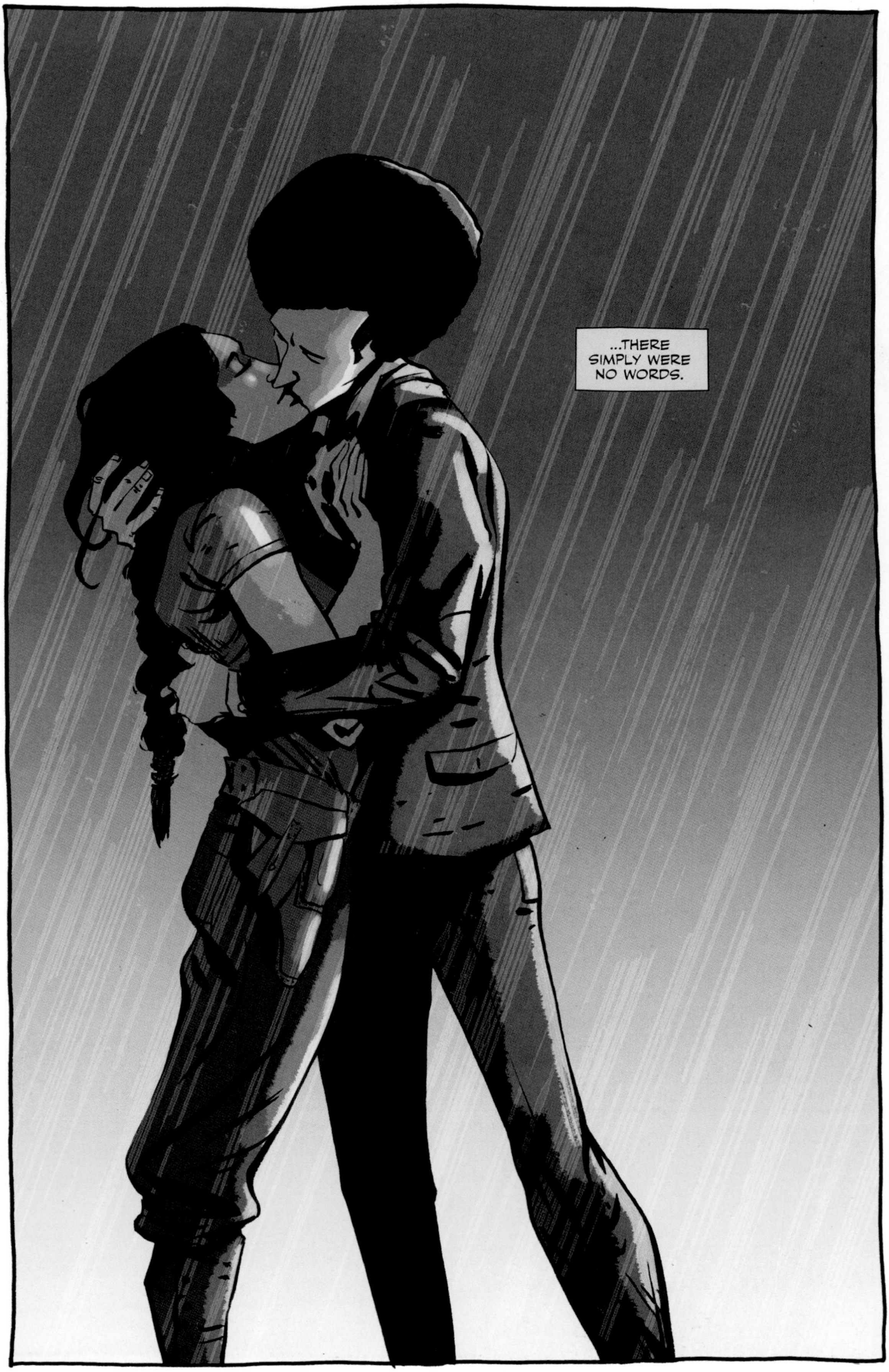
...THERE SIMPLY WERE NO WORDS.

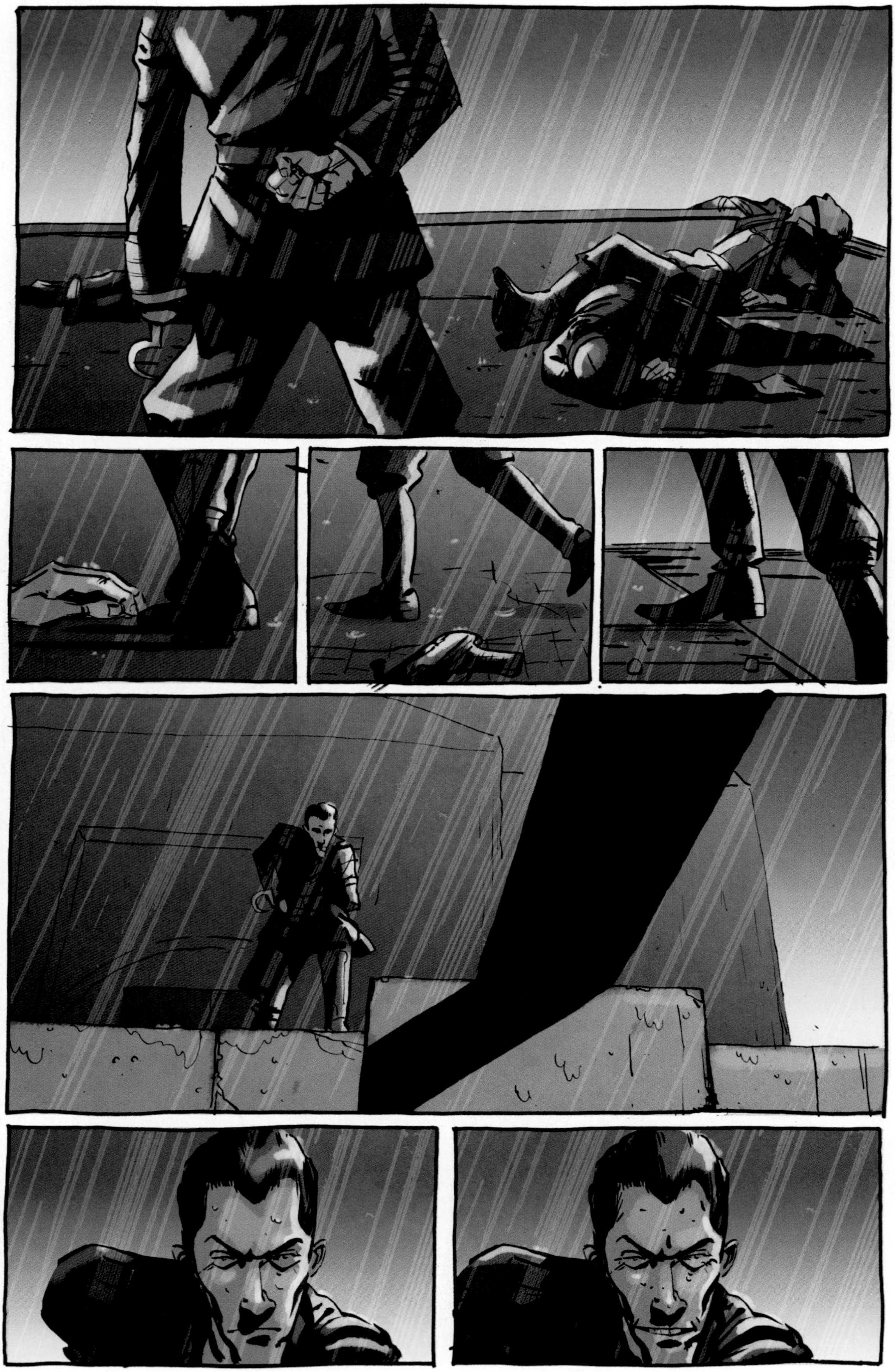

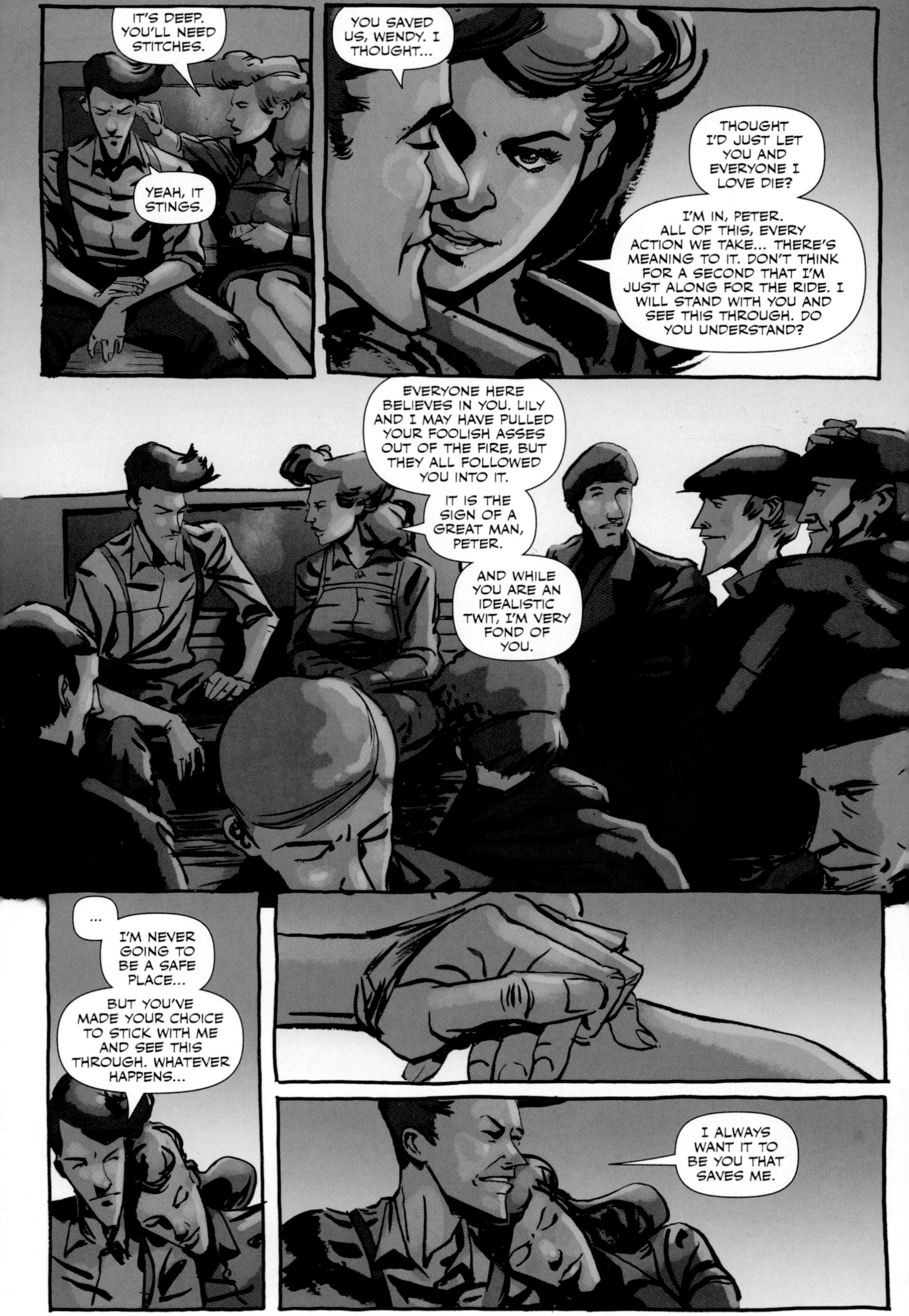
IT'S DEEP. YOU'LL NEED STITCHES.
YEAH, IT STINGS.
YOU SAVED US, WENDY. I THOUGHT...
THOUGHT I'D JUST LET YOU AND EVERYONE I LOVE DIE?
I'M IN, PETER. ALL OF THIS, EVERY ACTION WE TAKE... THERE'S MEANING TO IT. DON'T THINK FOR A SECOND THAT I'M JUST ALONG FOR THE RIDE. I WILL STAND WITH YOU AND SEE THIS THROUGH. DO YOU UNDERSTAND?
EVERYONE HERE BELIEVES IN YOU. LILY AND I MAY HAVE PULLED YOUR FOOLISH ASSES OUT OF THE FIRE, BUT THEY ALL FOLLOWED YOU INTO IT.
IT IS THE SIGN OF A GREAT MAN, PETER.
AND WHILE YOU ARE AN IDEALISTIC TWIT, I'M VERY FOND OF YOU.
...
I'M NEVER GOING TO BE A SAFE PLACE...
BUT YOU'VE MADE YOUR CHOICE TO STICK WITH ME AND SEE THIS THROUGH. WHATEVER HAPPENS...
I ALWAYS WANT IT TO BE YOU THAT SAVES ME.

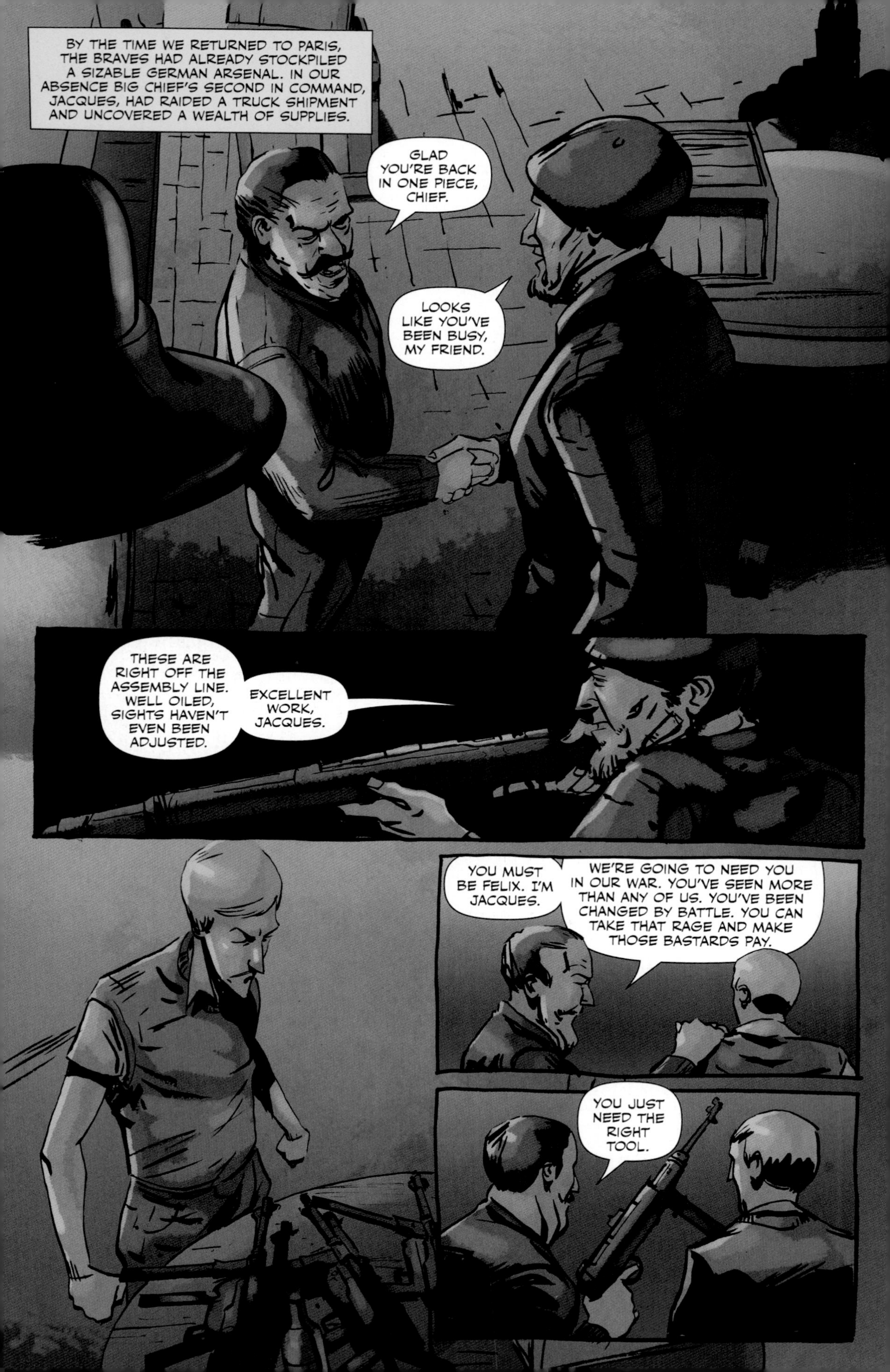
BY THE TIME WE RETURNED TO PARIS, THE BRAVES HAD ALREADY STOCKPILED A SIZABLE GERMAN ARSENAL. IN OUR ABSENCE BIG CHIEF'S SECOND IN COMMAND, JACQUES, HAD RAIDED A TRUCK SHIPMENT AND UNCOVERED A WEALTH OF SUPPLIES.
GLAD YOU'RE BACK IN ONE PIECE, CHIEF.
LOOKS LIKE YOU'VE BEEN BUSY, MY FRIEND.
THESE ARE RIGHT OFF THE ASSEMBLY LINE. WELL OILED, SIGHTS HAVEN'T EVEN BEEN ADJUSTED.
EXCELLENT WORK, JACQUES.
YOU MUST BE FELIX. I'M JACQUES.
WE'RE GOING TO NEED YOU IN OUR WAR. YOU'VE SEEN MORE THAN ANY OF US. YOU'VE BEEN CHANGED BY BATTLE. YOU CAN TAKE THAT RAGE AND MAKE THOSE BASTARDS PAY.
YOU JUST NEED THE RIGHT TOOL.

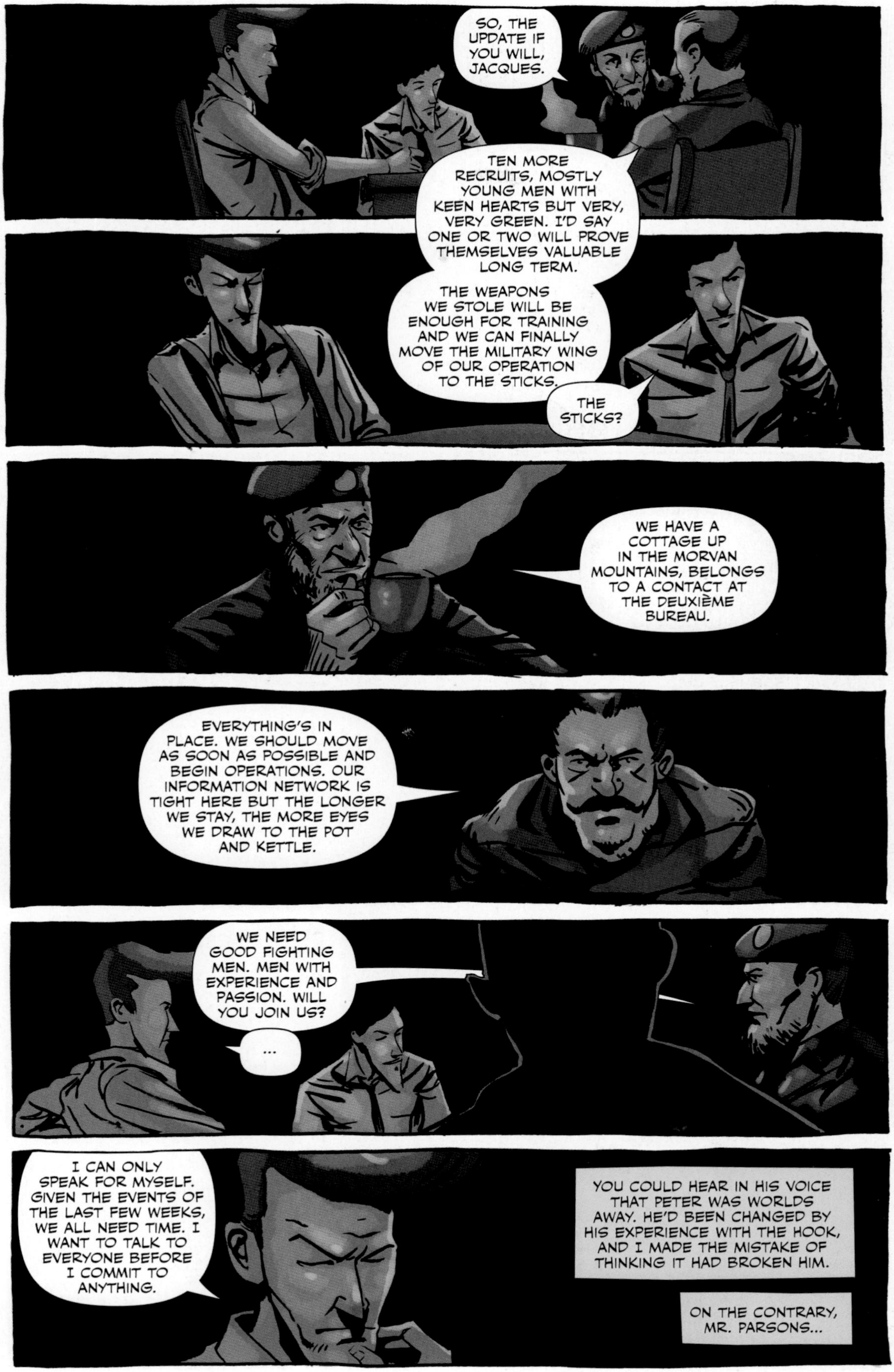

SO, THE UPDATE IF YOU WILL, JACQUES.
TEN MORE RECRUITS, MOSTLY YOUNG MEN WITH KEEN HEARTS BUT VERY, VERY GREEN. I'D SAY ONE OR TWO WILL PROVE THEMSELVES VALUABLE LONG TERM.
THE WEAPONS WE STOLE WILL BE ENOUGH FOR TRAINING AND WE CAN FINALLY MOVE THE MILITARY WING OF OUR OPERATION TO THE STICKS.
THE STICKS?
WE HAVE A COTTAGE UP IN THE MORVAN MOUNTAINS, BELONGS TO A CONTACT AT THE DEUXIÈME BUREAU.
EVERYTHING'S IN PLACE. WE SHOULD MOVE AS SOON AS POSSIBLE AND BEGIN OPERATIONS. OUR INFORMATION NETWORK IS TIGHT HERE BUT THE LONGER WE STAY, THE MORE EYES WE DRAW TO THE POT AND KETTLE.
WE NEED GOOD FIGHTING MEN. MEN WITH EXPERIENCE AND PASSION. WILL YOU JOIN US?
...
I CAN ONLY SPEAK FOR MYSELF. GIVEN THE EVENTS OF THE LAST FEW WEEKS, WE ALL NEED TIME. I WANT TO TALK TO EVERYONE BEFORE I COMMIT TO ANYTHING.
YOU COULD HEAR IN HIS VOICE THAT PETER WAS WORLDS AWAY. HE'D BEEN CHANGED BY HIS EXPERIENCE WITH THE HOOK, AND I MADE THE MISTAKE OF THINKING IT HAD BROKEN HIM.
ON THE CONTRARY, MR. PARSONS...

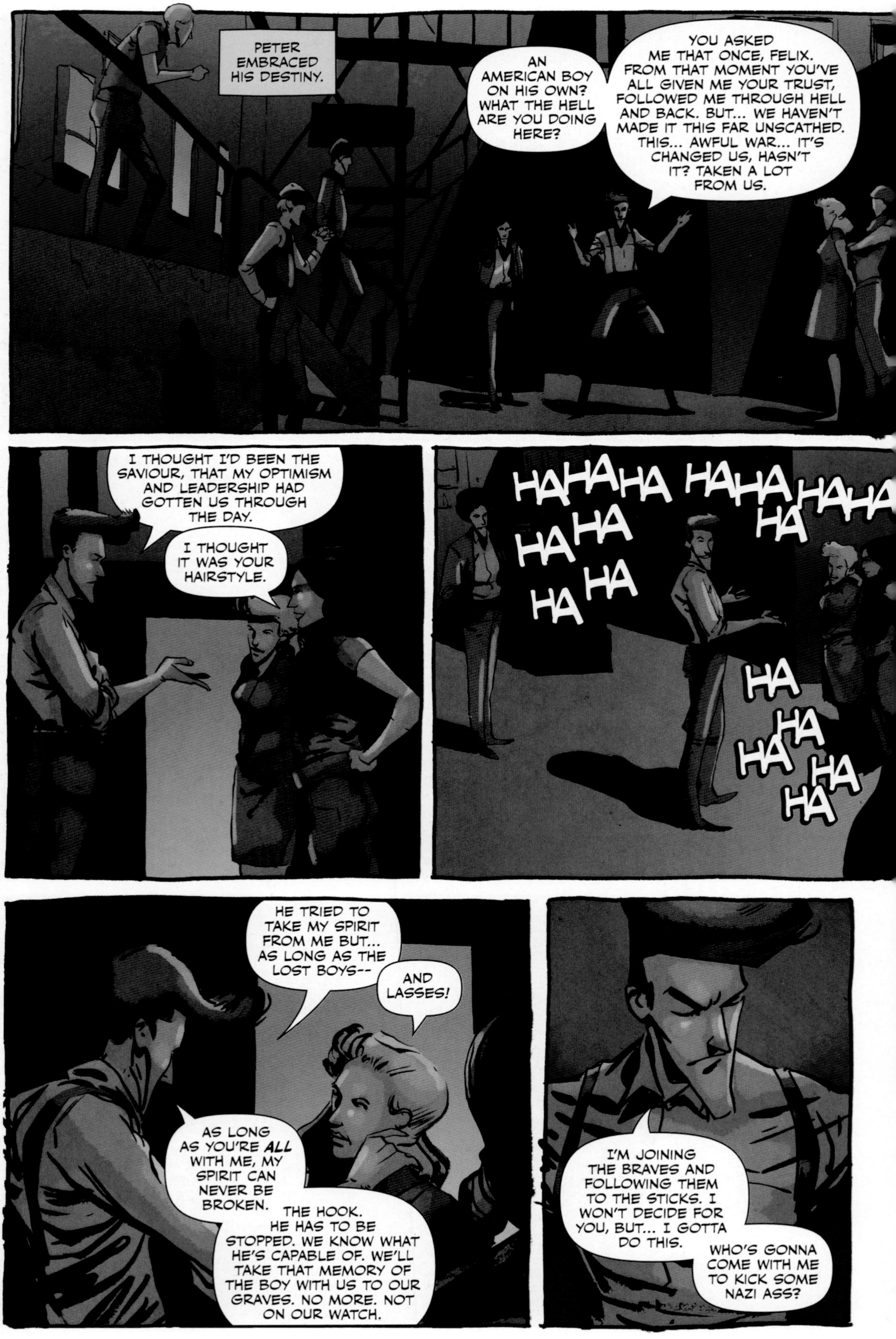
PETER EMBRACED HIS DESTINY.
AN AMERICAN BOY ON HIS OWN? WHAT THE HELL ARE YOU DOING HERE?
YOU ASKED ME THAT ONCE, FELIX. FROM THAT MOMENT YOU'VE ALL GIVEN ME YOUR TRUST, FOLLOWED ME THROUGH HELL AND BACK. BUT... WE HAVEN'T MADE IT THIS FAR UNSCATHED. THIS... AWFUL WAR... IT'S CHANGED US, HASN'T IT? TAKEN A LOT FROM US.
I THOUGHT I'D BEEN THE SAVIOUR, THAT MY OPTIMISM AND LEADERSHIP HAD GOTTEN US THROUGH THE DAY.
I THOUGHT IT WAS YOUR HAIRSTYLE.
HAHAHA HAHAHA HAHA HA
HA HA
HA HA
HA HA HA HA HA
HE TRIED TO TAKE MY SPIRIT FROM ME BUT... AS LONG AS THE LOST BOYS--
AND LASSES!
AS LONG AS YOU'RE *ALL* WITH ME, MY SPIRIT CAN NEVER BE BROKEN.
THE HOOK. HE HAS TO BE STOPPED. WE KNOW WHAT HE'S CAPABLE OF. WE'LL TAKE THAT MEMORY OF THE BOY WITH US TO OUR GRAVES. NO MORE. NOT ON OUR WATCH.
I'M JOINING THE BRAVES AND FOLLOWING THEM TO THE STICKS. I WON'T DECIDE FOR YOU, BUT... I GOTTA DO THIS.
WHO'S GONNA COME WITH ME TO KICK SOME NAZI ASS?

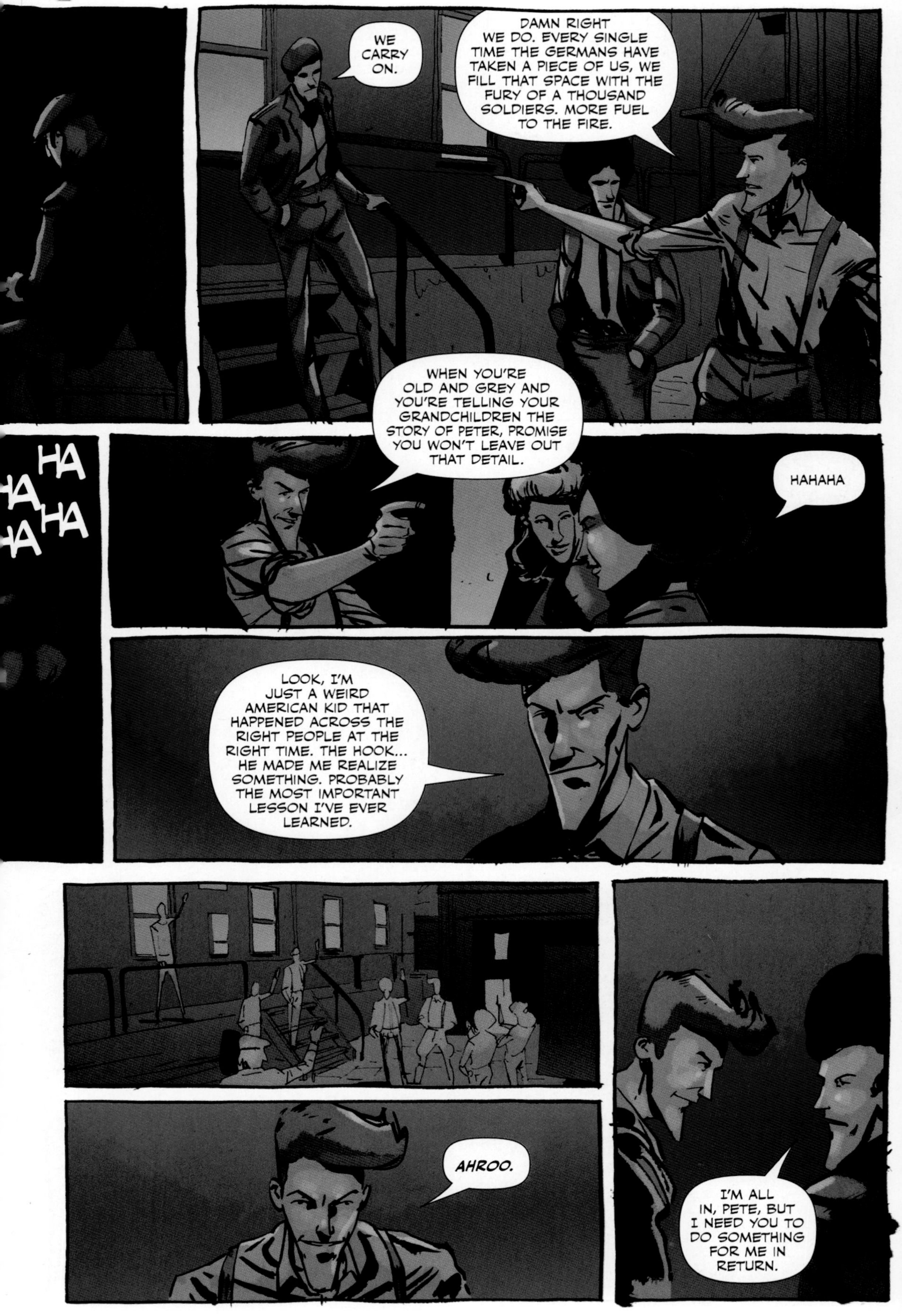
WE CARRY ON.
DAMN RIGHT WE DO. EVERY SINGLE TIME THE GERMANS HAVE TAKEN A PIECE OF US, WE FILL THAT SPACE WITH THE FURY OF A THOUSAND SOLDIERS. MORE FUEL TO THE FIRE.
WHEN YOU'RE OLD AND GREY AND YOU'RE TELLING YOUR GRANDCHILDREN THE STORY OF PETER, PROMISE YOU WON'T LEAVE OUT THAT DETAIL.
HAHAHA
HA HA HA HA
LOOK, I'M JUST A WEIRD AMERICAN KID THAT HAPPENED ACROSS THE RIGHT PEOPLE AT THE RIGHT TIME. THE HOOK... HE MADE ME REALIZE SOMETHING. PROBABLY THE MOST IMPORTANT LESSON I'VE EVER LEARNED.
AHROO.
I'M ALL IN, PETE, BUT I NEED YOU TO DO SOMETHING FOR ME IN RETURN.

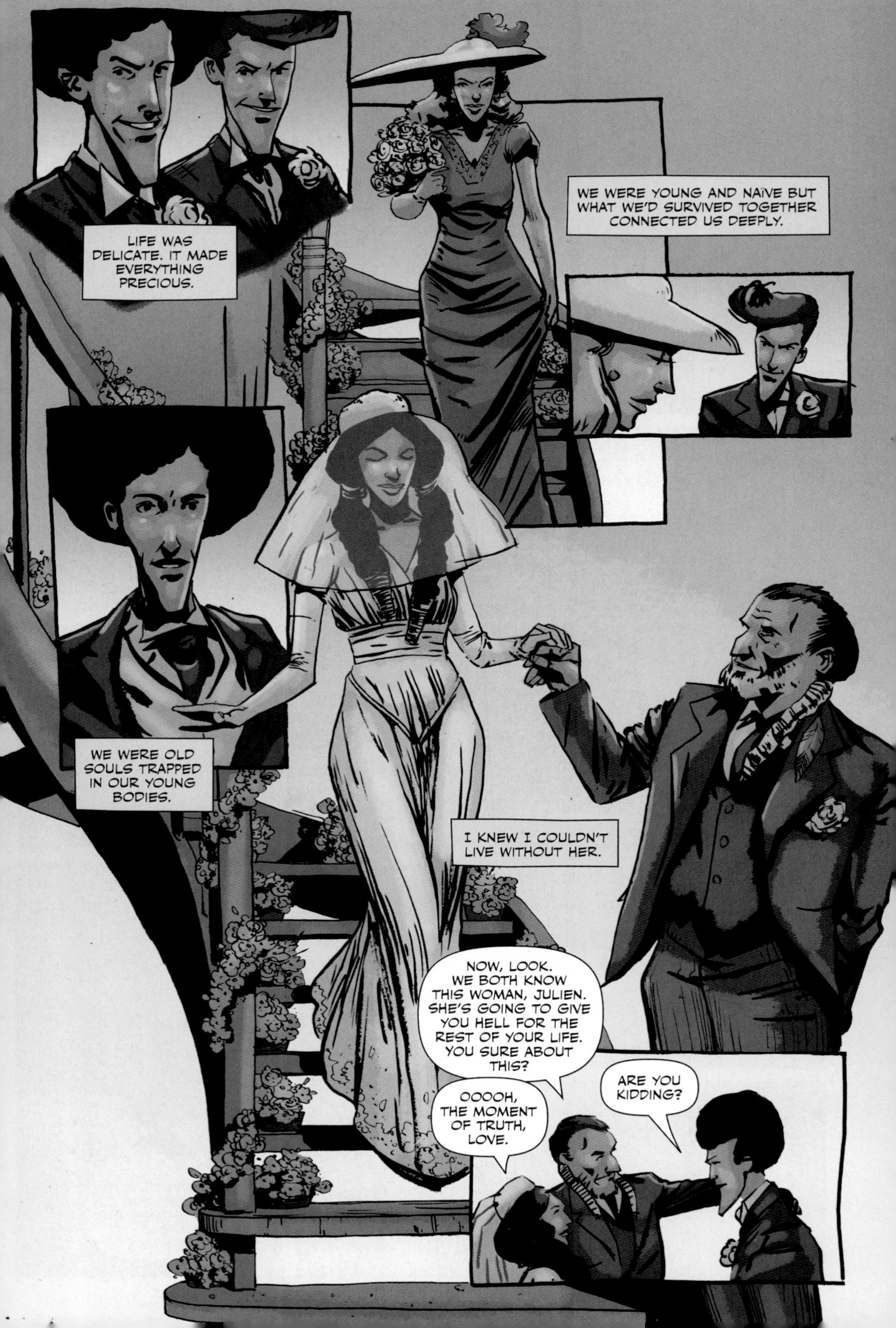
LIFE WAS DELICATE. IT MADE EVERYTHING PRECIOUS.
WE WERE YOUNG AND NAÏVE BUT WHAT WE'D SURVIVED TOGETHER CONNECTED US DEEPLY.
WE WERE OLD SOULS TRAPPED IN OUR YOUNG BODIES.
I KNEW I COULDN'T LIVE WITHOUT HER.
NOW, LOOK. WE BOTH KNOW THIS WOMAN, JULIEN. SHE'S GOING TO GIVE YOU HELL FOR THE REST OF YOUR LIFE. YOU SURE ABOUT THIS?
OOOOH, THE MOMENT OF TRUTH, LOVE.
ARE YOU KIDDING?

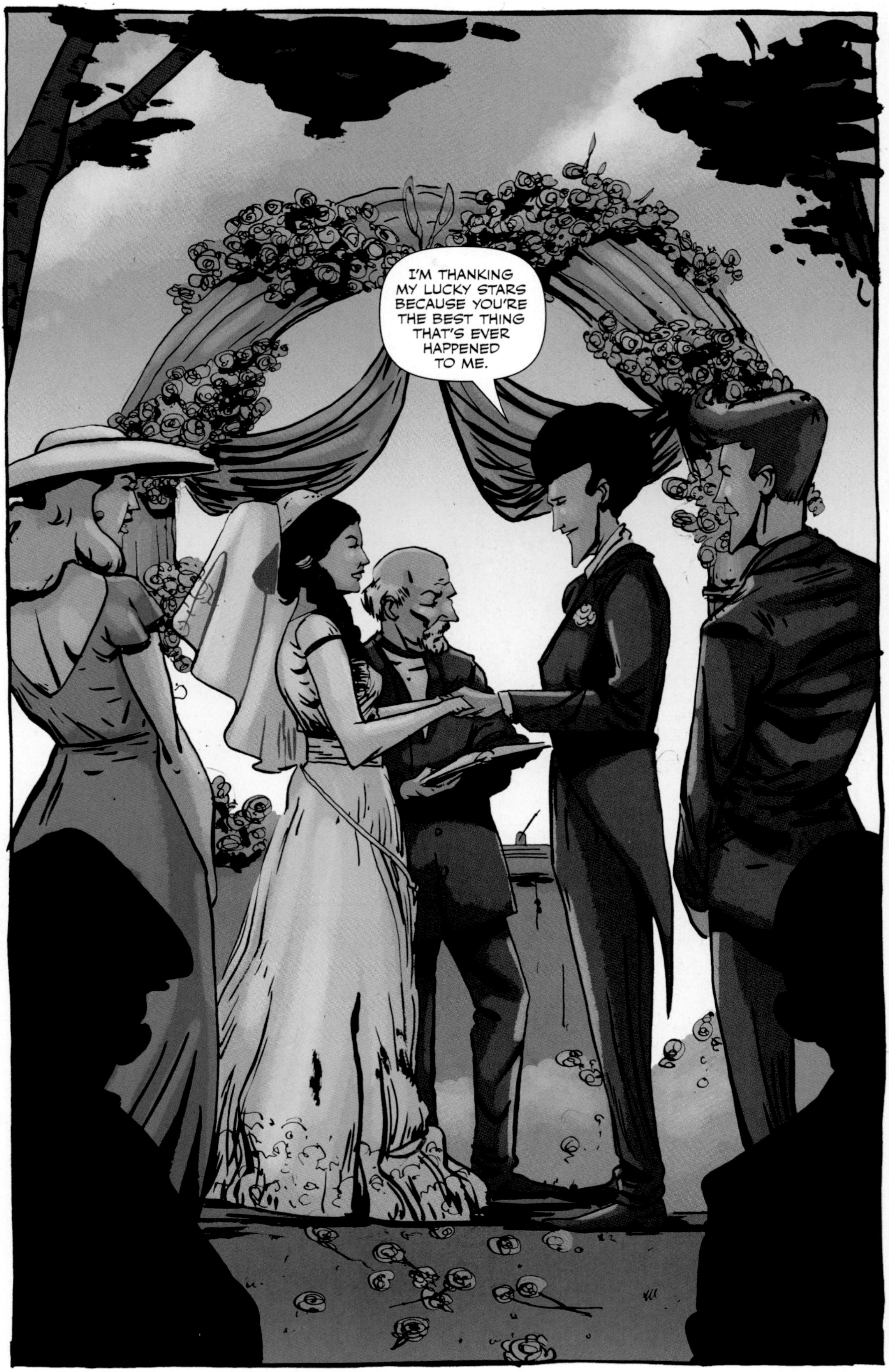
I'M THANKING MY LUCKY STARS BECAUSE YOU'RE THE BEST THING THAT'S EVER HAPPENED TO ME.

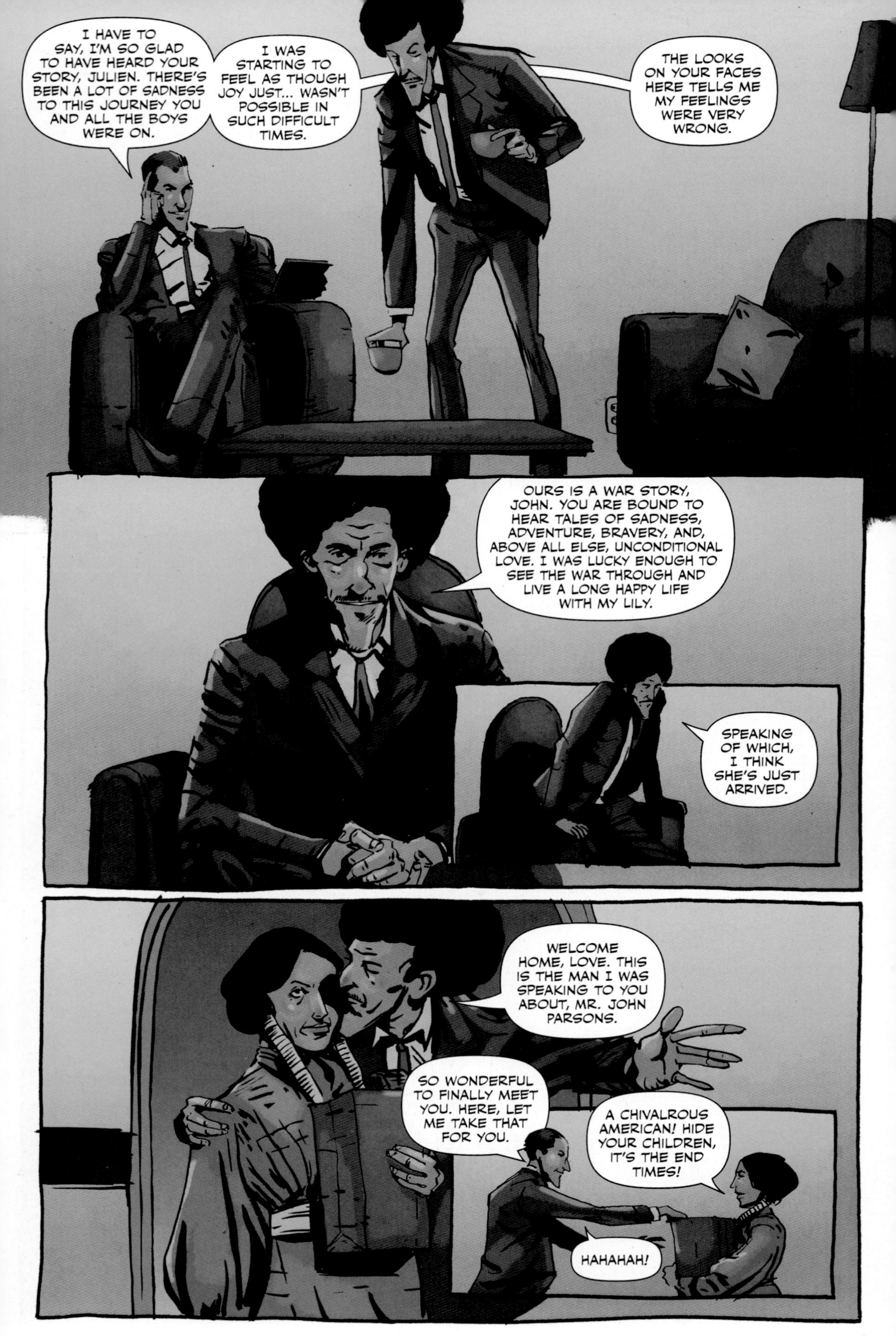
I HAVE TO SAY, I'M SO GLAD TO HAVE HEARD YOUR STORY, JULIEN. THERE'S BEEN A LOT OF SADNESS TO THIS JOURNEY YOU AND ALL THE BOYS WERE ON.
I WAS STARTING TO FEEL AS THOUGH JOY JUST... WASN'T POSSIBLE IN SUCH DIFFICULT TIMES.
THE LOOKS ON YOUR FACES HERE TELLS ME MY FEELINGS WERE VERY WRONG.
OURS IS A WAR STORY, JOHN. YOU ARE BOUND TO HEAR TALES OF SADNESS, ADVENTURE, BRAVERY, AND, ABOVE ALL ELSE, UNCONDITIONAL LOVE. I WAS LUCKY ENOUGH TO SEE THE WAR THROUGH AND LIVE A LONG HAPPY LIFE WITH MY LILY.
SPEAKING OF WHICH, I THINK SHE'S JUST ARRIVED.
WELCOME HOME, LOVE. THIS IS THE MAN I WAS SPEAKING TO YOU ABOUT, MR. JOHN PARSONS.
SO WONDERFUL TO FINALLY MEET YOU. HERE, LET ME TAKE THAT FOR YOU.
A CHIVALROUS AMERICAN! HIDE YOUR CHILDREN, IT'S THE END TIMES!
HAHAHAH!

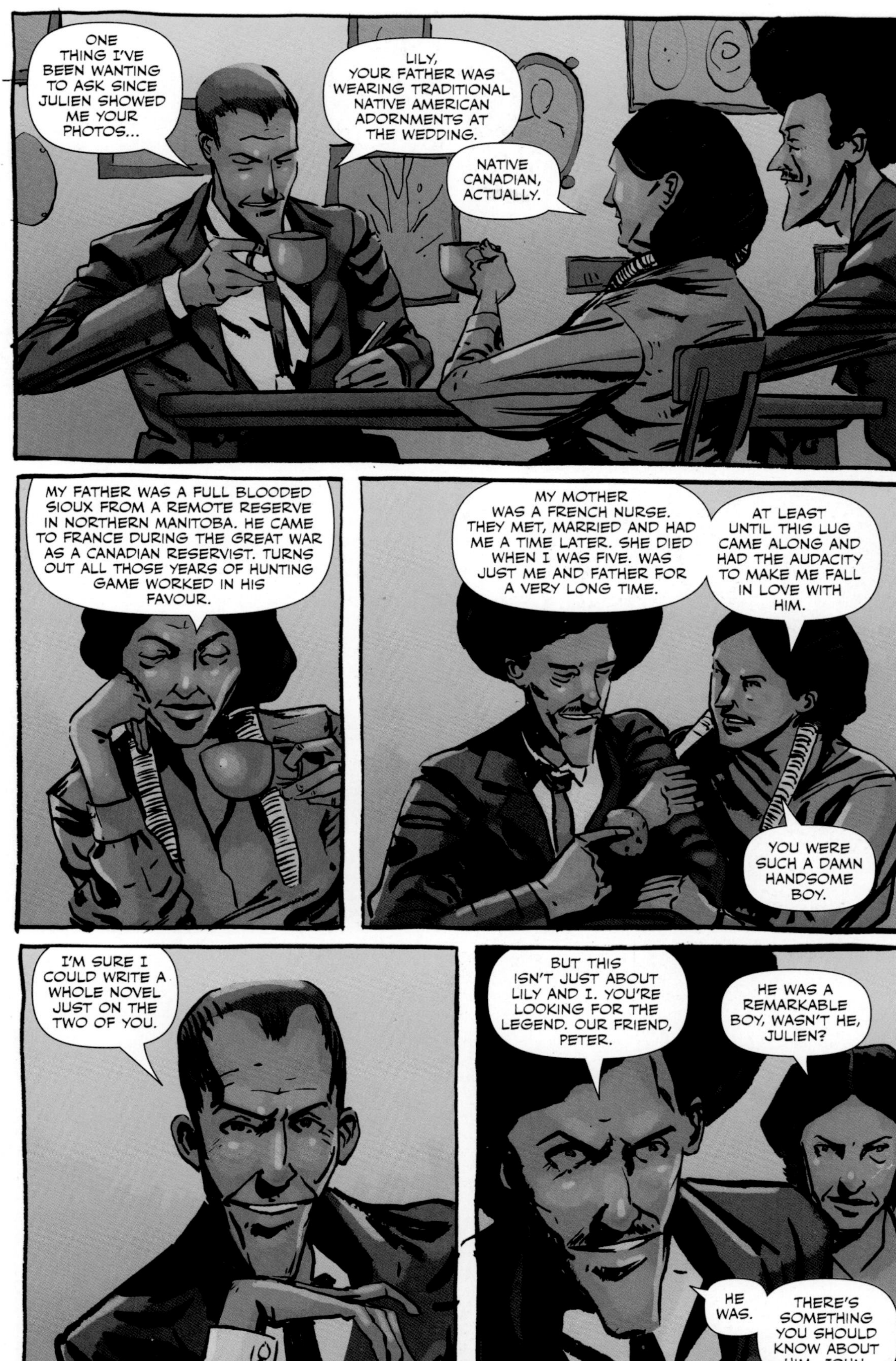
ONE THING I'VE BEEN WANTING TO ASK SINCE JULIEN SHOWED ME YOUR PHOTOS...
LILY, YOUR FATHER WAS WEARING TRADITIONAL NATIVE AMERICAN ADORNMENTS AT THE WEDDING.
NATIVE CANADIAN, ACTUALLY.
MY FATHER WAS A FULL BLOODED SIOUX FROM A REMOTE RESERVE IN NORTHERN MANITOBA. HE CAME TO FRANCE DURING THE GREAT WAR AS A CANADIAN RESERVIST. TURNS OUT ALL THOSE YEARS OF HUNTING GAME WORKED IN HIS FAVOUR.
MY MOTHER WAS A FRENCH NURSE. THEY MET, MARRIED AND HAD ME A TIME LATER. SHE DIED WHEN I WAS FIVE. WAS JUST ME AND FATHER FOR A VERY LONG TIME.
AT LEAST UNTIL THIS LUG CAME ALONG AND HAD THE AUDACITY TO MAKE ME FALL IN LOVE WITH HIM.
YOU WERE SUCH A DAMN HANDSOME BOY.
I'M SURE I COULD WRITE A WHOLE NOVEL JUST ON THE TWO OF YOU.
BUT THIS ISN'T JUST ABOUT LILY AND I. YOU'RE LOOKING FOR THE LEGEND. OUR FRIEND, PETER.
HE WAS A REMARKABLE BOY, WASN'T HE, JULIEN?
HE WAS.
THERE'S SOMETHING YOU SHOULD KNOW ABOUT HIM, JOHN.

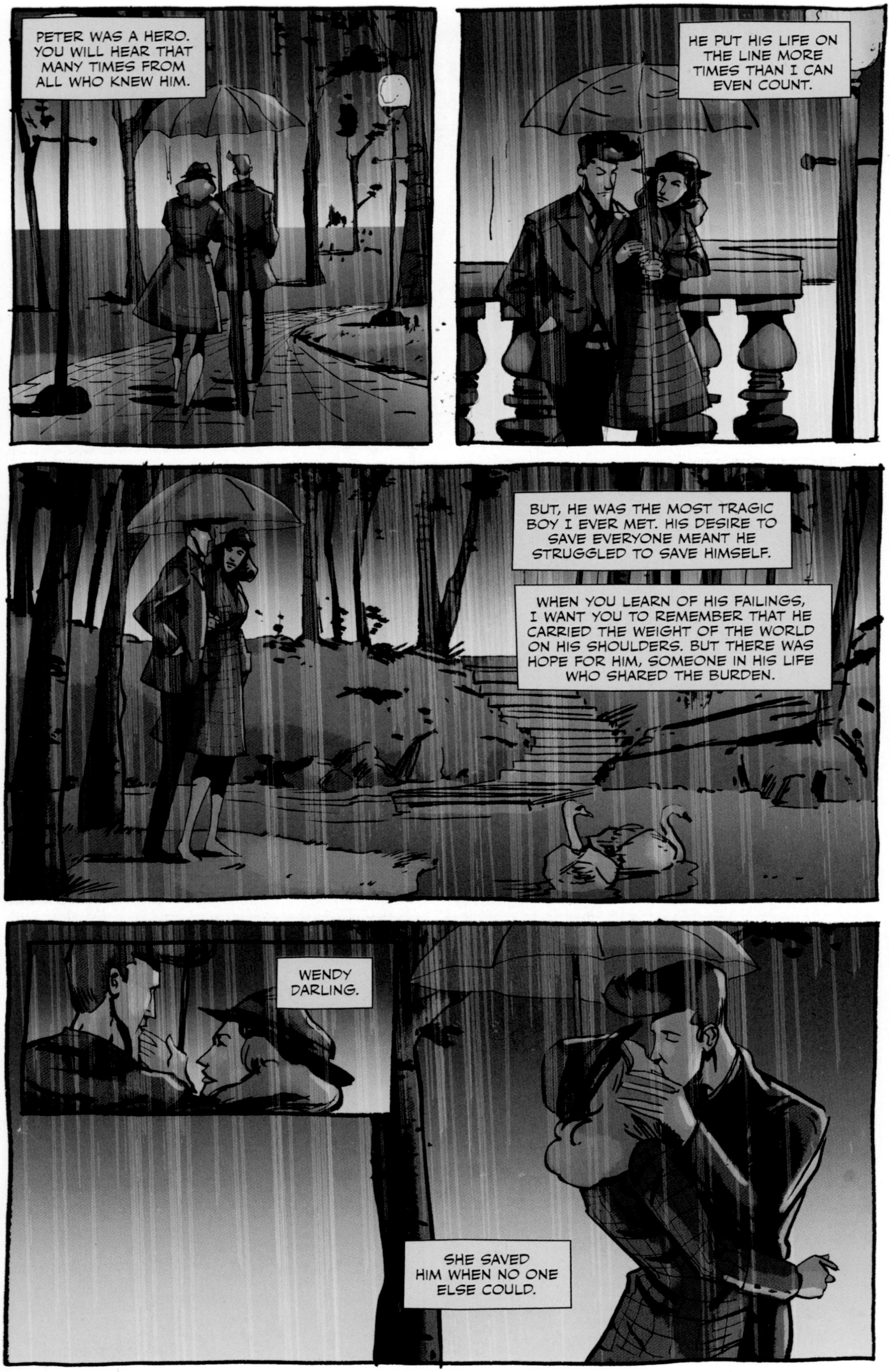
PETER WAS A HERO. YOU WILL HEAR THAT MANY TIMES FROM ALL WHO KNEW HIM.
HE PUT HIS LIFE ON THE LINE MORE TIMES THAN I CAN EVEN COUNT.
BUT, HE WAS THE MOST TRAGIC BOY I EVER MET. HIS DESIRE TO SAVE EVERYONE MEANT HE STRUGGLED TO SAVE HIMSELF.
WHEN YOU LEARN OF HIS FAILINGS, I WANT YOU TO REMEMBER THAT HE CARRIED THE WEIGHT OF THE WORLD ON HIS SHOULDERS. BUT THERE WAS HOPE FOR HIM, SOMEONE IN HIS LIFE WHO SHARED THE BURDEN.
WENDY DARLING.
SHE SAVED HIM WHEN NO ONE ELSE COULD.

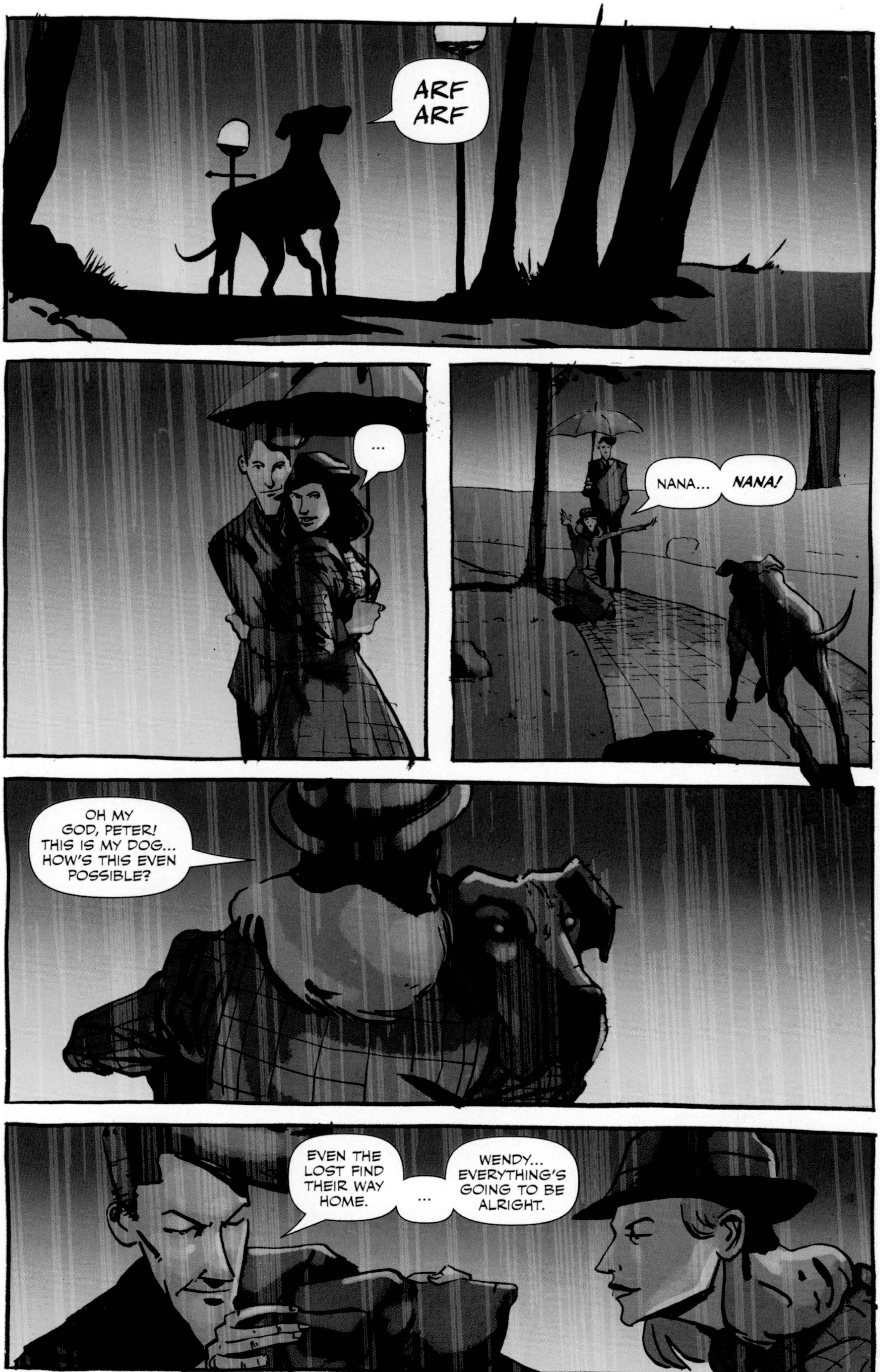

ARF ARF
...
NANA... NANA!
OH MY GOD, PETER! THIS IS MY DOG... HOW'S THIS EVEN POSSIBLE?
EVEN THE LOST FIND THEIR WAY HOME.
...
WENDY... EVERYTHING'S GOING TO BE ALRIGHT.

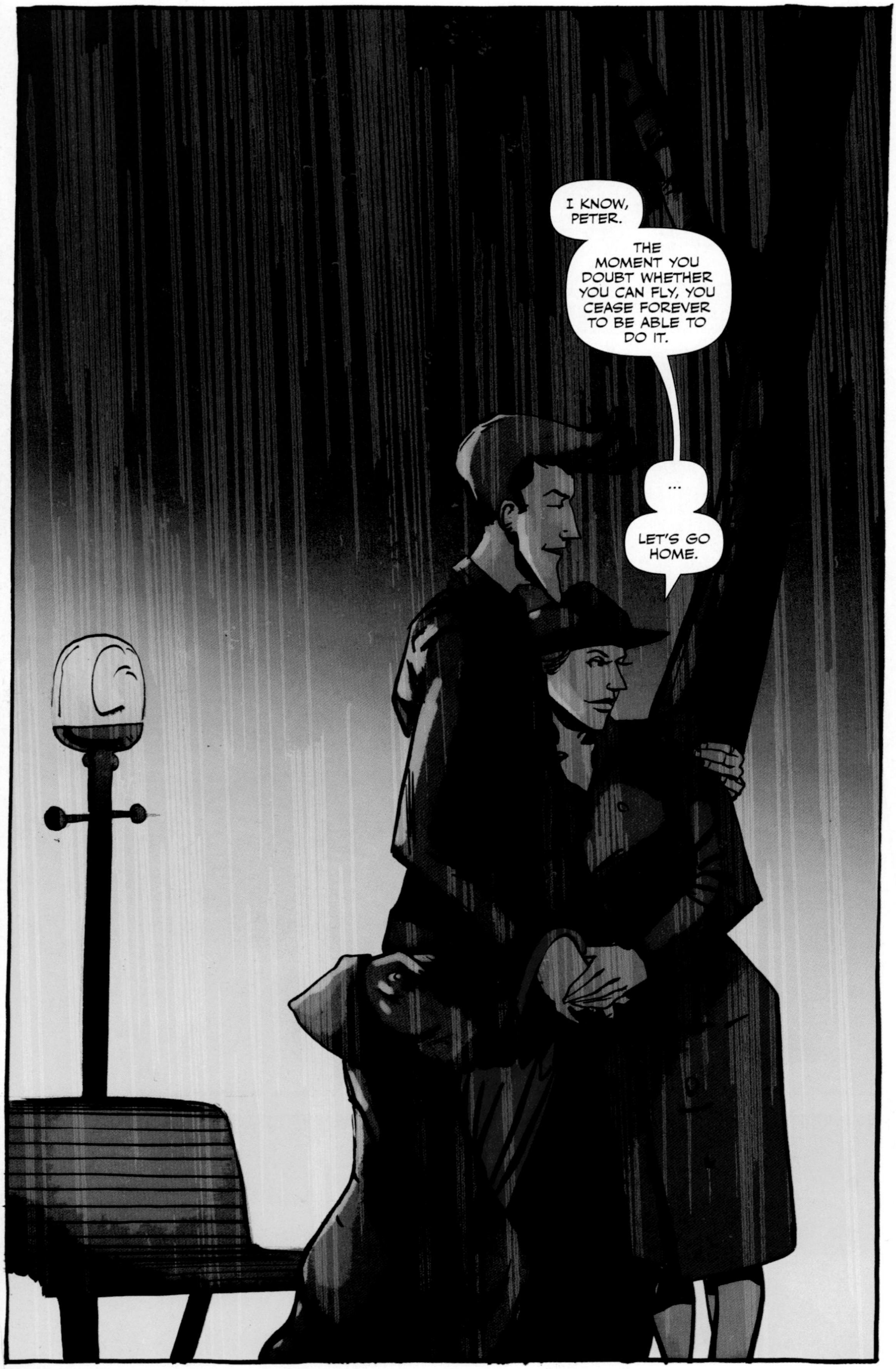
I KNOW, PETER.
THE MOMENT YOU DOUBT WHETHER YOU CAN FLY, YOU CEASE FOREVER TO BE ABLE TO DO IT.
...
LET'S GO HOME.

extras

ISSUE 10 SPECIAL EDITION COVERS

KURTiS J. WIEBE & TYLER JENKINS
PETER PANZERFAUST
Retailer Summit 2013
ISSUE TEN
Image

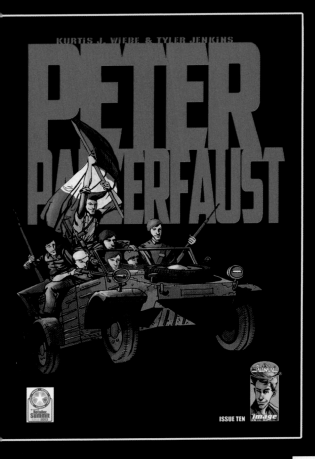

The 2013 c2e2 comic convention in beautiful downtown Chicago was going to prove significant for Peter Panzerfaust.
Not only were Kurtis and Tyler making a rare joint U.S. appearance (both are Canadian), but the cast for the upcoming BBC production (Elijah Wood, Summer Glau and Ron Perelman) was going to be announced at the show.

Issue 10 had just followed the four previous issues in selling out and going into a second printing (our regular second printing cover appears elsewhere in this volume) so we decided to do something very special.

We printed up THREE covers for issue 10's second printing!

Above is the limited editon cover that we gave to retailers as a way to thank them for their support. This was given away at the Diamond Retailer's Conference that was held just prior to the convention.

Then we ordered blank covers (right) for the show itself. Fans could get this special edition signed and get an original cover illustration from Tyler or any other artist of their chosing.

KURTIS J. WIEBE & TYLER JENKINS
PETER PANZERFAUST
ISSUE TEN CONVENTION SPECIAL
image

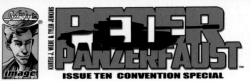

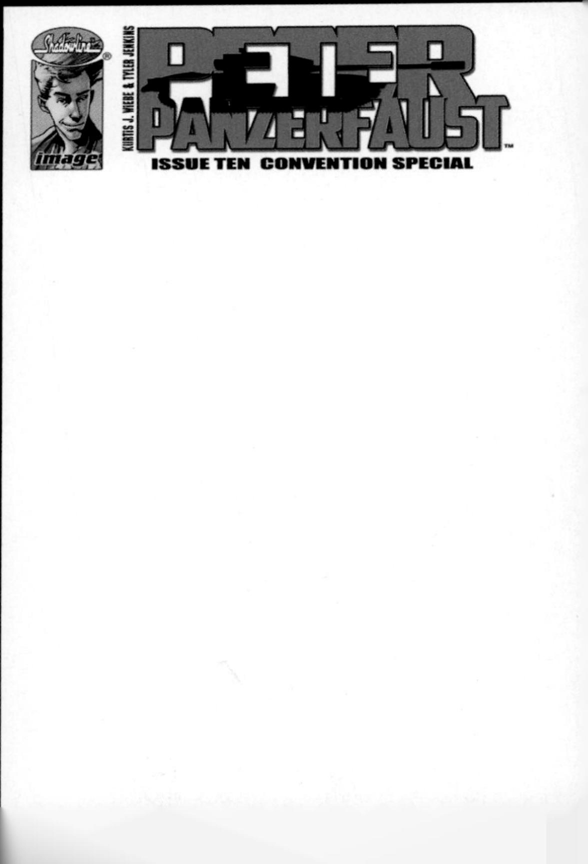

ISSUE 10 REGULAR EDITION COVER SKETCHES

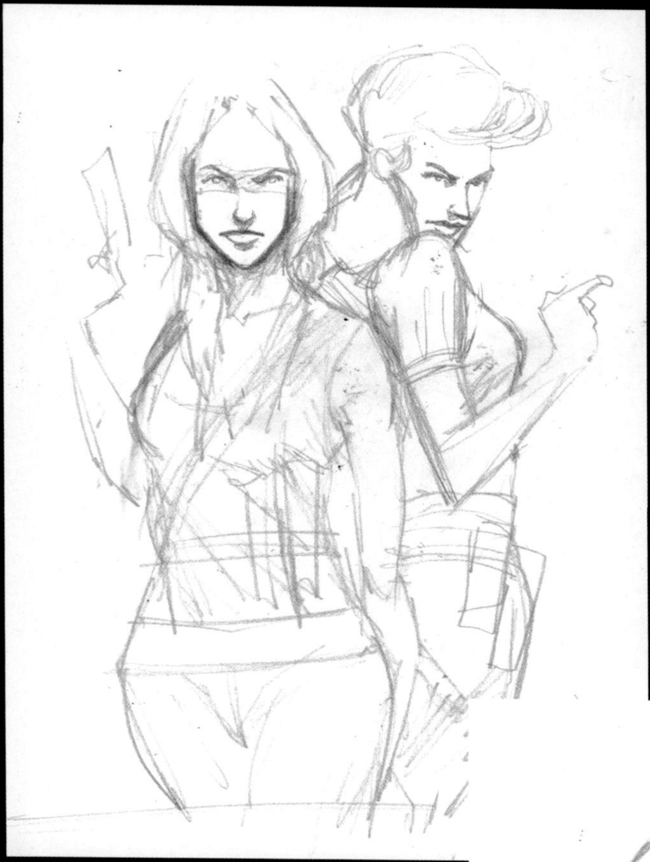

Tyler works up sketches for every cover. Subtle changes to the gesture or composition informs him of the best approach to each cover's unique challenge.

Compare these two skectches to the final cover elsewhere in this volume to get an idea of what the artist adds and omits on the way to the finished piece.

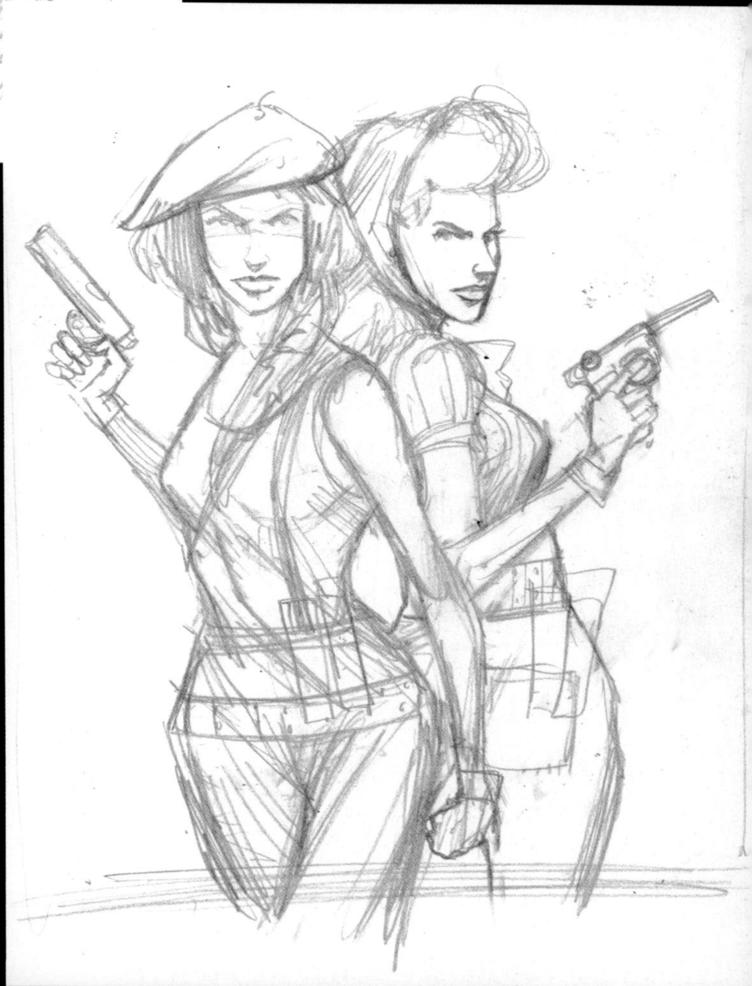

Over the next few pages we're going to show you the various stages a page goes through on its way to completion. The final, fully lettered pages appear elsewhere in this volume

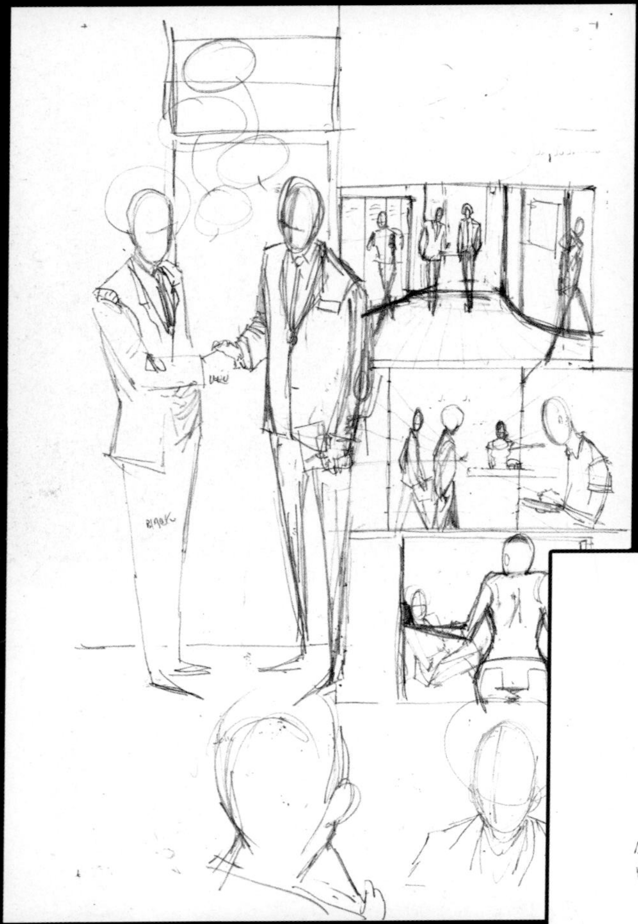

Tyler's original layout (left) is where he works out the composition (page layout, basic panel description), gesture of the characters and each panel's individual perspective.

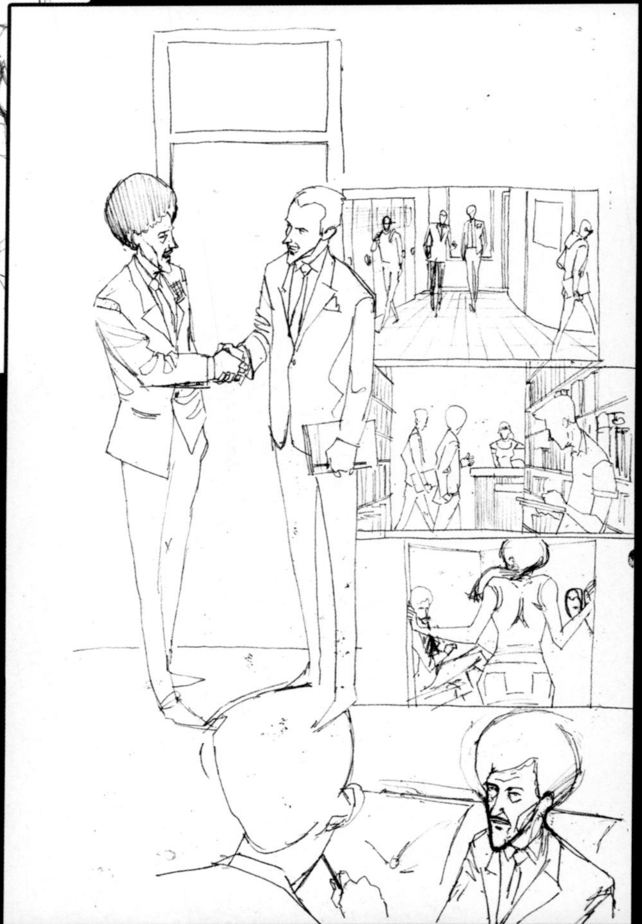

Once he's established the basic framework, he goes back in and tightens everything up in the pencil stage (right), still keeping just enough loose to allow for corrections and modifications.

This is page 3 from issue #6. We hope that you find this feature on the creative process both entertaining and informative.

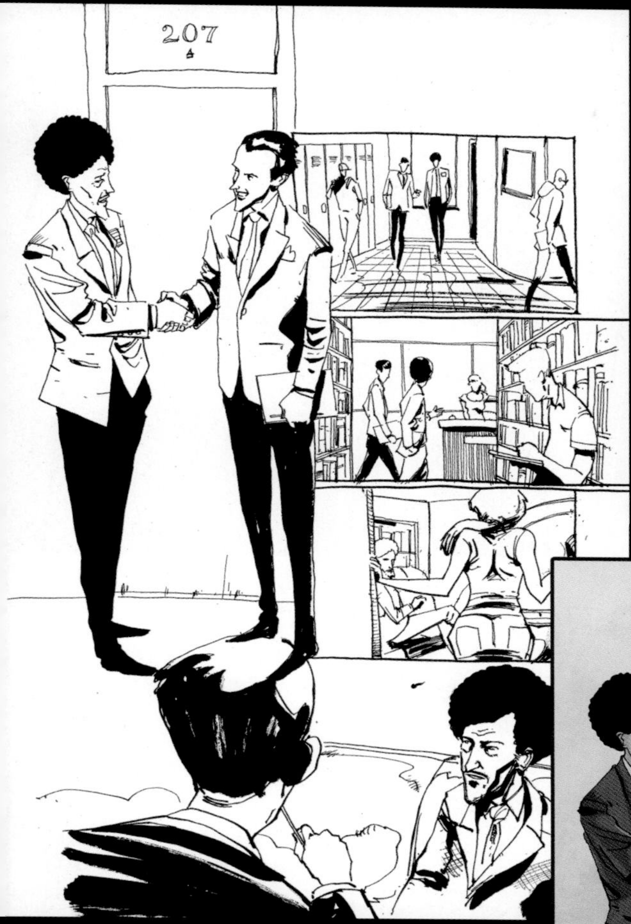
207

Tyler's final stage is inking (left) wherein he solidifies the holding lines and adds weight and volume to the figures.

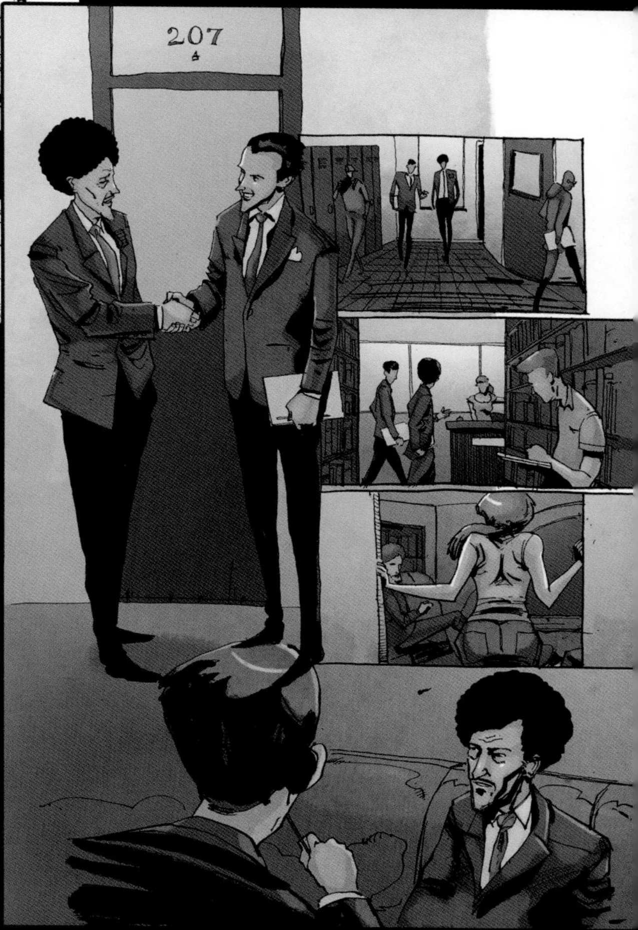
207

The inked pages are turned over to colorist Heather Breckel, who works her magic on them (right). Heather joined us with issue 6 and the book has been all the better for it!

This is the final stage before the pages are sent to letterer, Ed Brisson, then off to the printer (after Laura edits them).

This is page 6 from issue #13. Once again, you'll find the final, lettered page elsewhere in this volume.

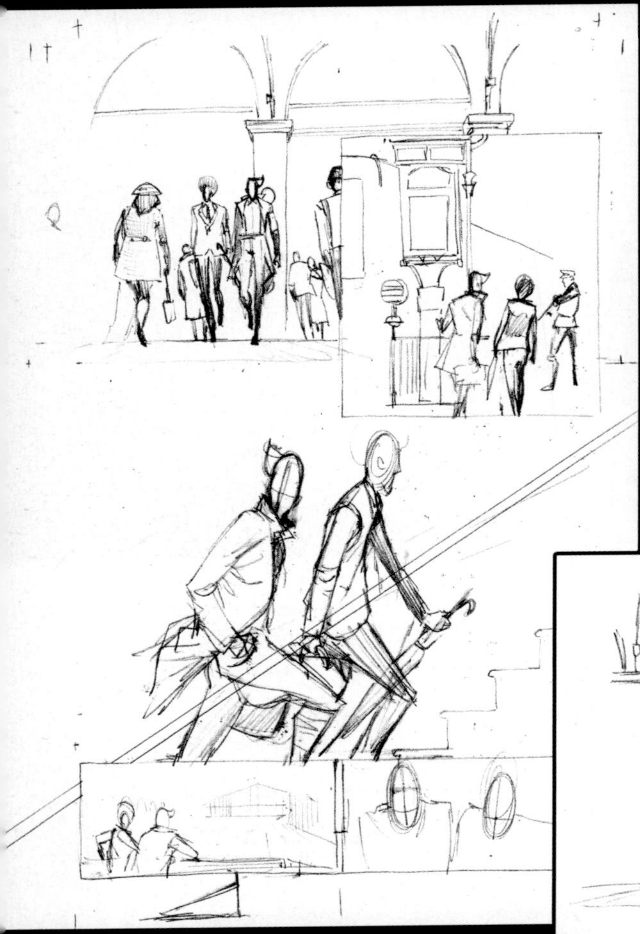

Tyler's original layout (left).

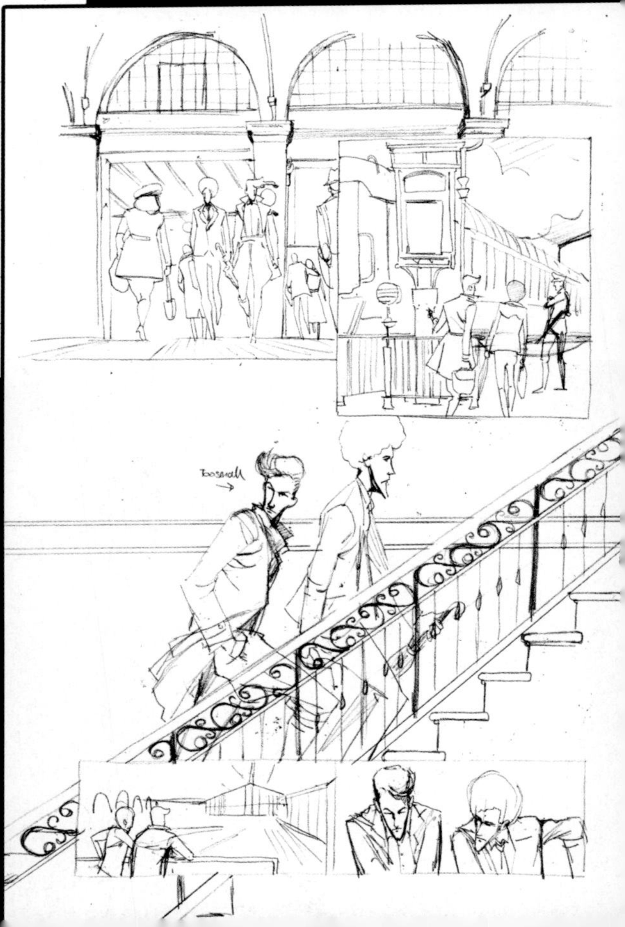

Pencil stage (right). Note that due to the elaborate backgrounds on this page that Tyler's pencils are a bit tighter than usual.

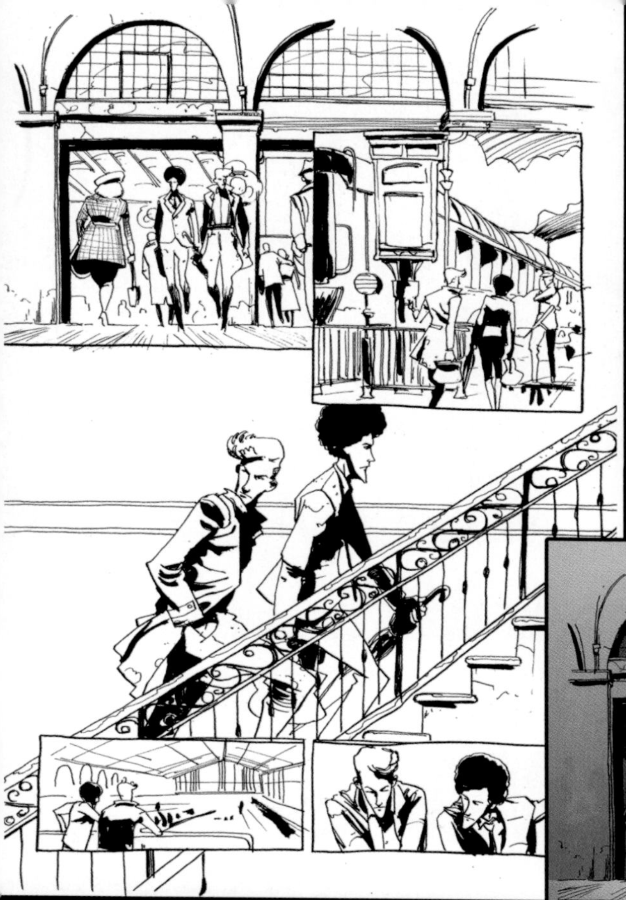

Inked page (left).

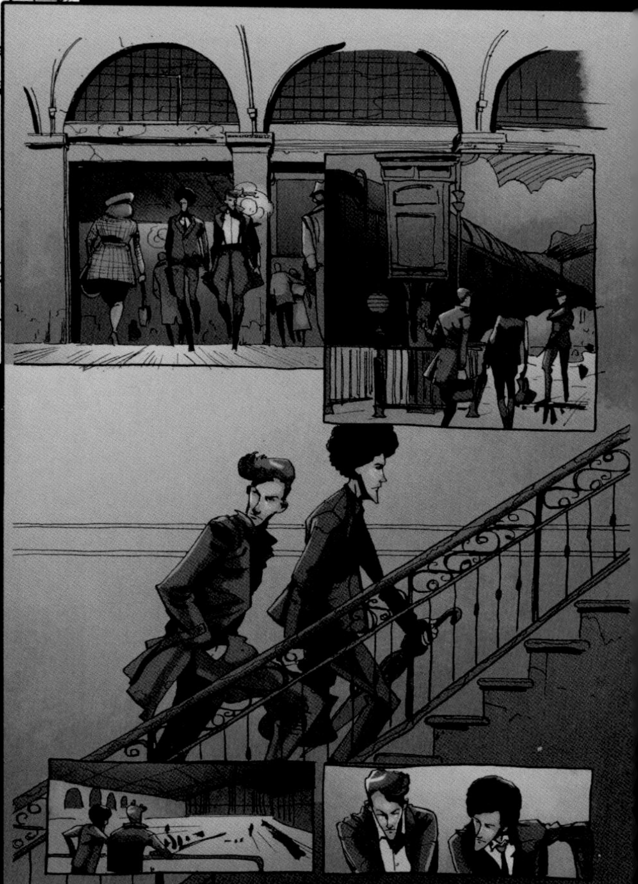

And, finally, Heather's colors (right).

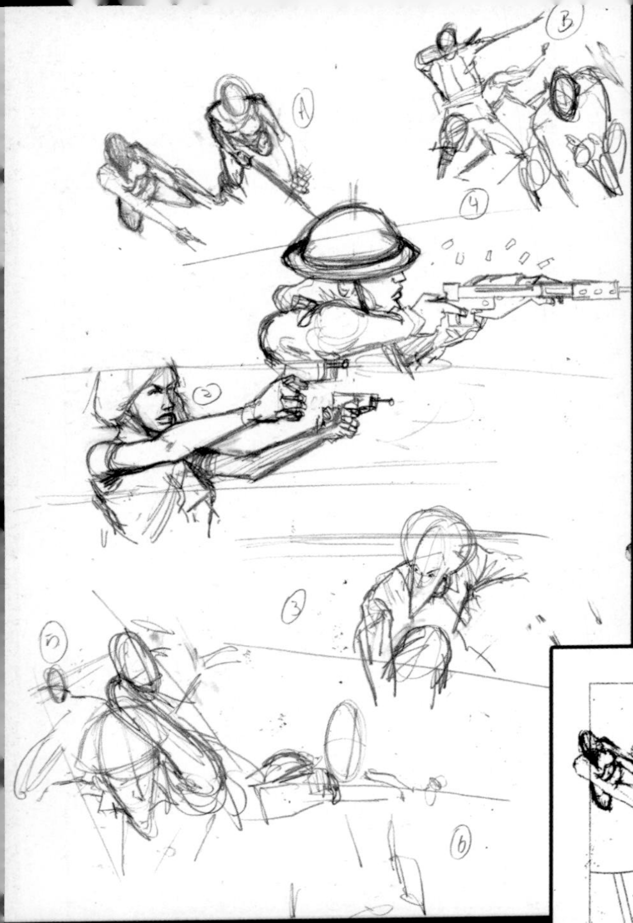

Tyler's rough sketch of the gestures required for this action heavy page.

For this second rough sketch, Tyler hits on the idea to give the page an unusual, but effective, layout. Diagonal panels connect the two semi-circles at page top and bottom. Note how the earlier gestures have been incorporated into the layout.

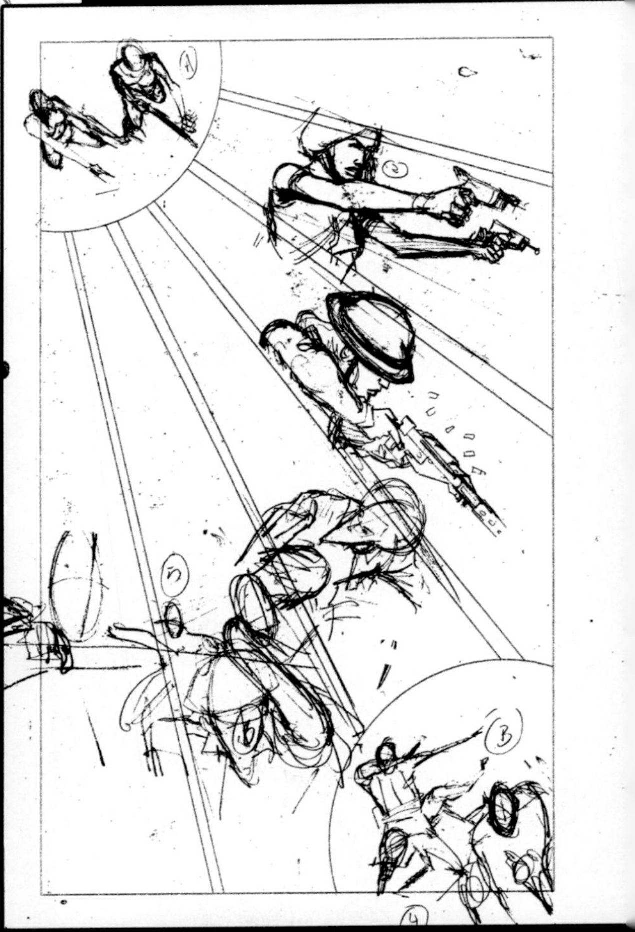

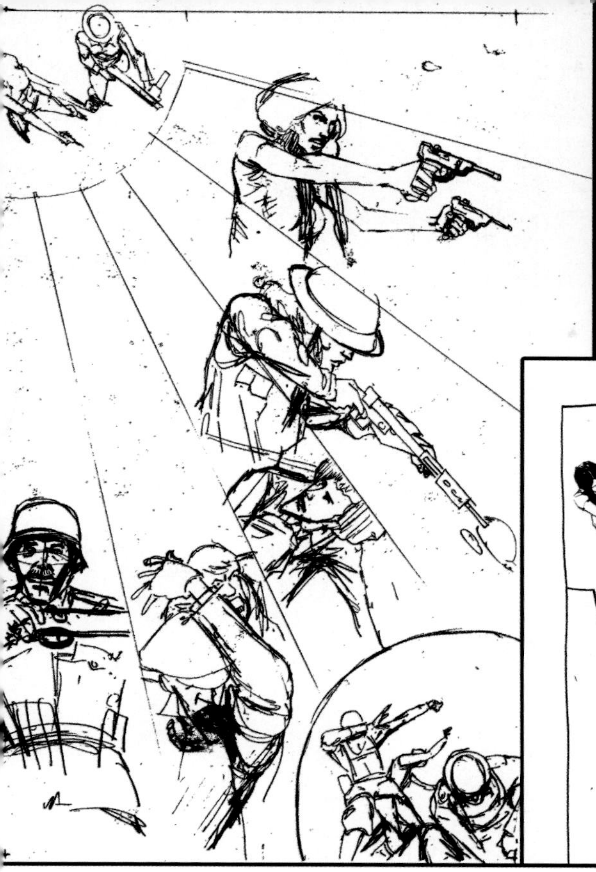

In the final pencil stage all figures are fleshed out within the panel borders (left) and the page is ready to be inked (below).

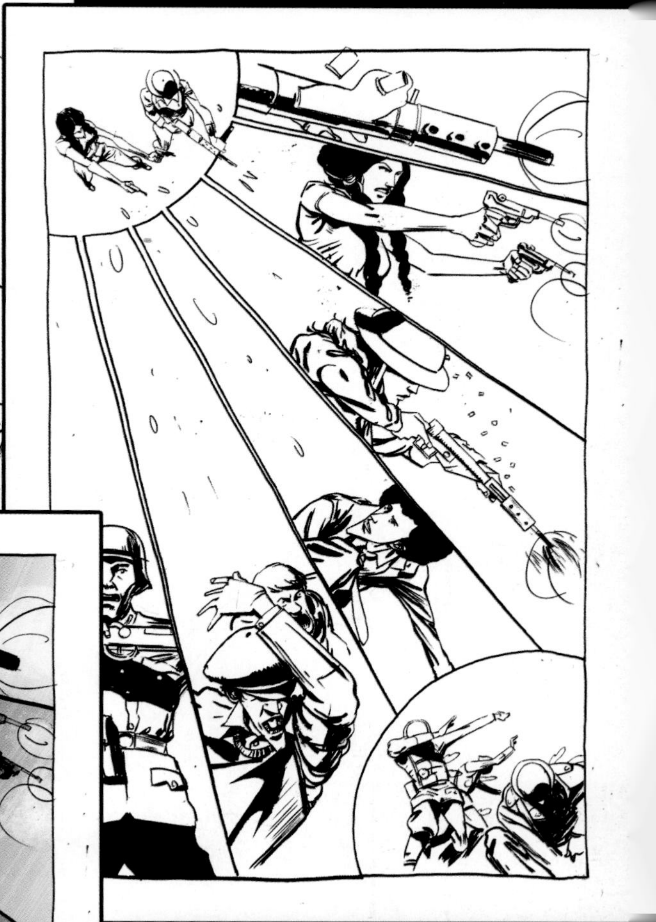

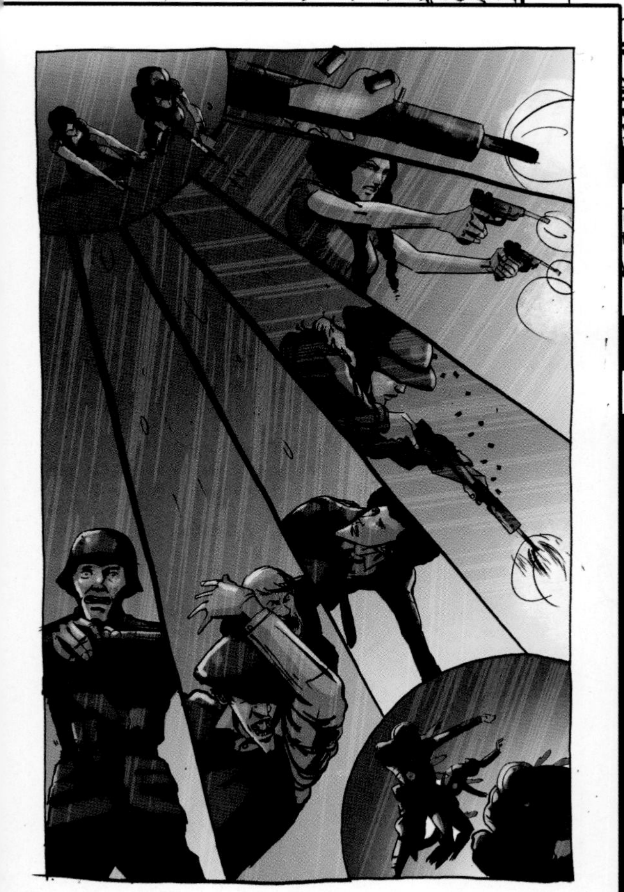

Heather's inspired color choices and effects give the page its heightened drama and adds richly to all of Tyler's hard work (right).

Very few (if any) characters emerge fully realized from its creator's hand. Most go through several iterations before arriving at a final, definitive version. And, even then, it will change and evolve as the series progresses over time. Here are some of Tyler's early sketches of Peter.

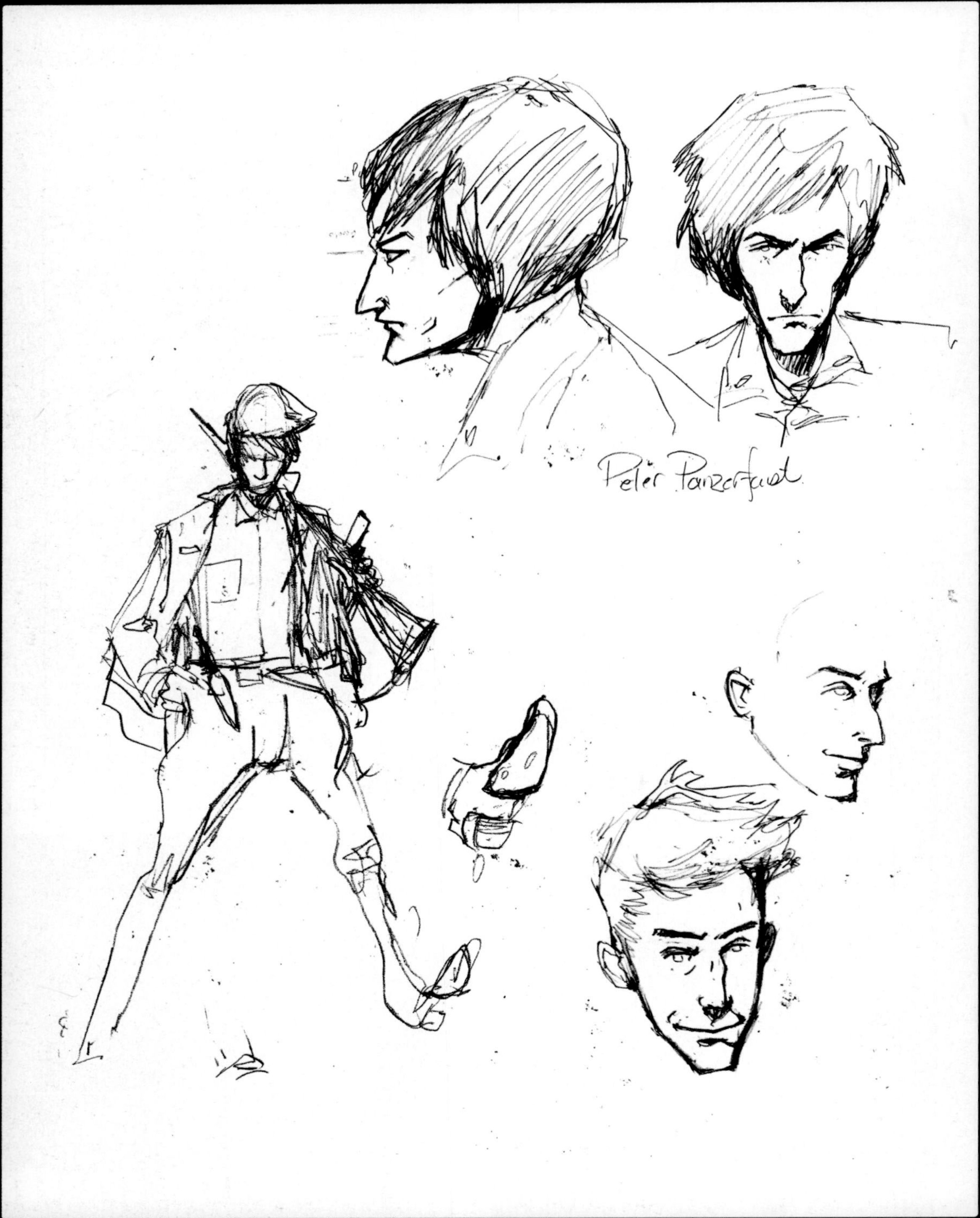
Peter Panzerfaust

IT ALL STARTS HERE:

VOLUME ONE: THE GREAT ESCAPE

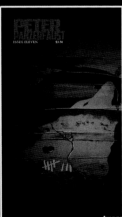

...k For Every Reader...

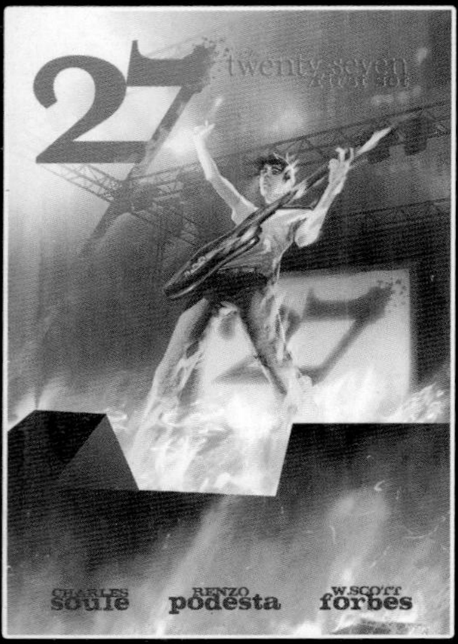
27
twenty seven
CHARLES soule
RENZO podesta
W. SCOTT forbes

SOULE/PODESTA/FORBES

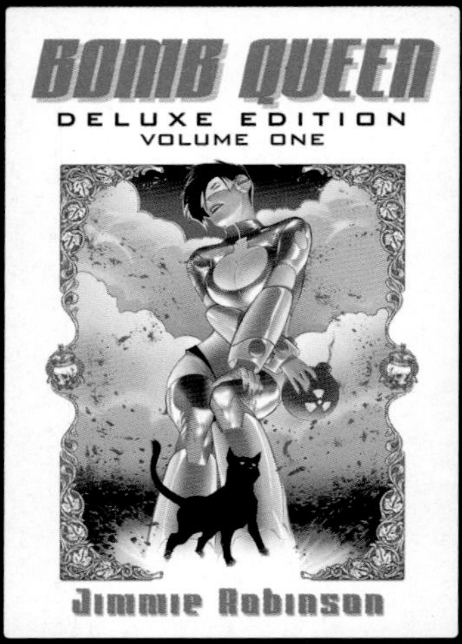
BOMB QUEEN
DELUXE EDITION
VOLUME ONE
Jimmie Robinson

ROBINSON

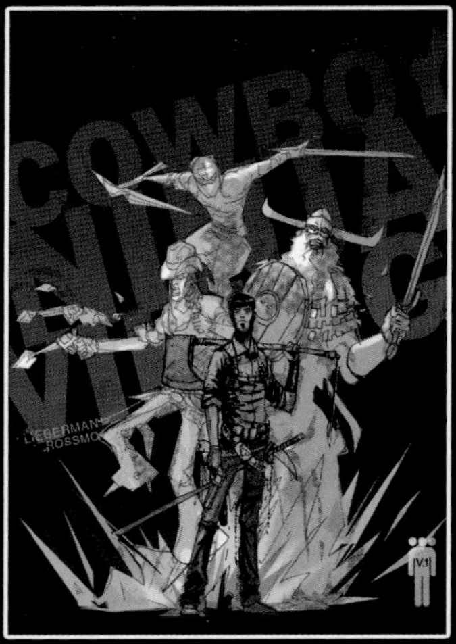
LIEBERMAN
ROSSMO

LIEBERMAN/ROSSMO

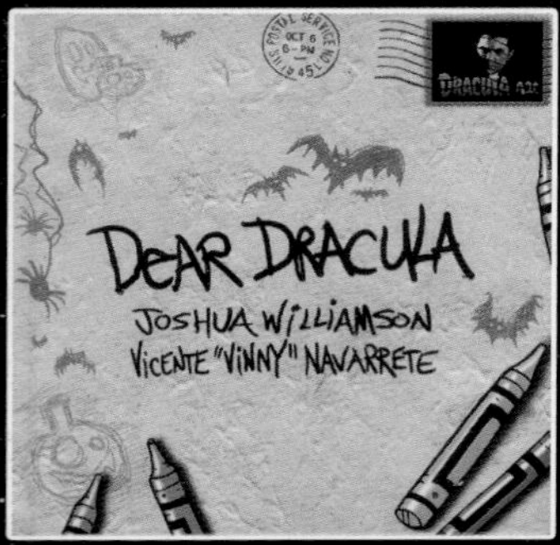
DEAR DRACULA
JOSHUA WILLIAMSON
VICENTE "VINNY" NAVARRETE

WILLIAMSON/NAVARETTE

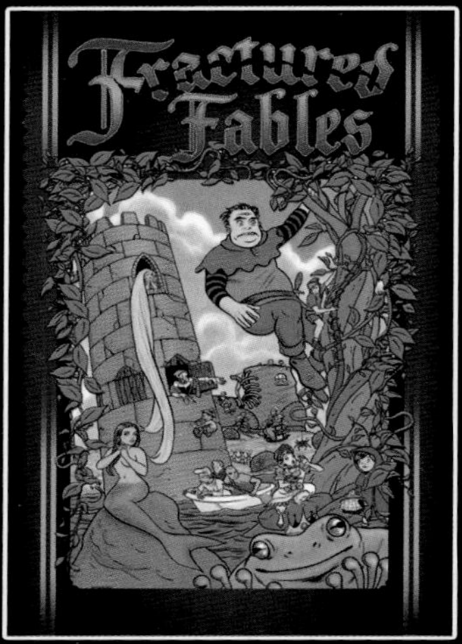
Fractured Fables

VARIOUS ARTISTS

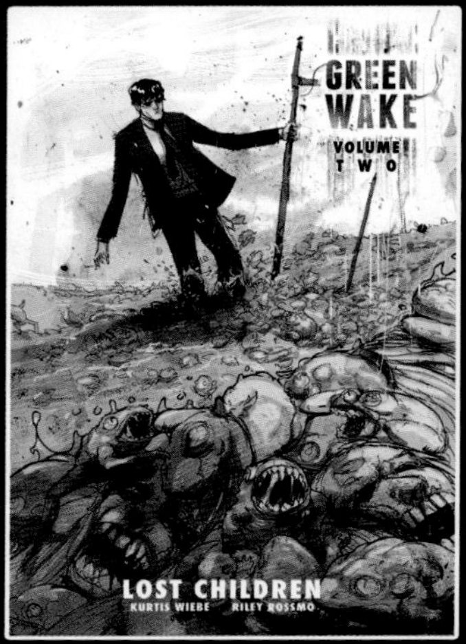
GREEN WAKE
VOLUME TWO
LOST CHILDREN
KURTIS WIEBE RILEY ROSSMO

WIEBE/ROSSMO

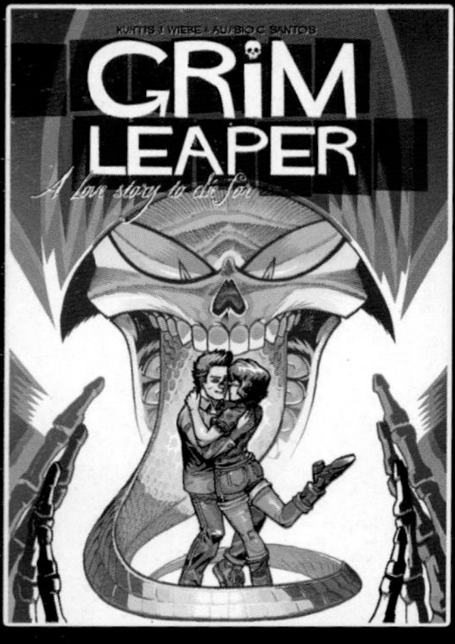
GRiM LEAPER
A love story to die for

WIEBE/SANTOS

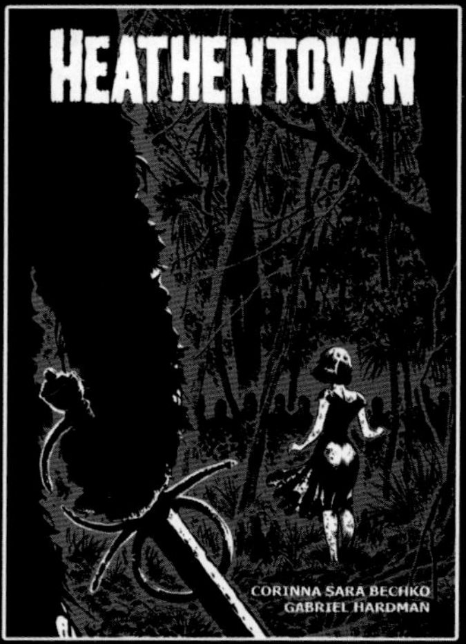
HEATHENTOWN
CORINNA SARA BECHKO
GABRIEL HARDMAN

BECHKO/HARDMAN

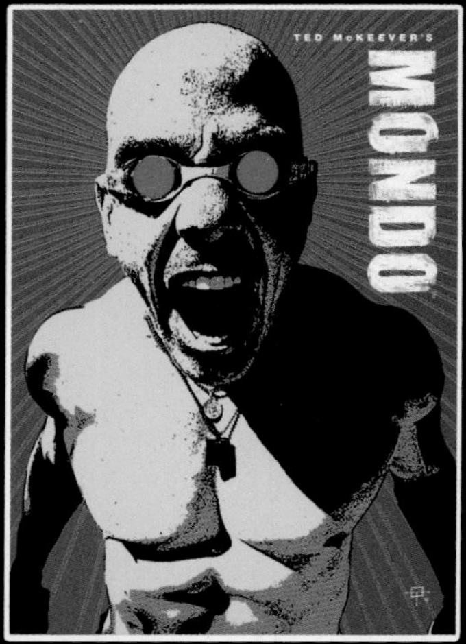
TED McKEEVER'S
MONDO

TED McKEEVER

FOR MORE INFORMATION ABOUT ALL Shadowline™ BOOKS AND WEB-COMICS, PLEASE VISIT US AT:

www.ShadowlineOnline.com